COUNSELLING SKILLS FOR MANAGERS

COUNSELLING SKILLS FOR MANAGERS

Second Edition

KAVITA SINGH

Professor
Faculty of Management Studies
University of Delhi
Delhi

PHI Learning Private Limited

Delhi-110092

2015

₹ 295.00

COUNSELLING SKILLS FOR MANAGERS, Second Edition
Kavita Singh

ISBN-978-81-203-5137-0

The export rights of this book are vested solely with the publisher.

Fifth Printing (Second Edition) . . . . . . **August, 2015**

Published by Asoke K. Ghosh, PHI Learning Private Limited, Rimjhim House, 111, Patparganj Industrial Estate, Delhi-110092 and Printed by Raj Press, New Delhi-110012.

Dedicated to the One who always shows me the way ahead and is always with me in whatever I do — "My God"

Contents

Preface

Revising *Counselling Skills for Managers* for the second edition, which was overdue, has been an interesting experience. As like its previous edition, the focus is still on being simple and approachable to the reader. It is hoped that the readers will find the new edition content also interesting, non-intimidating and of practical use.

In the second edition, an attempt has been made to take this journey of counselling further by focusing on the issues of termination and follow-up while discussing the issue of Counselling Procedures in Chapter 5. The concept of REBT (Rational Emotive Behavioural Therapy) has been examined in Chapter 8 to help the counsellor improve or enhance the behaviour of clients through counselling. While discussing Organizational application of counselling skills, in Chapter 9, a detailed analysis dealing with clients in crisis and trauma has been deliberated that has a great relevance in today's challenging environment. Further, a section has been specifically devoted to counselling women as they have to encounter different kinds of issues in both personal and professional lives. A comprehensive model of ethical decision-making has been added in the Chapter 13 on Ethics in Counselling.

KAVITA SINGH

Preface to the First Edition

If you sit down at the set of sun
And count the acts you have done,
And counting finds one self-denying deeds,
One work that eased the heart out of him who heard;
One glance most kind,
That fell like sunshine where it went—
Then you may count that day well spent.

— GEORGE ELIOT (Count That Day Lost)

This is the essence of Counselling. If you could make out a difference in one person's life, your life is worth it. And for this, you need not be a spiritual leader or a faith healer or a psychologist. You could do it in your capacity as a manager, as a supervisor, as a student. And believe it is not a difficult task. Just go ahead and try it!!

The work organization—a place where we spend approximately one-third of our lives—plays a very significant role in shaping our behaviours and personalities. Some of the basic human issues at work place, if not checked properly can destroy the system. You as a manager owe a great deal of responsibility to manage it more effectively. A little bit of inner drive, motivation and knowledge about the ways to handle human behaviour will make this process smooth. The present book is an attempt to provide some insight into handling behavioural issues at work place by developing counselling skills.

Unfortunately the concept of counselling is greatly misunderstood in our organizations. Some of us either assume that we are born counsellors, and therefore, do not require any guidance with respect to counselling skills or are simply not ready to accept this concept as an intervening variable in determining the effectiveness of an organization. This is hardly surprising, given that many people in business have not been exposed to a counselling style of operating. The techniques used by professional counsellors can be used by managers but only if he/she understands the concept of counselling, recognizing the implication of the skills that he or she is applying and knows when it is appropriate to use these skills.

The concept of counselling is quite unacceptable to the business world, and it may sometimes, threaten traditional business people. But one has to remember that key to success in any organization today lies in its ability to harness the potential of employees—which comes if managers begin to understand and utilize the skills of counselling. Use of counselling skills in business organization is still a relatively new concept and one that has tremendous potential for increasing individuals and their organizational effectiveness.

In the Indian context, we have an old age tradition and culture of counselling as an acceptable mode of human relationship, but we have yet to acquire the modern scientific tradition of professionally trained counsellors, especially for business organizations. It is, therefore, necessary to have a book that talks about approaches of counselling specially designed for business. With these forethoughts in mind, this book is an attempt to help the managers and supervisors in business organizations to develop their counselling skills, and be able to apply them appropriately in the right situations with the expected outcomes.

Many books business have been written on change management, management development, improving interpersonal relationship and communication and related fields. However, there are very few books on the techniques for achieving these goals in business organizations. One can find books on counselling in the discipline of psychology in the libraries and bookshops, but rarely on managers acquiring counselling skills, and applying them at workplace. The author hopes to bridge this gap through this book. This book is meant for established and aspiring managers of the corporate world, and the students of Management and Organizational Psychology.

The book comprises thirteen chapters. The first chapter 'Introduction to Counselling' introduces the concept of counselling to the readers, and includes the evolution of counselling, its definition highlighting the difference between counselling, psychotherapy and instruction. The second chapter on 'Approaches to Counselling' focuses on different approaches to counselling classifying them into psychoanalysis, behaviourism and humanism. The third chapter on 'Goals of Counselling' discusses the major goals of counselling, along with the role characteristics, and values of counsellors. The fourth chapter, 'The Process of Counselling' outlines different stages in the process of counselling and attitudes required at each of the stages. The fifth chapter, 'Counselling Procedures', highlights the intake procedures and referral procedures. Some guidelines for effective counselling and action strategies have also been suggested. The sixth chapter 'Counselling Skills', focuses on non-verbal and verbal communication and qualities of a counsellor. The seventh chapter, 'Role Conflicts in Counselling' dwells on the conflicts experienced by the managers, while they apply counselling skills at workplace. The eighth chapter 'Changing Behaviours through Counselling' outlines different principles to bring about change and specific techniques used by the counsellor. The ninth chapter, 'Organizational Application of Counselling Skills', specifies different area in which counselling skills can be used in business organizations. The tenth chapter, 'Dealing with Problem Subordinate' mentions different types of problem subordinates and the techniques of dealing with them. Eleventh chapter on 'Performance Management', discusses Performance Management System in an organization, and use of counselling skills for performance appraisal. The twelfth chapter 'Alcoholism and other Substance Abuse' cites the impact of alcoholism and substance abuse at work place and suggest ways to handle these problems. And, finally chapter thirteen, 'Ethics in Counselling' highlights the role of ethical principles in counselling employees in business organizations.

KAVITA SINGH

Acknowledgements

The process of acknowledgement is one of the most difficult activities in writing a book. The order in which the author is supposed to go, creates a lot of confusion. But I have total clarity that there are some significant people who have had a major impact on my professional and personal life. Amongst them, first of all, I would like to extend my heartfelt gratitude to Prof. Abad Ahmad, who helped me build my basic trust in people. It was he who has taught me to believe in everyone. I am thankful to Prof. J.K. Mitra, who gave me the opportunity to learn the intricacies of behavioural sciences at the time when I was new to this field. I would like to acknowledge Prof. M.L. Singla's contribution in helping me understand and internalize the value of sincerity and commitment. I acknowledge my past, present and future MBA students at the Faculty of Management Studies, University of Delhi, to whom I owe this book. It's their confidence in me that I have been able to carry out this task of putting my ideas on counselling together, in the form of a book.

My husband Dr. A.K. Singh, my daughter, Aditi and son-in-law, Akhil, deserve a special mention. This work would not have got completed without their constant support and accommodation to my odd routines. I would like to thank them for being my silent supporters. My father, S.K. Singh, has always been a pillar of strength for me; my sister Nivedita and brother Siddharth have always been by my side, whenever I need them. Thanks to all of you!

My thanks are also due for my publisher, PHI Learning and especially Ms. Pushpita Ghosh, for entrusting this responsibility of writing this book to me, and then taking this responsibility for publishing this book. Without my previous assistant, Ms. Anita Bisht's sincere dedicated efforts, this book would not be in its readable form today.

Finally, every effort has been made to trace references and quotations to their original source(s) in order to provide proper credits. I apologize any inadvertent omission(s), and welcome any correction or changes.

KAVITA SINGH

Chapter 1

Introduction to Counselling

Alvin Toffler (1970) predicted the rise of leisure time thirty-five years ago and his book *Future Shock* envisaged employees with two-third of their time devoted to leisure activities. But this has not happened. The reverse of this may be quite true. Today an organization demands more of the employee's time than ever before. There are fewer resources to do the work and more and more employees are suffering from 'presenteeism' (needed to be seen at work, while in spite of being overstressed doing the job). Levels of stress seem to be at an all-time high. A National Opinion Poll (*The Daily Telegraph*, 11th September 1995) reported that one-third of the workers feel so insecure in their jobs that they are afraid to go on a sick leave, 70 percent feel more in jeopardy than they did two years ago, and 44 percent are afraid to criticize their bosses. As employees struggle to cope, more and more employers, as well as their health experts, are struggling to find new ways to manage work place stress and its inevitable implications.

The problems arising due to stress at work place have been increasing with a rapid pace. Not only have learned journals published their research studies, but also stress has become such a constant feature in the popular press and glossy magazines that Newton (1995) remarks, "copy on stress would seem to be located in almost every editor's filing cabinet. Production is easy: include a stress check questionnaire, offer a ten-point plan to help readers attain 'stress fitness', and make a few telephonic calls to some academic luminaries on file." O'Leary (1993) and Cartwright and Cooper (1994) have documented some statistics around mental illness in the work place:

1. One in five of the working population (approximately 20 percent of the total working population) suffers some form of mental illness each year.
2. Some 90 million working days are lost each year as a result of mental illness.
3. Over half of the employees feet that emotional/personal problems and stress are the true reasons for their being absent from work.

4. Between 30 to 40 percent of all sickness at work is reported due to mental illness or emotional stress.
5. Alcohol abuse by employees to bust stress also poses a problem for the organization as it adversely affect its progress.
6. Approximately 20 percent of any workforces are affected by personal problems, which adversely affect their working performance.

There are several reasons why employers should be closely involved in the physical and mental well-being of employees (O'Leary, 1993, 1994). It makes sense to have a healthy and high-performing workforce. It not only creates happier individuals who provide quality service, but also contributes to the overall profits. But there is some incongruence in this. In a study it was found that while 94 percent of the companies surveyed felt that the mental health should be their concern, only 12 percent actually had a policy (O'Leary, 1993). With this kind of dichotomy, it appears to be a difficult task to introduce the ideas of counselling services in business organizations. But the other side of the dictum also holds true that today most of the organizations need work place counselling.

1.1 The Need for Work Place Counselling

There are several reasons why employers should turn to counselling as one of the techniques to take care of their workforce. Some of these reasons are as follows:

1. The welfare of employees is one of the major responsibilities of the employers. More and more employers realize that illness and productivity do not go well together.
2. The fact that harassed employees can take legal actions is another reason why organizations should introduce counselling.
3. Employers are turning to counselling as one way of helping the employees to cope with the changes taking place in organizations. Change is never easy—it disrupts, disorientates, causes anxiety and takes time. Support is needed for individuals and teams as transitions in organizations are managed. Counselling is one way of supporting employees as they reel under the pressure of organizational change.
4. Counselling can be seen as a way of improving mental health of the troublled persons. Employees do not leave their problems aside as they enter into work place. Egan (1994) has noted that the financial expenses borne by the organizations to deal with the psychological and social problems are quite high and has listed the kind of everyday problems that can prove costly to an organization, such as a poor relationship between two members of the team, a manager going through an impending divorce and an employee beginning to be abused by drug. If these problems go unnoticed and undealt with, the cost can be immeasurable.

5. More and more companies are realizing that their employees are one of their best assets. The direct link between the responsibility of taking care of their staff and the drive for achieving success and/or profit is a major factor in convincing employers to employ counselling services as one of the means to manage workforce constructively.

6. Counselling services can also be viewed as a preventive service. Counsellors are in a unique position within the organizational settings to offer the kind of training and education that prevents mental illness.

7. Organizations are realizing that a 'wholeness' approach needs to be adopted towards employees which implies that their physical, mental, emotional and social well-being go together and that they need to be worked with in totality. Emphasizing one element is not enough. Counselling process is a part of that package, where it is accepted that some individuals may require a professional counsellor's help at any critical stage of their lives and that for the majority it does prove quite helpful to enable them to deal with transitions and crises.

8. And finally, counselling can itself be a source of organizational change. Rather than just being an appendage to a company, counselling can bring the values, the energy for change, the vitality of acceptance, a realization of who we are and what we can be to the very dynamics of work place life. Counselling values are about the importance and process of change, how people can be empowered to manage their lives, how social responsibility can be built into life, and how decisions can be made. Counselling can influence organizational culture to work towards the ideal strong and adaptive culture that serves the company.

These are some of the reasons why employers need to introduce counselling into the work place. According to his research Cooper (1995) has divided the reasons into three main categories: (a) 76 percent of employees see counselling as a caring facility, (b) 70 percent see counselling as a way to help employees deal with work place changes, and (c) 57 percent view counselling as a means of managing stress. Counselling at work place makes sense when it is realized that employees spend about one-quarter of their lives in work settings; that, to many, key relationships are part of their work; that personal identity is often bound up with jobs; and that almost all people integrate personal and professional lives to a great extent. Having counselling available in the work place means that the problems can be dealt with fairly quickly and can be worked through in the environment from which they often emerge. The rate at which the counselling practices have grown over the years is the result of a number of experiments conducted over a period of considerable time. Section 1.2 traces the development of counselling to its present status.

1.2 Evolution of Counselling over the Years

The historical development of counselling may conveniently be classified into four periods.

1.2.1 Period 1

The first period in which the concept of counselling took shape can be traced back to somewhere between 1850 to 1900. During the latter part of the nineteenth century far-reaching innovations in the field of psychology were made. The very first Psychological Laboratory was set up at Leipzig by Wilhelm Wundt in 1879. It was followed by Stanley Hall (1844–1924) who started the first Psychological Laboratory in the USA in 1883. In 1895 George Merrill established the first systematic vocational programme in San Francisco. The first Psychological Clinic was founded by Lightner Witmer in 1896 which started the beginning of the counselling movement. J.B. Miner established and directed the free clinic in mental development at the University of Minnesota in 1909. However, it was Jesse B. Davis who first used the term *counselling*. He set up the Educational Career-counselling Centre in Detroit in 1898. President of Chicago University, William Rainey Harper, stressed the importance of guidance in his annual address in 1899 thereby giving importance to the guidance movement.

1.2.2 Period 2

The second period for the evolution of counselling can be marked from 1900 to 1930. During the first few years of the twentieth century following significant events took place:

1. The first convention of the International Congress of Psychoanalysis was held at Salzberg.
2. Stanley Hall invited Carl Gustav Jung to deliver a lecture on Counselling at the Clark University.
3. Mental Hygiene Movement was launched by Clifford Beers (1908) with his epoch-making book, *The Mind that Found Itself.*
4. Rev. Elwood Worcester advocated the use of psychological principles in pastoral counselling (Cunningham, 1967).
5. Binet-Simon tests of intelligence were adapted to American conditions about this time.
6. Progressive Education Movement was initiated by John Dewey (1910) with his epoch-making book, *How We Think.*
7. Mrs. Adolf Meyer started The School of Social Work, which also involved casework and psychiatry (Wirth, 1931).

These movements boosted the efforts to develop knowledge and services in order to assist individuals in need of help without which they would have wasted away. In the years that followed, these movements converged pointing to the need for the application of psychological insights for obtaining and providing a meaningful base and sense of direction for the efforts to become fruitful and rewarding.

Unfortunately, there is a wrong impression that counselling is a poor man's psychotherapy. It is hoped that with a greater degree of professionalization many of the prejudices and misconceptions concerning counselling will be dispelled.

The first decade of the present century saw the popularization of the Guidance Movement. Eli Weaver published, *Choosing a Career* in 1906. Frank Parsons started the vocational bureau of Boston in 1908 and published his book, *Choosing a Vocation* in 1909. The state of Michigan started the first citywide Guidance Movement in Grand Rapids in 1912. The National Vocational Guidance Association (NVGA) was founded in Grand Rapids in the following year. Thus, it can be seen that the Vocational Guidance Movement grew out of voluntary efforts in educational, civic and social work. These events not only signified growing public interest but also concern for the future welfare of the youth. Educationists and administrators began to recognize that it was hazardous to leave pupils to fend for themselves. There were cases of wastage and stagnation, evidences of under-achievement, instances of retarded learning, problems of handicapped children, special problems of school learning, truancy, delinquency and the like, which required close attention and supervision by the teacher concerned. In addition, remedial measures had to be devised and implemented. It is easy to see that this was a tall order for any individual teacher. Educational authorities became slowly but increasingly convinced that there was a genuine need for providing guidance to pupils to help them learn efficiently and effectively. With this recognition of the need for guidance at school, it was evident that the school-leaving youth and the out-of-school youth also required appropriate guidance in their choice of occupation. Thus, Guidance Movement was started out of society's concern for the youth.

In the early years, guidance consisted of giving the necessary occupational information to the young to decide for themselves what would be most appropriate for them. With the outbreak of World War I (1914–1918) and the entry of USA on the side of the Allies, Psychology in general, and Guidance in particular, received tremendous impetus. As a part of the war effort, E.L. Thorndike (1874–1949) and Robert Yerkes (1876–1956) helped develop the Army Alpha and Army Beta tests in 1917 for screening the defense personnel. James Burt Miner developed the first ever known questionnaire in 1908. It was closely followed by R.S. Woodworth and F.L. Wells association tests and psychometric inventory in 1911, which was specifically developed as a screening device for the army recruits. This was published later as Personal Data Sheet (1920). The cessation of hostilities resulted in an unprecedented situation, which helped the Guidance Movement to consolidate its position and make further progress. The war had uprooted thousands of young as well as middle-aged men from their normal occupations and lives. They had been engaged as defense personnel at different theatres of war in Europe and the Middle East. When the hostilities ended, the servicemen were repatriated and they had to be rehabilitated. Thousands of jobs had to be found. The Vocational Guidance Movement, which was already in existence at several places, was pressed into service for this purpose. The problems of the war veterans were different from those of the young. The former had once been gainfully employed but the war had torn them away from their traditional occupations in which they had acquired a certain degree of competence. In addition, as members of the defense services, they had received a different kind of training that had also to be taken into account in finding them suitable jobs. All these factors afforded ample opportunities for the development of the Guidance Movement. There was a great need for its services and the movement braced itself to meet the demand.

1.2.3 Period 3

The third period in the growth of counselling is classified from the year 1930 to 1940. In catering to guidance needs, guidance workers looked around for suitable tools and techniques. The Psychometric Movement, with its fascinating and interesting tests of mental functions and abilities, attitudes, interests, etc. began to attract attention. They took advantage of the new innovations and pressed them into service with great success. The Guidance Movement thus developed a vocational bias. It came to be recognized as the Vocational Guidance Movement as distinct from vocational selection. In the Vocational Guidance Movement the subjects were to be apprised of their assets and liabilities (their abilities and skills) so that they would have a fuller and healthier appreciation of themselves and choose occupations that were congruent with their abilities. It was appreciated that vocational maladjustment resulted from an inappropriate choice of jobs in the absence of a proper and adequate understanding of one's own capacities and potentialities. Donald Paterson in 1930 of Minnesota remarked that when Parsons launched his vocational bureau he found his psychological cupboard bare, i.e., there were no psychological tests he could have readily used in guidance work (Lofquist and Dawis, 1991). This was owing to the obvious fact that the influence of psychometric was not yet appreciably felt. There were very few psychological tests available and few persons were trained to use them at that time. Consequently, Parsons had to be content with providing only the occupational information basic to proper vocational choice. Thus, in the first few decades, the Guidance Movement was only aimed at providing educational and vocational guidance.

The post-war situation remarkably changed the character of the Guidance Movement. The period, 1918–1939, from the end of World War I to the outbreak of World War II, saw the publication of books and important psychological tests, such as Harry Kitson's *Psychology of Vocational Adjustment* in the year 1925, Clark L. Hull's *Aptitude Testing* in 1927 and E.K. Strong Jr.'s *Strong Vocational Interest Blank* (SVIB) in 1943. The

National Vocational Guidance Association (NVGA), founded in 1913, formed the American Council of Guidance and Personnel Association (ACGPA) in 1934, which later merged with NVGA to become the American Personnel Guidance Association (APGA). Robert Hoppock, a former Secretary of NVGA published his book, *Job Satisfaction*, in 1935. With Hoppock's (1935) work, the guidance movement tended to become more psychologically oriented, unlike the earlier period in which it was more concerned with school education and provision of career information. Another milestone in the progress of the Guidance Movement in this direction was marked by the publication of L.L. Thurstone's (1887–1955) *Tests of Primary Mental Abilities* in 1938. The following year, i.e., 1939 saw the publication of the Dictionary of Occupational Titles (DOT), which listed 18,000 jobs (Morton, 1969). The Guidance Movement made tremendous progress in the hands of Donald Paterson and E.G. Williamson during 1930–1940 at the University of Minnesota. Their work was largely concerned with the objective assessment of the individual's abilities, to help him gain adequate self-knowledge so that he is able to make meaningful choices in his career and get maximum job satisfaction.

1.2.4 Period 4

The fourth period in the growth of counselling is marked with the Second World War and the years that followed. But the major breakthrough which finally established counselling as a science in its own right was achieved through Carl Rogers' book, *Counselling and Psychotherapy* (1942). Until about the publication of this book in 1942, there was a certain amount of hesitation regarding the acceptability of counselling as a form of psycho-therapy. In 1944, by an act of Congress, the Army Separation and Classifi-cation and Counselling Program was initiated and the United States Employment Services (USES) published the General Aptitude Test Battery (GATB) in 1945. The Veterans' Administration Authority had become more concerned with the provision of counselling as part of the rehabilitation programme. However, counselling has not only stood the test of time but also obtained recognition by the American Psychological Association (APA). Owing to the efforts of Profs. C.G. Wrenn, D.E. Super, P. Robinson, E.S. Bordin and other psychologists, a meeting was convened at the North Western University, Evanston in 1951 prior to the Annual Convention of the American Psychological Association of September 1951. At this conference, 60 leading psychologists currently involved in guidance and counselling, were invited to participate. They recommended, among other things, the starting of an independent division for counselling. The report of the conference was published in the *American Psychologist* in June 1952. The American Psychological Association also introduced certification and professional examination for counselling psychologists to be held by the American Board of Examiners in professional psychology. The first *Journal of Counselling*

Psychology was published in 1954. This conclusively established counselling psychology as a specialized field of psychology.

There has been a growing awareness of the need for professionalism. For a long time the medical men and general public had serious reservations about the credibility of psychological techniques of therapy. Mesmer's (1734–1815) work had two-fold effects, while it popularized mesmerism: it also raised serious doubts in some circles. Since then the need has been felt for a sound professional basis for psychotherapy. In course of time, the need for improving the efficiency of training led to scientific selection procedures. To exercise healthy supervision, a scheme of certification or licensing was introduced as in the other professional fields like medicine, law, accountancy, etc.

Over the past five decades counsellors have gained overwhelming acceptance from society; consequently, a large number of sub-specialties have developed to serve in settings such as schools, mental health clinics, rehabilitation centres, community agencies, college personnel services, etc. They incorporate the important findings of the personality theory, social psychology, counselling psychology and therapeutic techniques.

The early innovators were mostly preoccupied with practice and were impatient for the practical results. Perhaps because of their preoccupation with results they adopted a pragmatic approach in the first two to three decades after inception of the Guidance Movement. Little effort was made towards theory building. When the early Guidance Movement, which was pragmatic in its outlook, developed into a powerful Counselling Movement, the importance and need for a sound theory came to be acutely felt. Therefore, the attention of counsellors was naturally drawn to this lacuna. The different approaches adopted by the guidance workers and counsellors have led to different approaches to counselling. Psychoanalysis, as a theory of human personality, was like a Copernican revolution in psychology and was perhaps the first systematic attempt to explain human behaviour—both normal and abnormal. Theory building in counselling began with the adoption of the psychoanalytic approach to counselling needs. However, the different views concerning human nature and man's philosophic concerns significantly influenced theory building. Thus, several theoretical approaches to counselling are in vogue today, which would be discussed in Chapter 2.

1.3 Defining Counselling

Counselling as a fast growing dynamic movement has rapidly progressed from its modest beginning in the early part of the present century to its current dynamic status in a brief period of six decades. In the rapidity of its growth, counselling has overlooked many issues, causing apparent confusion with psychotherapy, psychoanalysis, behaviour conditioning, guidance, advising, etc. Yet it is all these things in one-way or the other. The counselling function is claimed to be performed also by ministers, physicians, social workers, teachers, managers and many others whose number is ever on the increase. Though counselling, like any other science, is based on scientific principles of objectivity and verifiability it cannot proceed in the absence of subjective aspects, such as rapport, warmth and trust.

Counselling has earned recognition through its service in enhancing and in preserving human happiness. It is found to be of service by different organizations for increasing their efficiency and productivity. In the history of its growth, as a science and as a profession, it has changed its emphasis, aims and roles as can be seen from its expanding range of activities in diverse settings.

Since counselling has already become an important part of the organizational life so it becomes necessary to understand and to define the concept. Different experts have tried to capture the essences of counselling in different ways. Some of these viewpoints are expressed hereinafter:

Good (1945) defined counselling as the "individualized and personalized assistance with personal, educational, vocational problems, in which all pertinent facts are studied and analyzed, and a solution is sought, often with the assistance of specialist, and personal interviews in which counselee is taught to make his own decisions with emphasis on cognitive material, immediate decision making and use of external resources (Sreedhar, 2001).

English and English defined it as a relationship in which one person endeavours to help another to understand and solve his adjustment problem. The area of adjustment is often indicated such as educational counselling, vocational counselling and social counselling. Counselling is a two-way affair involving both counsellor and counselee. Unfortunately, both noun and verb *Counsel* retain an older meaning of advice giving, which is now conceived as only part of the counselling process (Sreedhar, 2001).

According to **Pepinsky and Pepinsky**, counselling is seen (a) as a diagnosis and treatment of minor (non-embedded, non-incapacitating), functional (non-organic) maladjustment and (b) as a relationship primarily individual and face-to-face, between counsellor and client (Sreedhar, 2001).

Wrenn defines counselling as a dynamic and purposeful relationship between two people in which procedures vary with the nature of the client's need, but in which there is always mutual participation by the counsellor and the client with the focus upon self-clarification and self-determination by the client (Sreedhar, 2001).

Hahn says that there is difference in perception of people on counselling because counselling itself has three different bodies of supporters as follows:

1. The social welfare advocates who have primarily an ideographic interest (Coombs and others in phenomenological school).
2. Those who are more medically oriented or more nomothetic in their position (Thorne).
3. Those who are primarily concerned with student personnel administration and who have great interest in measurement (Strong, Bingham and Williamson).

Although they may be each patting the same element, they are getting quite different notices of what the beast is like (Sreedhar, 2001).

Tyler presents the clearest view. According to him counselling is a kind of psychological helping activity that concentrates on the growth of clear sense of ego identity and the willingness to make choices and commitments in accordance with it. It is a process in which client is helped to understand himself more completely in order to correct an environmental or adjustment difficulty.

Common element in all definitions is that the main aim of counselling is to help people make the right choice and to motivate them to act towards its achievement. It is basically to help the counselee answer the question—what shall I do?

Based on all these definitions, it can finally be rightly said that counselling is a process, a relationship that is designed to help people take right decision. Underlying better choices are matters of learning, personality development and self-knowledge, which can be translated into better role perception and more effective role behaviour.

Section 1.4 pertains to the inter-relationship between counselling, psychotherapy and instruction.

1.4 Counselling, Psychotherapy and Instruction

The terms *counselling* and *psychotherapy* were generally used as disparate terms. However, an increasingly large number of writers are tending to use them interchangeably. Also the terms, advising, guidance and counselling have been for some time used rather loosely. But with increasing specialization and professionalization, some amount of clarification of the terms is made. Clarification of the inter-relationship between the terms, namely, *advising* and *guidance*, clears the ground for a discussion of the terms, *counselling* and *psychotherapy*. Advising has now come to be understood as academic advising provided by the faculty members to students who seek assistance concerning their curricular choices. Guidance is used mostly in educational settings with vocational import. It also involves the provision of educational and vocational information to enable students to make a proper choice of courses leading to appropriate vocational goals. Guidance services understood in this sense have been increasingly found to operate in high-school settings.

Chronologically speaking, psychotherapy existed long before the emergence of counselling as a helping service. Psychotherapy can be said to have had its origin in the work of Mesmer (Söderlund, 2000). However, Freud laid sound and scientific foundations for it. Psychoanalysis was acclaimed as psychotherapy par excellence. In the years that followed, many other techniques were introduced into psychotherapy. Different critics have tried to explain psychotherapy:

Wolberg (1977) defines psychotherapy as a form of treatment for problems of an emotional nature, in which a trained person deliberately establishes a professional relationship with the patient with the object of removing, modifying or retarding existing symptoms of mediating disturbed pattern of behaviours and of promoting positive personality growth and development.

Eysenck (1952) defines psychotherapy as an unidentified technique applied to unspecified problems with unpredictable outcomes. It contains elements like (a) a prolonged interpersonal relationship, (b) involvement of trained personnel, (c) a self dissatisfaction with emotional and/or interpersonal adjustment on the part of the client, (d) the use of psychological method, (e) an activity based on theory of mental disorders and (f) an aim through this relationship of ameliorating self dissatisfaction.

Counselling emerged as a field of psychotherapy. Both counselling and psychotherapy aim at changing individuals rather than institutions. Social reform movements are specifically concerned with the latter. Further, the kind of change sought to be brought about is different from the change a salesman or an executive or a priest seeks. Counselling intends to make individuals more self-directed and autonomous. Thus, the function of counselling is to facilitate the development of self-actualization in persons. Counselling and psychotherapy are often distinguished in terms of the situations they tackle. In the case of psychotherapy, there is an element of pathology present in the client. Section 1.4.1 dwells on the distinction between counselling and psychotherapy.

1.4.1 Distinction between Counselling and Psychotherapy

The distinction between counselling and psychotherapy was sought to be made in terms of the nature of the clientele catered to by them. It was argued that the counselling concerns itself with the normal individuals and intends to prevent the occurrence of emotional breakdowns. On the other hand, psychotherapy, it was claimed, deals with the individuals who are not normal. Some element of psychopathology was involved and clinical treatment was indicated to remedy the situation. But this distinction was considered unacceptable, as abnormality could not be defined in irrefutable terms. The problem of distinguishing the terms became so involved that the American Psychological Association (APA) felt it necessary to entrust the problem to its Committee on Definition, Division of Counselling Psychology. Counselling, as it is pointed out, is essentially concerned with the psychological development of the individual and it contributes to the total development of personality.

Counselling is not, as it is claimed, an emergency treatment. Psychotherapy, on the other hand, is concerned with the individual whose emotional growth has become severely distorted. Bordin (1979) makes a quantitative rather than a qualitative distinction between the terms. According to him, counselling is concerned with emotional cases of less intensity and he emphasizes cognitive and rational factors in their treatment. In cases requiring psychotherapy, however, there is a greater distortion of reality and cognitive and rational factors may not be of much avail (Hobbs and Seeman, 1955).

Sanderson (1995) stresses that the counsellor deals with a particular area of difficulty while the psychotherapist is interested in the total personality structure. Mowrer (1961) holds that the techniques of counselling and psychotherapy differ from each other. In the former counsellor gives information, guidance, etc., while in the latter the psychotherapist seldom uses these. The distinction between counselling and psychotherapy has unnecessarily created confusion. What is important to bear in mind is that the counselling is one type or kind of psychotherapy. Besides counselling, there are several other types of psychotherapy. At one extreme we have the Freudian psychoanalysis as an example of psychotherapy, which is concerned with the depth analysis but counselling, on the other hand, is not essentially concerned with the depth analysis. In the case of counselling, no pathology is ever involved. It deals with the normal persons who have problems, which do not require prolonged intervention as in the field of psychotherapy. Here, the counselling assistance consists of providing *intrapsychic* insight. Our age has been characterized as an age of anxiety. Anxiety has a prime role in our civilization. The socialization process inculcates a certain amount of anxiety. A civilized man has to curb some of his spontaneous impulses which lead to inhibition and anxiety. Perhaps the absence of anxiety would itself be a kind of pathology or abnormality. The most important function of counselling is to reduce, if not eliminate, anxiety by helping the counselee overcome his inhibitions and make more rational decisions both for himself and for others. Counselling is both preventive and restorative in its function.

It is more likely that a continuum may exist from one activity (counselling) to another (psychotherapy). Just as first aid may shade into the practice of medicine so counselling may shade into psychotherapy. In general, counselling would be characterized by the terms as educative, supportive, situational, problem solving, conscious awareness, with an emphasis on 'normal, while psychotherapy would be characterized by the terms, such as reconstructive, depth emphasis, analytic, focus on unconscious with an emphasis on neurotic or other emotional problem.

Common goal of counselling and psychotherapy is the reduction of psychological discordance. To visualize the difference between the two we shall look at their respective goals, clients, practitioners, settings and methods being stated in Table 1.1 to 1.4.

On the basis of these tables, it can be concluded that all the psychotherapists should have the following qualities:

1. The ability to build a rapport with the patients.
2. The ability to accept and appreciate the basic human worth of the individual.
3. The quality to maintain a supporting relationship with the patients.
4. The quality to maintain the status implicit or explicit of the psychotherapists.
5. The ability to draw a line of control and limit the relationship between psychotherapist and patients.

Table 1.1	Differences between Counselling and Psychotherapy with Respect to Goals	
Sl. no.	*Counselling*	*Psychotherapy*
1.	Counselling deals with normal individuals and intends to guide an individual towards a better life.	Psychotherapy deals with abnormal individuals and intends to prevent the occurrence of mental or emotional breakdown.
2.	The goals of counselling are more limited, more concerned with the immediate situations as helping the individual function adequately in appropriate roles.	The goals of psychotherapy usually are more vast and hard to attain. It involves a complete change of basic character structure.
3.	Counselling prepares an individual to deal with the development task appropriate for his age. Adolescent who is being helped out regarding sexual problems, emotional independence from parents, preparation for an occupation and other tasks typical of his age, would receive counselling. It helps people to deal with emotional breakdown, which might arise due to failure in examinations, maladjustment in office, dissatisfaction with the job, etc.	Psychotherapy provides help to an individual suffering from emotional and nervous disorders such as a sexually harassed employee or a molested woman or a child facing the same problems.
4.	Counselling is more concerned with providing cure for narrowly situational matter, i.e., more peripheral issues.	Psychotherapy is more concerned with providing cure for mental illnesses; it is more central. Its aim is to help client handle not only the present but also future problem, i.e., more central.
5.	Normal anxiety is the business of counselling.	Neurotic anxiety is the business of psychotherapy.
6.	Counselling helps to attain a clear sense of identity. It deals with the utilization of resources.	Psychotherapy attempts to make change in the basic developmental structure. It deals with the personality changes.

Table 1.2	Differences between Counselling and Psychotherapy with Respect to Settings	
Sl. no.	*Counselling*	*Psychotherapy*
1.	Counselling permits reality testing in a somewhat sheltered situation.	Psychotherapy allows reality testing in a completely sheltered situation.
2.	Counselling may more often occur in educational settings or business organizations.	Psychotherapy occurs more in medical settings and is confidential.
3.	The session takes less duration as compared to psychotherapy and occurs less frequently.	The session takes longer duration and occurs frequently.

Table 1.3	Types of Clients Seeking Counselling and Psychotherapy	
Sl. no.	*Counselling*	*Psychotherapy*
1.	Counselling deals with the normal people. Counsellor is basically trained to deal with normal people.	Psychotherapy deals with the neurotic or psychotic patients. Psychotherapist is primarily trained to deal with abnormal clients.
2.	The concern with conscious is more characteristic of counsellor.	The concern with unconscious is more characteristic of psychotherapist.

Table 1.4 Qualifications Required and Methods followed by Counsellor and Psychotherapist

Sl. no.	Counsellor	Psychotherapist
1.	The counsellor should be qualified to deal with the conscious, i.e., which is apparent.	The psychotherapist should be qualified to deal with the unconscious i.e., which is not apparent and can be understood only with skilled analysis.
2.	A counsellor is relatively untrained and will have master's degree in social work or clinical psychology.	A psychotherapist will have a formal internship of two or more years and will be apt to hold a doctor's degree.
3.	A counsellor has basic training in personality theory, interviewing, research method, considerable background in biological and physical science, in sociology, mathematics and in community organization.	A psychotherapist has basic training in psychotherapy, personality theory, interviewing, research method, considerable background in biological and physical science, in sociology, mathematics and in community organization.
4.	A counsellor is concerned with preventive medical health with emphasis on prevention of disruptive deviation.	A psychotherapist is concerned with remediation with primary emphasis on present deviation with secondary attention to prevention.
5.	The counsellor may frequently make use of psychometric tools.	A therapist is more apt to make his individual assessment or diagnosis chiefly through a clinical interview.

Similarly, counselling too involves rapport, acceptance, support, status, control and limit on the relationship. The counsellor should possess the following qualities:

1. The ability to devote full attention to the counselee.
2. The quality to win the confidence of the client.
3. The ability to maintain the ethics of the relationship.
4. The right expertise and the willingness to guide the client in the right direction.
5. The ability to motivate and facilitate the development of the client.

When a counsellor moves towards a more ambiguous subject in his counselling he is moving towards psychotherapy. Ambiguity can occur with regard to topic, relationship or goals. Ambiguity leads to anxiety and anxiety leads of therapeutic relationship.

Section 1.4.2 is about the difference between Counselling and Instruction.

1.4.2 Difference between Counselling and Instruction

If the thunder on the left of counselling is psychotherapy, the thunder on the right is instruction. Some people like educational theorist treat them as same. In broad sense, both are concerned with helping an individual to develop so that he can take responsibility for himself and live a satisfied life. Some of these differences are discussed in Table 1.5:

Sl. no.	Counselling	Instruction
	Table 1.5 Differences between Counselling and Instruction	
1.	The individual determines goals as he sees them. In counselling, one has fewer preconceptions about what will be needed to help the individual.	Goals of instruction are determined by the society. What has to be covered in an algebra class is defined by the society.
2.	Counselling is given only to those who voluntarily request for it, perhaps to those who require it.	Instruction is beneficial to all and is basically imparted for the educational purposes.
3.	Counsellor undertakes additional training in the interviewing, psycho-metrics, occupational information and other competencies.	The instructor is trained in specific instructional technique and subject matter.
4.	Counsellor is responsible for an individual and so can be less judgmental.	Instructor is required to be judgmental and to operate as a representative of an educational institution with certain responsibilities determined by the institute.

1.5 Summary

It wouldn't be wrong to say that the rate at which the counselling services have grown prove that these services are in great demand. Life in present time has become full of stress and strain that it naturally gives rise to the need for seeking professional help. Counselling can provide answers to those anxieties resulting from stress and strain. An individual's personal and professional life suffers due to stress, which might be the result of lack of adjustment with his personal life or life at the work front. This may cause either mental or physical problems like deviation of mind, degeneration of body and other psychosomatic disorders. Psychotherapy and counselling are interrelated. The former helps the person deal with more serious pathological disorders and help him gain his/her mental balance, while the latter helps the person enhance the quality of his/her personal and professional life by providing right guidance. The people taking up these professions like counsellors, psychotherapist, and instructors have to be well qualified and well experienced to provide their services. They should be responsible enough to honour the ethics of their profession.

The chapter that follows will discuss the various approaches to counselling with their goals, procedures and skills required to attain the objectives of these theories.

Review Questions

1. With the consistent increase in the mental illness at work, the challenges before the corporate is manifold. Identify and discuss some of these challenges and rationalize the need for workplace counselling in business organizations today.

2. Outline and discuss the evolution of the concept and the practice of counselling in the last century. How has the perception of society changed towards counselling from the past to the present?

3. Highlight the similarities and the differences between Counselling, Psychotherapy and Instruction? Is it advisable to use these three terms interchangeably? Why or why not?

Chapter 2

Approaches to Counselling

In keeping with the complexity of human nature and the varying attempts to explain it as lucidly and succinctly as possible, several theories of human behaviour have been proposed. Each theory seeks to integrate its postulates consistently with the specified hypotheses constructed. The theory is then verified in terms of experimental findings or observational data. Further, a theory is integrated in what is known as a meaningful framework. Within this framework it predicts new relations and outcomes and seeks to obtain solutions to the anticipated problems. Scientists have stated most of the criteria of a good theory with great care. A theory is considered acceptable if it meets the stated criteria, the most important being precision, clarity and comprehensiveness, i.e., it should include within its scope as many facts or phenomena as possible, provide for empirical verifiability and stimulate research. The usefulness of a theory is considerably enhanced if it defines its terms operationally. These definitions help in developing suitable procedures for testing the derived propositions.

The substantive elements of a counselling theory include:

1. Assumptions regarding the nature of man
2. Belief regarding learning theory and change in behaviour of people
3. Commitment to certain goals of counselling
4. Definition of the role of the counsellor
5. Generic contribution made by the theory

Counselling theory may not necessarily derive from a specific philosophy, some assumptions must be made about what kind of a creature man is in order to construct a theory about counselling him. As we discuss theories, we will be able to identify, whether the theorist is assuming the innate goodness or evil of man, the problems attendant upon the human condition and the pliability of man, i.e., whether he is sufficiently plastic in nature that he can be shaped in one way or another by the interaction of genetic elements and environment or not.

Counselling theories also include beliefs about how people change or how people learn. Counselling constitutes a learning process, but theorists may agree or disagree on how learning occurs. Is it furthered by general atmosphere or by specific stimulus response situation? Change is the goal of counselling, but how it is brought about, there are different opinions about it.

Goals of counselling are related to providing a cure to various emotional afflictions in order to improve the mental health of the people. The goals of one theorist might be totally different from the goals of another theorist. A person could be considered to have been successfully treated by advocate of one theory but at the same time be seen in need of therapy by advocates of another theory. A good theory will be explicit and clear regarding its goals.

Role of a counsellor will differ with respect to the place and the manner in which the diagnosis is conducted. For example, some counsellors while diagnosing might make use of tests; case histories and screening interviews while other may not. There may be difference in terms of extent to which interpretation, advice and persuasion are thought to be the proper methods for the counsellor. There may be differences in terms of basic styles. These differences can be with regard to such special problems as dependency of the client, the communication problems and other elements, which may appear of help, define the role of the counsellor.

A theory that is completely abstract is a poor theory not because it is wrong but because it does not help us to understand the facts, which are already available. Different approaches to counselling are based on the varying conceptions of human personality structure and dynamics, and are subject to the limitations to which the personality theories are prone. The term *approach* is used in preference to theory as no single theory has yet been able to encompass all the aspects of counselling. The approaches to counselling have been classified in three main categories, which are being discussed in the following sections.

2.1 Psychoanalytic Approach to Counselling

Psychoanalysis was originated by Sigmund Freud, who developed his theory from his experience as a therapist and wrote about his work for a period of nearly fifty years prior to 1939. An edited multi-volume collection of Freud's complete works (Freud, 1953–1974) facilitates reference to this important germinal material. Psychoanalytic theory, is also sometimes referred to as *dynamic theory*, because of its emphasis on the interactions (dynamics) of unconscious processes "where conflicts arise between the need for tension reduction and the inhibition of basic instinctual drives." (Baker, 1985)

Freud's works were not initially considered important for the practice of counselling. His work focussed on the alleviation of serious emotional problems; counselling in its early years centred on decision-making, mainly about career choices. The introduction of *person-centred counselling*, opened the door for counsellors to deal with a broader range of human concerns and emotions, and since then the counselling profession has subsequently moved steadily towards increased involvement with clients suffering from emotional disturbances. As a result today counsellors are licensed to diagnose and treat emotional disorders in some states. Counsellors have embraced psychoanalytic theory as an important stream of thought, and many psychoanalytic concepts, for example, the unconscious, the ego and the defenses, have, in fact, entered the common man's language.

Freud's form of psychoanalysis was a very thorough, long-term helping process that placed heavy emphasis on the client's historical psychosexual development; the goal was for the client to gain insight on all aspects of his or her personality. Today, few practitioners, even psychoanalysts, practice that kind of treatment. But modern psychotherapists generally question whether in some cases such total analysis of the client's personality is necessary for the time and the money spent in such a process exceed most people's resources. Consequently, shorter-term counselling based on psychoanalytic theory is now a much more common form of treatment, and many counsellors who practice with one or more other theories as a base also use some psychoanalytic principles.

It would be difficult to overestimate Freud's contributions to the understanding of the human psyche and to the process of helping people resolve emotional problems through talking about them. Burke (1989) points out that much of the theoretical basis for today's psychotherapy is either a further development of Freud's work (Adler, 1927; Alexander, 1963; Erikson, 1963; Fromm, 1941, 1976; Jung, 1954; Sullivan, 1953) or a reaction against it in the form of the person-centred, Gestalt, cognitive, and behavioural systems. Psychoanalytic counselling and psychotherapy account for a very large proportion of helping services. The next section will explain Freud's conception of psychoanalysis and how it helps in resolving person's personal problems.

2.1.1 The Nature of People

Freud saw humans as biological beings driven by an instinctual desire for personal pleasure (gratification). The life force or libido was postulated as the energy source that propels people toward behaviour that satisfies the pleasure motive. Only through the process of socialization humans are redirected toward behaviour that allows satisfaction of personal needs in ways that are not destructive or unacceptable to others. If allowed to grow and develop without control, people would serve their own selfish pleasures without regard for the rights of others or the accomplishment of useful work. There is no element in Freudian theory related to any tendency on the part of humans toward self-actualization; rather, humans are seen as operating by the pleasure principle and in need of shaping toward positive endeavours. Let us examine Freud's Psychoanalytical principles one by one:

Psychosexual Development: In Freud's theory, pleasure is linked with sexuality, and libido is a driving force toward gratification. Freud postulated that the desire for sexual pleasure is a lifelong drive that begins in infancy and is first satisfied by sucking the mother's breasts. This first stage is called the **oral stage**; if the baby's oral needs are not met, greediness or acquisitiveness may result later (Corey, 1996). Anal, phallic, latency and genital stages each follows in turn, bringing needs that, if satisfied, allow growth toward psychological maturity. If the child's needs are not accepted by the parents and are not satisfied in acceptable ways, the probable consequence will be fixation on meeting these needs at a later period in ways that are not effective.

Freud's views on sexuality have resulted in a great deal of controversy over the years. Many people object to the idea that all pleasures have a sexual component and that sexuality is experienced from birth. To many, the idea that humans are sexually motivated beings who begin seeking satisfaction at birth is offensive. Some are of the opinion that Freud is not only incorrect but perverted. Others see truth in the theory of infantile sexuality but place less emphasis on sexual pleasure as the primary motivator of all human behaviour. Many women have seen his views of female sexuality, heavily influenced by the social strictures of the nineteenth century, to be offensive and inaccurate.

Whether or not one chooses to accept Freud's ideas about psychosexual development, there is much to be learnt from his work on the unconscious, the structure of personality and the defense mechanisms. Unfortunately, many counsellors have discounted this important work because his views on sexuality seem extreme to them or because his views on women and mental health, developed in Victorian times, do not pass muster today. The suggestion is that instead of rejecting Freud's contributions, a counsellor should use his work selectively in those areas where it can be applied in a contemporary context.

The Unconscious: One of the most important ideas introduced by Freud was the concept that people are unaware of much of their mental processes—that mental activity can be unconscious. A person's unconscious motivation is based on instinct as modified and socialized by the interaction with significant others, mainly parents, during the formative years. If the satisfaction of instinctual needs is blocked through ineffective parenting so that the acceptable means of expression cannot be found, then unconscious motivators will propel the individual to satisfy those needs by whatever means available. The key concept is that people frequently do not understand why they behave as they do, since motivation can be unconscious. This may be true even when a person seems to have a plausible explanation for particular behaviours. The plausible explanation may simply be a socially acceptable defense covering a motive of which the person is not aware. All behaviour is understood to be purposeful (as a means of satisfying drives) though the individual may not be aware of the purposes. Discovering motives and developing effective means of meeting needs is one of the tasks of counselling.

The Structure of Personality: The personality structure comprises the id, the ego, the superego and the gratification of libidinous urges. The id functions on the pleasure principle and is subject to the predicate error, i.e., it confuses the idea or image of an object for the object itself. The ego is essentially a part of the id which has been socialized as a result of its contact with reality. The ego, therefore, functions on the reality principle and has to often turn down the demands of the id. Consequently, tension develops between the id and the ego. Just as the ego develops from the id and is a part of it, the superego also develops from the id. However, the superego and ego are not the same and do not serve the same purpose. The superego is the moral governor of the individual. It is the individual's conscience. A very important distinction between the ego and the superego is that the former is conscious while the latter is not conscious. The id, owing to its primitive and unsocial zed nature, is raw, infantile and irrational. The superego partakes of the characteristics of the id. When the id desires gratification of its urge or wish, its energy is drawn and expended by the ego. The superego also uses the libidinal energy of the id for its activity. The ego and the superego have no independent source of energy. In all action, there is a transfer of energy from one to another. The sum total of all energy remains constant and this explains the principle of equilibrium of energy in the psychic system comprising the id, the ego and the superego. The libidinal urges emanating from the region of the id are gratified through the ego. Therefore, without the ego, the id is blind and helpless. But the demands of the id are not always manageable. Sometimes they may be grotesque and bizarre. They may even be incestuous. The ego cannot gratify such demands and turns them down. This process is known as **inhibition**. Inhibition is a normal process and it is one of the defense mechanisms commonly employed by the ego. Often the libidinal urges may come into direct conflict with the injunctions of the superego. The result is repression. A repressed idea, wish or desire is relegated to the depths of the unconscious or id but does not become extinct. A repressed wish or idea is dynamic and ever active and wants to thrust itself into the region of the conscious.

The human personality has two basic urges, namely, *Eros*—the urge to live, the life instinct, and *Thanatos*—the urge to die, the death instinct. The Eros is the creative force and the Thanatos is the destructive or self-destructive force. The ego has to deftly balance these two instinctual urges and personality development is a result of this process. Freud assumes that the early part of childhood is the most important in the personality development of the individual. The highly emotionally charged ideas called **complexes** are repressed during this early part of life and Freud explains that what the adult individual experiences as a problem is only the result of repressed complex in his early childhood. Psychotherapy or psychoanalysis is a method of unearthing these repressed complexes and this process is called **catharsis**. When a repressed idea is brought to the conscious and interpreted, it ceases to be a problem. The symptom caused by it disappears.

The psychoanalytic point of view, as explained by Freud, looks upon the individual as a biological entity craving for the gratification of instinctual urges. The present state or condition of the individual is determined by the active forces (libidinous gratifications, fixations, repressions, etc.) operating in his early childhood. The present environmental conditions as represented by the social forces, which have little, if any, role to play in the manner, in which libidinous urges are expressed.

Defense Mechanisms: When an individual is confronted with demands for which the ego has no solutions, anxiety results. The person becomes afraid because without ego-mediated solutions, he or she may directly express unacceptable impulses. The resulting behaviour may be both ineffective and embarrassing. In such circumstances, defenses come into play to soften the blow on the ego and reduce stress. For example, a student who is lagging behind in school may use the defense of denial to dismiss the problem or the defense of rationalization to explain why he or she can't do better. A defense mechanism works in the sense that it takes the pressure off the individual. Unfortunately, if the defense mechanisms are used repeatedly, the result is that the person dismisses many demands to perform and thus misses many opportunities to succeed at life tasks. According to psychoanalytic thinking, neurosis is said to occur when an individual uses defense mechanisms in interaction with other people to such an extent that few or no rewarding relationships are experienced. Psychosis results if the ego becomes so overwhelmed that its contact with external reality is severed and distorted thought patterns result.

Defense mechanisms are employed as a part of the unconscious process of a person's mental functioning. Therefore, it would rarely be useful to tell a client, "You are just being defensive." Counsellors must be able to recognize defenses and to help clients explore troublesome circumstances to find coping responses that can replace or reduce the defensive ones. But it is important to realize that there are times when everyone needs the temporary respite that a defense provides and that moderate defensiveness in the face of tough circumstances is healthy and necessary.

Common defense mechanisms include denial, rationalization, intellectualization, projection and regression. To get a further explanation and clarification on defensive mechanisms any general psychology text can be referred.

Freud described humans as instinctually motivated beings, seeking pleasures that have sexual roots. Development through the psychosexual stages in a nurturing environment allows the individual to develop a healthy personality in which the ego is strong. When the ego is not strong enough to face life's challenges, defenses are developed to protect the ego. Defenses serve a useful purpose, provided they are not overused as substitutes for coping with challenges. The dynamic process of personality includes unconscious thought; thus, people are not fully aware of all the motives behind their behaviour.

2.1.2 The Counselling Process

Fundamental of the psychoanalytic counselling process is the belief that people relegate material they cannot tolerate to the unconscious, using defense mechanisms (for instance, repression). Because crucial issues have been pushed out of awareness without being resolved, unmet needs keep intruding into the fabric of life. The process of counselling, then, encourages the client to dislodge unconscious material and resolve the conflicts contained therein.

The client is encouraged to talk as freely as possible about troublesome situations. Talking about these issues often leads to the recall of related thoughts that were repressed. In some cases, free association is used. In free association, the client is asked to suspend control over what he or she says and just let speech flow—regardless of how disconnected or bizarre the material seems. Sometimes dreams are also analyzed for clues to the unconscious.

Regardless of the methods of disclosure namely, problem discussion, free association or dream analysis, the counsellor tries to understand the client's motives and to interpret to the client his or her thoughts, feelings and behaviours. The counsellor depends on the knowledge of psychodynamics to lead the client toward new insights. The counsellor also uses events in his or her own relationship with the client as samples of the client's behaviour that can be interpreted. There is often substantial discharge of emotion by the client (referred to as catharsis), as painful circumstances are explored but the new insights are achieved.

With interpretation serving as an important counselling lead, psychoanalytic counselling depends heavily on the counsellor's knowledge of personality dynamics. Psychoanalytic counselling places the major emphasis on the in-depth exploration stage of counselling.

2.1.3 Contribution to the Generic Model of Counselling

The greatest contribution of the psychoanalytic approach to the practice of contemporary counselling is the theory of personality and its application to the diagnostic process. The structure of personality as posited by Freud provides a convenient framework for analyzing human functioning and unconscious motivation. It helps the counsellor consider the comparative contribution of impulse, reason and conscience to the behaviour of a given client. Along with the tripartite structure of personality comes the concept that the ego develops strength through positive experience with the external world (environment). At times, the strength of the ego is not equal to the demands placed on it, and the client becomes defensive. The nature of defense mechanisms, the purposes they serve and the problems they cause are all issues that are important to the diagnostic process. Transference, counter transference and resistance are manifestations of the process of ego defense.

Elements of Freud's original methods of conducting therapy certainly survive today. Many counsellors use interpretation as a predominant lead, attempting to help clients see their experiences using a psychodynamic structure of personality. Such counsellors work heavily with clients' reports about their experiences in everyday life and also make use of observations of the client's interaction with the counsellor as material for interpretation. Dream analysis and free association are used less as material for the interpretive process than they once were, but they remain a window of the unconscious experience of the client. Much of the psychoanalytic counselling is in-depth exploration, with comparatively less emphasis on relationship building or action plans. However, all the three stages of the counselling process will receive some attention from most psychoanalytic counsellors.

Psychoanalytic counselling focuses on both cognitive and affective material and both the counsellor and the client are active in the process of counselling. A psychoanalytic counsellor will not be content by simply listening to a client talk about his experiences but he will try to explore the depth of the client's subconscious. It is the client's responsibility to reveal self. Psychoanalysis is not about building relationship with the client but is about trying to find a cure for disturbed. It is the counsellor's responsibility to interpret the client's experiences so that the client will gain greater insight into his personality and his ego will increase its coping capacity, directing effective rather than defensive responses to environmental demands.

Psychoanalysis was found to have varying degrees of success with different types of clients plagued by different kinds of psychological ailments whereas counselling is concerned with clients who have problems that do not compare by any stretch of imagination with those of psychoneurosis or psychosis. Most of the problems that require counselling are simple, mild to moderately disturbing and are usually of a brief duration. The psychoanalytic technique, as practiced, requires enormous time and most counselling clients cannot spare that much time for therapy. Due to such practical reasons, the psychoanalytic approach is not usually employed in counselling situations.

Some of the major criticisms levelled against psychoanalysis are as follows:

1. The deterministic view of man portrays him as a nasty person driven relentlessly by animalistic instincts, unconscious needs and repressed urges.

2. Freud's system implies the dualism of the body and the mind as distinct phenomena, which emphasized psychosomatic phenomena or reaction formations.

3. Too much emphasis is placed upon childhood experiences and the present maladjustment is sought to be explained on the basis of some experience in early childhood. This makes the individual feel helpless and incapable of overcoming his difficulties.

4. In Freud's system all behaviour is determined by the psychic energy, which can flow into or towards one object or another. This explanation minimizes the importance of situational events.

5. Freud minimizes the role of rationality in human behaviour. But in his practice of therapy Freud appears to unwittingly take recourse to rationality. In psychoanalysis, the repressed material is brought out and interpreted for the client and this makes him understand his irrational fears, complexes, etc., that is, the individual becomes more knowledgeable.

6. The constructs have not been shown to be empirically demonstrable or verifiable.

2.2 Behaviouristic Approach to Counselling

Counselling and psychotherapy are concerned with behaviour change and, therefore, according to some theorists, must involve the applications of the principles of learning or learning theory. Learning here is understood as changes in behaviour which are relatively longlasting and which are not due to maturation or due to physiological factors like fatigue, effect of drugs, etc. However, counselling, by and large, has developed outside the learning theory. It is only in recent times that the principles of learning theory have been sought to be applied in the counselling technique. One such application is in the form of behaviouristic approach to counselling.

The purpose of behavioural counselling is to change ineffective and self-defeating behaviour into effective and winning behaviour, and only measurable behaviour change is regarded as evidence of successful counselling. Generally, behavioural counsellors do not regard hypothetical concepts about mental functioning, such as the unconscious, as important to the counselling process. Self-understanding is not an outcome goal.

No single author is credited with the development of behavioural counselling. Joseph Wolpe's (1958) work on reciprocal inhibition applied the principles of classical conditioning to changing neurotic behaviour. B.F. Skinner (1971) is widely recognized for his work in developing operant conditioning techniques used in behavioural counselling, although he was not a therapist himself. Together with modelling, operant conditioning and classical conditioning are the principal methods employed in behavioural counselling. Lazarus (1989), Wolpe (1990) and Kazdin (1995) offer contemporary applications of behavioural methods. Interest in behavioural methods increased during the late 1960s, when many people became dis-enchanted with Rogerian methods as a predominant approach to counselling. During 1970's, narrowly conceived behavioural approaches declined in popularity, and some behavioural counsellors (for example, Meichenbaum, 1977) turned their attention to the thought processes that mediated behaviour, blending their work with that of cognitive counsellors. Lazarus (1989) has described a broad array of behavioural techniques, each of which provides clients with new opportunities for learning strategies of self-management.

The learning approach employed in the behaviouristic model could be either the classical conditioning or the operant conditioning model. While it is not necessary to go into the details of conditioning, it is essential that the basic principles be grasped. From the behaviouristic point of view, all behaviour—adjustive or maladjustive—is primarily learnt in the same manner. Hence, it should be modifiable by employing suitable learning principles. All behaviour of organisms, including human beings, ranging from simple to complex behaviour, is learnt. Four basic principles (DCRR) are involved in all types of learning. The first is *drive* or motivation, which impels the organism to act. The drives could be primary (tissue needs) or secondary (learnt). Without drive there can be no action; consequently, no learning can occur. The second principle is *cue* or stimulus. For instance, an organism is hungry and is stimulated by a variety of different objects, including food. The stimulation by food would be effective while the other stimulations in this situation would not be effective. Thus, drive and cue together determine the response of the organism. The third principle of all learning is *response*. Stimulation leads to responses. The relevance of a response to a situation at a given time is determined by its survival value or its serviceability or usefulness to the organism. For example, the ringing of a bell elicits different responses like the turning of the head in the direction of the sound, the pricking of ears, salivation and so on. Among these, salivation is the relevant response because it has survival value or its serviceability or usefulness to the organism. If there is danger then running or flight would be the relevant response. Usually the relevant responses are reinforced. *Reinforcement* is the fourth principle of learning. It is of the nature of a reward. A response that is reinforced or rewarded is acquired; while a response that is not rewarded is not acquired.

The behaviouristic approach to counselling employs the four principles of learning namely, drive, cue, response and reinforcement. Every response is considered modifiable by the use of an appropriate system of reinforcement. The behaviouristic approach differs from the psychoanalytic approach and medical approach with regard to its attitude towards maladaptive or maladjusted behaviour. In psychoanalysis approach or clinical approach, the concern is with the past, i.e., as to how a particular symptom or syndrome has been caused. The therapist delves deep into the life history or case history of the client to identify the causes. The dispelling of these causes is expected to rid the client of the undesirable symptom(s). In sharp contrast to this view, the behaviour therapist is least concerned with the past. He is not interested in knowing what caused the symptom. He is concerned with treating the present symptoms. The past for him is something, which cannot be changed. It is irrelevant. But the future can be modified. Past, however, is not existent and, therefore, unmodifiable. There is no need for delving into the past life history of the client. It serves no real purpose. Therapy essentially consists of several simple steps such as: (a) identifying the undesirable, unwanted, maladjusted and maladaptive behaviour; (b) careful analysis of the maladaptive behaviour into small units; and (c) eliminating the maladaptive unit by using an appropriate technique involving an operant conditioning procedure. There are different approaches stressing different aspects of the learning theory.

Dollard and Miller's (1950) reinforcement theory is a thought provoking approach. They define neurosis as learned behaviour. What is more interesting is that, according to them, neurotic conflicts are taught by parents and learnt by children. Thus, unwanted and maladjusted behaviour is acquired or learnt. This includes phobias, compulsions, hysterical symptoms, regression, reaction formation, alcoholism, etc. In the long run many behavioural reactions become maladaptive. They increase the misery though in the beginning the results appear favourable. In the treatment of the clients, therapy involves the creation of a new type of social situation, which is the opposite of that responsible for inducing repression. The new social situation provides for gradually over-coming the repressions under permissive social conditions. The therapeutic situation is characterized by permissiveness, which leads to the removal of repression. Rogers (1951) underlines the importance of the permissiveness of the counselling situation. The therapeutic process is a slow and difficult one because fear and anxiety accompany the repressed ideas and even though the therapist is permissive and neutral, the client cannot help experiencing these unpleasant emotions. The client is encouraged to verbalize his/her experiences, i.e., talk about things and events related to his/her life, and in this process give vent to his/her emotions.

2.2.1 The Nature of People

Behaviourists see human behaviour as a function of heredity and environment. This view is often called **deterministic**, because both elements that shape behaviour are largely beyond the individual's control. One is born with certain inherited equipment that cannot be changed, so the only variable left that can be altered after birth is the environment. What one learns from the environment determines one's behaviour; changing the environment changes behaviour.

Behaviourists hold no general view that humankind tends toward good or evil. Given adequate hereditary characteristics, any individual can become good or evil depending on what he or she learns from the environment. Constructs such as the self-concept, the ego and the unconscious have no meaning in describing human nature in a strict behavioural system. Behaviourists do not necessarily deny that such mechanisms exist but say that, if they do exist, it is impossible for the counsellor to observe or manipulate them. The description of humans as capable of learning is sufficient to behavioural counselling. A lot of knowledge about how people learn exists, and it makes sense to use it to influence them toward effective behaviour.

2.2.2 The Counselling Process

The important steps involved in the counselling process are:

Goal Setting: Behavioural counselling places great emphasis on clear definition of goals. Goals are stated in terms of behaviour change so that the observation will provide evidence that can be measured. A goal such as "I'd like to get along better with my parents" would not be acceptable. A more specific goal, such as "I will be home for dinner at least four nights a week to share some part of my life in pleasant conversation", would be seen as a step toward a better relationship with parents. Because the goal is specific, behaviour, counsellor and client are able to assess the extent of accomplish-ment. Krumboltz (1966) states that many behavioural counselling efforts fail because of lack of specific goals.

Frequently, clients are referred for counselling by *significant others* who are dissatisfied with their behaviour. The counsellors following behavioural approach are perhaps more amenable than the other counsellors to the suggestions of significant others that the problematic behaviours of the client needs to change. For example, a child may be referred to counselling because he or she fails to meet the curfew standards of her parents. A behavioural counsellor might centre his or her goal on changing the unwanted behaviour without devoting extra time to understand the client's affective experiences in the historical relationships with parents or peers.

The client is usually provided with the opportunity to participate in the goal-setting process, even when problem behaviours are quite obvious to the counsellor from the outset. In some instances, the client may set his or her own goals in mind, as in the case of a person trying to gain control over eating habits or a person who is trying to free himself from some fears like fear of heights.

Because goals are specific, the counsellor and the client have direct means for documenting change. It is possible to identify and count specific target behaviours that are to be eliminated or increased as a result of counselling. The frequency of occurrence of the target behaviour at the outset of counselling is considered to be the baseline against which progress is measured.

Strategies for Change: Counselling strategies are based on the principles of learning. In cognitive-behavioural approaches, the client is taught to think differently about his or her behaviour or is simply conditioned to behave differently. Operant conditioning is one of the most common procedures used in behavioural counselling. The procedure, which can be used to eliminate undesirable behaviour or to develop positive behaviour, uses reinforcement techniques. If the counsellor is attempting to help the client eliminate an undesirable behaviour, he or she first of all determines what environmental conditions are supporting the behaviour and then arranges for the reinforcers to be eliminated. A child who misbehaves at home or in school is frequently seeking the attention of parents or teachers. Often parents and teachers pay attention to the child only when he or she is misbehaving. In an operant conditioning plan, the counsellor teaches parents or teachers to withhold attention to misbehaviour but to pay attention to the child when he or she does something positive, such as doing his or her chores or homework. If significant others consistently reward positive behaviour with attention and fail to respond to negative behaviour, which is just a child's way of seeking attention, the child will learn good manners and behaviours. In operant conditioning, the client's behaviour is selectively reinforced to increase desired behaviour in a variety of way—for example, through positive attention, awarding free time to children after completion of tasks, rewarding them for free candies and so forth. Undesirable behaviour may be discouraged through negative consequences, such as isolation or withholding of privileges.

Desensitization training (Wolpe, 1958, 1990), used to help clients reduce or eliminate irrational fears or phobias, is based on the principles of classical conditioning. First, the client is asked to be as specific as possible about the condition that produces the anxiety, such as fear of heights. A list is then made that arranges frightening conditions in a hierarchy from least frightening (for example, standing on a chair) to most frightening (for example, standing at the edge of a cliff though safely behind a railing). The client is then taught to relax his or her body through breath and muscle control. When completely relaxed, the client is asked to think about the frightening circumstances, starting with the least frightening, while the counsellor continues to encourage relaxation and the positive feelings that accompany relaxation. Finally, the client can be encouraged to experiment with real feared circumstances while practicing self-relaxation techniques.

Modelling is yet another process whereby the client is taught new behaviours. A model (may be a counsellor or a peer in group counselling or an assistant) demonstrates to the client how to behave in a situation with which the client has difficulty, and the client observes his or her performance, giving the client access to the thought processes that lead to behavioural consequences. This procedure may be applied more informally by placing the client with effective models in real-life situations, such as work place or school.

The discussion on behavioural procedures presented here is far from exhaustive. The common thread in these and other behavioural strategies is the establishing of conditions for new learning to take place. This often requires the manipulation of conditions in the client's life external to counselling, and significant others may become involved in consultation on how to support behaviour change in the client.

2.2.3 Contribution to the Generic Model of Counselling

Behavioural counselling places very little emphasis on the history of how a problem has developed, except for an assessment of the learning conditions in the environment that have sustained an unwanted behaviour or failed to support a desired one. This approach depends on learning theory, rather than personality theory, as a basis for understanding a client's behaviour. In that respect, it is substantially different from the other approaches discussed in this chapter. Self-understanding and insight into developmental issues are not the main focus of behavioural counselling.

The process of behavioural counselling moves quickly from the first stage (initial disclosure) to the third stage (action planning). The first stage is accomplished without special emphasis on empathy, acceptance or genuineness. These conditions are simply helpful in learning what the client's problems are. Once the problems are identified, goals are set rather quickly as specifically as possible. Goals address specific target behaviour, and behavioural counsellors emphasize the development of specific goals more than any other system of counselling. The main emphasis of behavioural counselling is to deal with the present problems without digging up the past and is very effective in relieving irrational fears (phobias), in modifying the behaviour of children who have difficulty adapting to and making use of classroom environments, and in helping clients overcome various addictions. Counsellors whose primary allegiance is to approaches that are more insight oriented often use behavioural strategies for these specific problems.

Behavioural counselling has been presented in its most conservative conception in this chapter to show how much it can contrast with some of the other theoretical orientations presented. However, it is important to understand that the notion that behavioural counsellors are cold and mechanistic toward their clients is unfounded. Their procedures are dictated by their belief that the most effective means of helping is through setting conditions for new learning rather than through extensive discussion of emotions rooted in developmental experiences.

2.3 Humanistic Approach or Person-centred Counselling

Carl Rogers (1942, 1957, 1961, 1980, 1986) is known as the founder of the **person-centred approach** to counselling. Two other names, nondirective counselling and client-centered counselling, were attached to this approach in Rogers' earlier writings, and a majority of the references to the system are to be found under client-centred counselling or client-centred therapy. The change to a person-centred approach reflects Rogers' (1980) later recognition that his system worked in any setting in which a helper sets out to promote human psychological growth and that many of those who are helped (for example, students in a classroom) do not think of themselves as clients.

Rogers' approach to the helping process was presented initially as an alternative to psychoanalytic psychotherapy, in which he was first trained. Because his views of human nature (1942) appealed to educators and his method of counselling did not require extensive psychological training, the person-centred approach was adopted by many then-practicing counsellors and it had a great influence on the preparation of new counsellors. Rogers' work is regarded as one of the principal forces in shaping current counselling and psychotherapy.

Rogers did not present his approach as a systematic theory until 1947 when he presented it in his Presidential address to the *American Psychological Association*. The approach caught the attention of psychologists because it was related to psychology more than to medicine. The course of treatment proposed was relatively brief compared to that of psychoanalysis. The major concepts of client-centred theory thus do not arise from psychopathology. Its aim was not to cure sick people but to help people live more satisfying and creative lives. Rogers was influenced to a considerable extent by the phenomenological psychology popular during that period. He is also counted as one of the important protagonists of the humanistic approach popularly known as the *third force* in psychology.

Client-centred therapy, i.e, the practical application of humanistic psychology made a great impact on the academic scene. According to Rogers, in any kind or type of psychotherapy the underlying basic theme is the helping relationship. In all human interactions, such as mother-child, teacher-pupil, manager-subordinate, therapist-client, etc. the helping relationship is fundamental. This relationship is intended to facilitate the growth of the person receiving help. Such a growth in individuals is aimed at improving their functioning and/or accelerating their maturity. This is usually called **psychological growth** or **psychological maturity**. Counselling aims at bringing about psychological growth or maturity in the client. The helping relationship is also generally a one-to-one relationship. It could also be in some specific cases an individual-group relationship.

2.3.1 The Nature of People

In person-centered counselling, human beings are seen as possessing positive goodness and the desire to become fully functioning, i.e., to live as effectively as possible. This view of human nature contrasts with the Freudian view that the people possess such impulses, which, if inadequately socialized, will lead to behaviour, that is destructive to themselves and others. According to Rogers, if people are permitted to develop freely, they will flourish and become positive, achieving individuals. Because of the faith in human nature expressed in Rogers' theory, it is considered a humanistic approach to counselling.

Person-centred counselling is based on a theory of personality referred to as *self-theory*. One's view of oneself within the context of environment influences one's actions and personal satisfactions. If provided with a nurturing environment, people will grow with confidence toward self-actualization—becoming all they can be. If their development is restricted and if they do not receive the love and support of significant others, they will see themselves as lacking in worth and regard others as untrustworthy. Behaviour will become defensive (self-protective), and growth toward self-actualization will be hampered.

An important principle of self-theory is the belief that person's perceptions of himself or herself in relation to the environment including significant others are reality for that person. Thus, if an individual sees himself or herself as incompetent or parents as mean, he or she will act on that belief, even if others view the person as brilliant or the parents as kind. Telling an underachieving student that he or she is capable seldom makes much difference because the assessment probably is in conflict with the student's personal reality. Personal reality may be changed through counselling but usually not by such a direct intervention as substituting the judgment of the helper for that of the client.

Rogers attaches enormous importance to helping relationships. These may often be looked upon as nurturing and uplifting contacts among people. This can be exemplified by enumerating the basic characteristics of all helping relationships. The main characteristics of the helping relationship are as follows:

1. Helping relationship is meaningful to the persons involved—it implies mutual self-commitment.
2. It has a marked tone of feeling, i.e., the individuals who are involved experience certain emotional states.
3. It implies integrity—the persons involved are intellectually and emotionally honest with each other.
4. It can exist by mutual consent only, i.e., there is no compulsion. No one can be compelled to be helpful and similarly no person can be compelled to receive help.
5. It comes into existence or becomes necessary when one is in need of some kind of help, which another can reasonably provide. For instance, an individual may need information, advice or assistance in a particular situation while another individual may have the necessary knowledge and capacity to provide him with the required help owing to his experience, position or situation.
6. It involves communication and interaction. This may involve non-verbal behaviour, such as facial expressions, gestures and the like and also direct verbal communication.
7. It is often structured, i.e., it is not vague and amorphous. The helping individual knows what sort of help he could possibly provide and the individual receiving help knows what kind of help he is in need of.
8. It is sustained through mutual co-operation and collaboration. If a certain kind of help provided is not useful, the receiver will indicate the same, and the helping person will naturally modify his approach.
9. The helping person must have a sense of security. An insecure person obviously cannot be of much help to the individual who is in need of help.
10. The goal or the object of the helping relationship is to change the client positively.

2.3.2 The Counselling Process

Rogers viewed humans as positive and self-actualizing by nature, and so he conceived the counsellor's role as providing conditions that would permit self-discovery and that would encourage the client's natural tendency toward personal growth. If the counsellor completely accepts each client as a person, relates empathically to the client's reality, and behaves in a genuine way (behaviour is congruent with feelings), the client will be free to discover and express the positive core of his or her being. As clients come to perceive themselves more positively in the nurturing environment, they will be able to function more effectively. Counsellors not only provide the nurturing environment that may be missing elsewhere in clients' lives but also serve as a role model of how fully functioning persons relate with others.

The underlying philosophical view of human nature is far more important to the practice of person-centred counselling than is any particular set of techniques or any body of knowledge. It has been said that in person-centred counselling, the helpers learn how to be a counsellor rather than how to do counselling. Counsellors must be comfortable enough within themselves to become fully involved with the worlds of their clients without fear of losing their own sense of wholeness. Besides this counsellors must care enough for their clients to be willing to experience their pain. Through all this, counsellors must be able to retain their own sense of separateness and emotional perspective over the client's difficulties. Because clients are seen as having the potential to solve their own problems, counsellors are not perceived as having expert knowledge to share with clients.

There is extensive use of silence, acceptance, restatement, empathy and immediacy, with the client taking the lead on what is discussed and being responsible for outcomes. If a need for further information is perceived in the course of a discussion, the counsellor may encourage the client to seek information outside the counselling session. A purely person-centred counsellor would not be likely to use tests, although a counsellor who uses some person-centred procedures might include some testing at the client's request. Person-centred counsellors encourage careful self-exploration but they tend to avoid confrontation and interpretation as tools for hastening insight. There is little focus on specific action planning except as initiated by the client. It is assumed that as the client becomes free to actualize his or her potential through the exploration process, behaviour change will occur naturally and without prompting from the counsellor.

However, sometimes the term client-centered is somewhat misleading. All therapies—the orthodox psychoanalytic and the more recent approaches—are basically client-centred. The goal of all therapy is to help the client. So the object of every system of therapy is the betterment and well being of the client. It is not as if the other therapists are disinterested in the well being of clients. On the contrary they also have the same objectives but make use of the different techniques to achieve those objectives. Rogers uses the term client-centred therapy to emphasize the role the client has to play. In psychoanalytic therapy, for example, the client has a passive role. The therapist is at the centre of the stage. It is he who directs the course of the therapy, interprets the client's communications and terminates the sessions. In the context of the client-centred therapy, the therapist is not supposed to play the big brother role. He does not direct the course of therapy nor does he offer interpretations. The client, in the client-centered approach, is always encouraged to rely on himself.

2.3.3 Essential Conditions for Personality Change

According to Rogers (1957), the conditions necessary to change the personality of the clients are as follows:

1. The counselee and the counsellor should be in psychological contact with each other.
2. The counselee is in a state of incongruence and hence is vulnerable and anxious (vulnerability is the condition of the individual whose experience is discordant with his self-structure and thus capable of creating tension and psychological disorganization).
3. The counsellor is congruent and integrated, that is, he is free from anxiety and tension. Hence relationship with the counselee should be genuine and should not cause any disharmony in counselee.
4. The counsellor should have unconditional positive regard for the counselee. (The counsellor should not have any reservations. He should accept the counselee as he is and should not impose any preconditions.)
5. The counsellor experiences an empathic understanding of the counselee's internal frame of reference and so he tries to communicate his experience to the counselee. (By internal frame of reference is meant the subjective world of the individual, which is available to himself and to no one else.)
6. The counsellor should exhibit empathy and warmth to counselee so that he (counselee) appreciates and understands the counsellor's unconditional positive regard towards him to a reasonable extent. (The client has some understanding of the counsellor's position.)

2.3.4 Contribution to the Generic Model of Counselling

The work of Carl Rogers has made a great contribution to the generic model of counselling presented in this book. The obvious contribution is his clear description of the helping relationship that forms the substance of the first stage of the counselling process and sustains trust through the next stages as well. Because of Rogers' work, counsellors have learned to become better listeners. Even counsellors who prefer more active and counsellor-initiated methods have come to recognize the importance of employing relationship-building conditions to encourage their clients to reveal significant elements of their personal reality. It has been said that the counselling must begin where the client is—and to learn where the client is, most counsellors employ methods that Rogers defined.

A second important contribution, which owes its origin to Rogers' statements about the nature of people, is that the clients are ultimately responsible for their own lives. Even though some counsellors may not be as optimistic as Rogers in believing that all persons are fundamentally good, most counsellors recognize that the counsellor cannot and should not attempt to control a client's actions (except in instances in which physical safety is a real concern). Counsellors of essentially all theoretical persuasions now maintain that they are working to help clients achieve their own goals.

Person-centred counselling is based on a positive view of human nature that is consonant with views of freedom and self-determination. Rogers has described a methodology that can be learned relatively easily by persons who are themselves fully functioning. Because Rogers and his colleagues have demonstrated through a strong research program that person-centred counselling works with a wide variety of clients, many of his ideas have been incorporated into other counselling models.

2.4 Summary

Different approaches to understand counselling have been categorized into psychoanalysis, behaviourism and humanism. Each of this theory has been discussed with reference to assumptions regarding the nature of man; belief regarding learning theory and change in behaviour of people; commitment to certain goals of counselling; definition of the role of the counsellor; and generic contribution made by the approach discussed.

Chapter 3 focuses on the goals of the counselling and how a counsellor with specific personality traits helps in achieving these goals.

Review Questions

1. What is good theory? Highlight and discuss some of the substantive elements of a counselling theory.

2. Psychoanalytical approach to counselling emphasizes on the interaction of the unconscious processes. How does this approach help in resolving the personal problems of the clients?

3. Behaviouristic approach to counselling relies on the present state of the client's situation rather than relying on the past as in the case of Psychotherapy. Do you think it is better strategy to handle client's problems? Why or why not?

4. Which of the major learning theories govern the behaviouristic approach to counselling? Discuss with examples.

5. According to humanistic approach to counselling, what are the main characteristics of helping relationship? How does the counsellor try to bring a positive change in the client's personality and behaviour?

Chapter 3

Goals of Counselling

What is the expected result from counselling? There is an element of uncertainty attached to the results expected from counselling services as the results of these services are not measurable. Therefore, different individuals have different perceptions of what can be expected. Individuals preparing to become counsellors, those who seek counselling, parents, teachers, school administrators and governmental agencies all differ in what they hope will result from the counselling experience. Such expectations are, of course, germane to the counselling process. However, the ultimate decision about what the goals of counselling shall be should rest with the counsellor and the client as a team. In the following section we will discuss the major goals of counselling.

3.1 Five Major Goals of Counselling

As we have already discussed in Chapter 2 on the various approaches to counselling that counselling theorists do not always agree on appropriate counselling goals and so statements of counselling goals are bound to be general, vague, and saturated with implications. However, the following five major goals are often stated: (a) facilitating change in client's behaviour, (b) improving the client's ability to establish and maintain relationships, (c) enhancing the client's effectiveness and ability to cope, (d) promoting the decision-making process, and (e) facilitating client potential and development. Now, let us discuss these goals in details:

Facilitating Behaviour Change: Almost all theorists indicate that the goal of counselling is to bring about a change in client's behaviour which will enable the client to live a more productive, satisfying life as the client defines it within society's limitations. However, the way theorists talk about changes in behaviour varies greatly. Rogers and Dymond (1961) see changes in client's behaviour as a necessary result of the counselling process although specific behaviours receive little or no emphasis during the counselling experience.

Dustin and George (1977), on the other hand, suggest that the counsellor must establish specific counselling goals. They believe that a shift from general goals to specific goals enables both the client and the counsellor to understand precisely the specific change that is desired. They point out that specific behavioural goals have an additional value. The client is better able to see any change that occurs.

Krumboltz (1966) suggests three criteria for judging counselling goals. They are: (a) the goals of counselling should be capable of being stated differently for each individual client, (b) the goals of counselling for each client should be compatible with, though not necessarily identical to, the values of his counsellor and (c) the degree to which the goals of counselling are attained by each client should be observable.

Improving Relationships: Much of one's life is spent in social interaction with other individuals, yet many clients have a major problem relating to other people. This problem may be conceptualized as the result of the client's poor self-image, which causes him or her to act defensively in relationships, or it may be seen as the result of inadequate social skills. Whatever the theoretical approach, counsellors work with clients to help them improve the quality of their relationships with others. Difficulties in relationships can range from the family and marital problems of adults to the problems at work to the peer group interaction difficulties to the adjustment problems of an elementary school child. In every case the counsellor is striving to help the clients improve the quality of their lives by becoming more effective in their interpersonal relationships.

Enhancing Coping Skills: Almost all individuals run into difficulties in the process of growing up. Few of us completely achieve all of our developmental tasks, and the various unique expectations and requirements imposed on us by significant others often lead to problems. Certainly, inconsistency on the part of significant others can result in children's learning behaviour patterns that are inefficient, ineffective or both. These learned coping patterns may serve the individual well in most situations, but in time, new interpersonal or occupational role demands may create an overload and produce excessive anxiety and difficulty for the individual. Helping individuals learn to cope with new situations and new demands is an important goal of counselling.

Promoting Decision-making: To some, the goal of counselling is to enable the individual to make critical decisions. It is not the counsellor's job, they say, to decide which decisions the client should make or to choose alternate courses of action. The decisions are the client's, and the client must know why and how the decisions were made. Client learns to estimate the probable consequences in personal sacrifice, time, energy, money, risk, and the like. The client also learns to explore the range of values that are related to the situation and to bring these values into full consciousness in the decision-making process.

Counselling helps individuals obtain information, clarify and sort out personal characteristics and emotional concerns that may interfere with or be related to the decisions involved. It helps these individuals acquire an understanding not only of their abilities, interests and opportunities but also of the emotions and attitudes that can influence their choices and decisions.

Facilitating the Client's Potential: Developing the client's potential is a frequently emphasized, although ambiguous, counselling goal. Certainly few theorists would disagree with the idea that counselling seeks to promote the growth and development of clients by giving them the opportunity to learn ways to use their abilities and interests to the maximum. This goal can be viewed as one of improving personal effectiveness. Blocher (1966) suggests that first, counselling seeks to maximize an individual's possible freedom within the limitations set by himself and his environment, and second, counselling seeks to maximize the individual's effectiveness by giving him control over his environment and the responses within him that are evoked by the environment.

Such an emphasis means that counsellors work to help people learn how to overcome excessive smoking or drinking, to take better care of their health, and to overcome shyness, stress and depression. They help people to learn how to overcome sexual dysfunctions, drug addiction, compulsive gambling, overweight, and fears and anxieties. At the same time, counsellors can help people with their interpersonal problems, with emotional problems, and with the development of learning and decision-making skills (Krumboltz and Thoresen, 1976).

3.1.1 Commonality of Goals

The previous description of the kinds of goals that various counsellors emphasize fails to recognize certain points about counselling goals. First, as Shertzer and Stone (1980) pointed out, the goals expressed by differing counselling theorists may reflect their own needs rather than those of the clients. Blackham (1977), however, suggests that while the counsellor does provide some direction for the counselling process, both counsellor and client decide which goals are to be pursued and how.

Second, perhaps there are more likenesses than differences among the statements of counselling goals. Certainly all of the theorists seem to recognize the broader goal of helping the client to feel better, to function at a higher level, to achieve more and to live up to his or her potential.

Third, the focus of all counselling goals is the achievements of personal effectiveness that is both satisfactory to the individual and within society's limitations. Thus, many of the presumed difference in counselling goals shrink in importance and become simply differences in terms of the criteria used to judge the counsellor's effectiveness. In addition, the differences in the way counselling goals are formulated may result from the differences in the way counsellors attempt to help clients.

3.2   Role of a Counsellor

The counsellor's role has been redefined and expanded from that of an expert or specialist who deals with his clients exclusively on a one-to-one basis to that of a staff-consultant and agent of institutional change. This is a very significant development. The counsellor can be seen in the role of a consultant-counsellor, and he is increasingly involved with consulting academic staff and teaching them skills ancillary to counselling. The consultant-counsellor attempts to:

1. Enhance teachers' sensitivity to student problems of personal growth (Rao, 1967).
2. Demonstrate the application of psychological principles of learning to human problem solving.
3. Improve the effectiveness of the academic faculty in institutions of higher learning.

Another welcome trend is the extension of counselling services to new areas. The early counselling services were primarily concerned with younger people, especially students in schools and in colleges. The interesting feature of modern demographic trends is the increase in the proportion of the population in the older age groups in almost all countries and this poses several pertinent problems, which have not been sufficiently researched. While counselling does not underestimate the importance of its service to growing people it is now also looking towards assisting middle-aged and older people. There is another group of clients whom counsellors are getting actively interested in. This group comprises women, especially young and middle-aged. The high-risk students, i.e., those who are not likely to make good grades, are also drawing the counsellor's attention. They appear to be in greater need of intensive academic counselling. Similarly, family counselling and counselling of minority people and immigrant populations are also promising areas in which counselling is branching out.

A couple of decades back there was a dramatic rise in the use of behavioural counselling. Notwithstanding the enormous experimental research using the principles of reinforcement, shaping, desensitization, aversive conditioning, etc., behavioural counselling has still not been found to be quite acceptable and applicable in all situations. This has given rise to a lively controversy, which centres on behavioural counselling and appears less related to its ability ·to produce changes in people than to the moral and ethical questions involved. Humanistically oriented counsellors are distressed by the notion of the control of behaviour and they frequently make the charge that advocates of behaviour modification are not sufficiently sensitive to needs, such as personal goals and freedom of growth of the clients. Behavioural counsellors maintain that their methods do not entail any threat to individual freedom of choice. However, the limitations of behavioural counselling, such as failure to demonstrate the durability of the changes produced, amelioration of the self-defeating behaviour of such groups as alcoholics, drug addicts and the like, have dampened their enthusiasm and there is revived interest in the humanistic-oriented approach.

3.3 The Counsellor as a Person

Before we can focus on what happens with the client during the counselling process, we should consider the other person involved in therapeutic intervention—the counsellor. In his professional behaviour, counsellor draws on three somewhat different areas, such as personal qualities, professional knowledge and specific counselling skills. These three areas combine to determine counselling effectiveness. The qualities of the counsellor as a person, as opposed to what he actually does during counselling, require special attention. So is it important to find out the answers to the questions like, what are certain individual characteristics of a counsellor that will make him more effective in providing counselling as compared to others? Let us try to unravel some of these characteristics of an effective counsellor.

Counselling theorists and researchers have given this question as much importance as any other question in the field of counselling. Despite the vast amount of research, the exact qualities that distinguish an effective counsellor from an ineffective one still remain somewhat uncertain. Part of the difficulty is semantic. Words to identify clearly the specific human traits essential in effective counselling are still lacking. Such words as accepting, open, warm, genuine, flexible and sincere are the closest we can use to discuss counselling, and the meanings of these words have been polluted by their everyday usage. Such terms no longer have specific meanings; meanings often overlap and are ambiguous.

We also continue to have difficulty defining and measuring counsellor's effectiveness. Despite these problems, a great deal is known about qualities that significantly contribute to counsellor's effectiveness. The basic premise is that while effective counselling requires certain behaviours or core conditions, the personal traits of the counsellor are also extremely important variables.

3.4 Personality and Background of the Counsellor

To be effective in the process of counselling, the counsellor needs to develop the qualities of maturity, empathy and warmth. These qualities, in addition to many, will go a long way in determining the effectiveness of the counsellor. It is also important for them not to get disturbed easily by the adverse situations, and keep a positive frame of mind. However, sometimes the spirit of counselling as a profession gets lost when people come to join the same for wrong purposes.

3.4.1 Negative Motivators for Becoming a Counsellor

Everyone who aspires to be a counsellor may not be the right person for the same. The reason to be a counsellor has to do a lot with the extent to which the individual has the inner motivation to be in this role and the degree of congruency between the personality characteristics of the counsellor and demands of the counselling roles.

A number of people "attracted of professional counselling . . . appear to have serious personality and adjustment problems" (Witmer and Young, 1996). An individual willing to play the counsellor's role should try to explore the reason for doing so. According to Guy (1987), there are a few dysfunctional motivators for becoming a counsellor. These are as follows:

- *Emotional distress:* Individual might have his or her own un-resolved personal stresses and in order to avoid dealing with it might want to enter this activity.

- *Vicarious coping:* This happens when individuals, instead of living a meaningful life of their own, try to live the life of others whom they identify as perfect.

- *Loneliness and isolation:* Sometimes isolation in one's own life pushes individuals to take up this profession so that they can be in continuous contact with the other people.

- *A desire for power:* A desire to exert power on others in order to escape the insecurities of their own lives, may propel people to begin the practice of counselling.

- *A need for love:* This is belief that all problems are resolved through the expression of love and tenderness, especially with individuals who are narcissistic and grandiose, and this forces them to take up counselling.

3.5 Positive Motivators for Becoming a Counsellor

But there are a few individuals who join this profession for positive reasons too and have advocated that it seems to be some form of "calling" for them to be in this role (Foster, 1996). Counsellors and counsellors-in-training should always assess themselves on the parameters of who they are and what they are doing. Such introspection carried out by them may help them examine their developmental histories, their best and the worst qualities and personal/ professional goals and objectives (Faiver, et al., 1995).

CASE EXAMPLE: SUPRIYA'S ROTATION

Supriya had been a business student pursuing an MBA, but during her course she found most of the subjects very dull and number based. So she left her course. She always found that she liked working with people, and use to help them out in times of crisis. While examining her interests, she found that counselling would be one area where she would be able to satisfy this interest of hers. "That's it!" she said excitedly. "I'll become a counsellor! Thats way I can 'help' these business minded people who are bored to death in their jobs. And I think all I have to do is to listen. Interesting!"

Do you think Supriya would make a good counsellor? What else she should consider while choosing to go ahead with this profession?

Foster (1996) and Guy (1987) have given a list of factors which play significantly important roles, and propel these individuals to assume the role of a counsellor and take up this profession confidently. Although this list is not exhaustive, it focuses on an individual's personal life that makes him or her best-suited to function as a counsellor. An effective counsellor should have the following skills:

- *Inquisitiveness:* A basic desire of search in people
- *Listening skills:* To be able to give a patient hearing to what people speak
- *Conversation skills:* A basic interest in communication with people
- *Empathy:* The ability to fit into another person's shoe and look at the situation from his or her perspective
- *Emotional intelligence:* Ability to deal with wide variety of emotions
- *Self-search:* The skill to question oneself and look from within
- *Self-denying capabilities:* The capacity to deny ones own require-ments and take care on the needs of other people
- *Tolerance of intimacy:* To be able to handle emotional and physical proximity with the clients and maintain professionalism
- *Ability to handle power:* The ability to handle the power relationship with utmost care and caution
- *Sense of humour:* The capacity to find out and reflect humour in the worst possible scenario and to help the client deal with it

In addition to these, there are a few qualities that are essential for an effective counsellor. These include qualities like stability, harmony, constancy and purposefulness. Overall, the potency of counselling is related to counsellors' personal togetherness (Gladding, 2004; Kottler, 1993). It is a well-accepted fact that the counsellor's personality is sometimes a more important factor in assisting the change in the client's behaviour as compared to his knowledge, aptitude and skills (McAuliffe and Lovell, 2006; Rogers, 1961). It has also been found that the individuals who are able to have a control of their self-biases, and are able to listen and ask for clarification from others are able to grow professionally and personally as persons, and also help others grow (Ford, et al., 1993).

To be able to heal the pain of others it is important for an individual to be able to resolve one's own experiences and to be sensitive to the feelings of self and others (May, et al., 1985). It is paradoxical that individuals who have gone through pain in their lives and have learnt to deal with them are able to help others who are trying to deal with the same or similar emotional problems (Miller, et al., 1998). Since it enhances the ability to feel the pain of others, it is relatively easier for them to connect with the clients, and be more genuine with them as they have gone through the experiences that their client is going through now (Foster, 1996). Effective counsellors are both personally and professionally qualified. They have interest in people, and are also sound as far as the technical knowledge is concerned. They become a perfect blend of the technical competencies and the ability to relate with other people (Cormier and Cormier, 1998).

3.6 Personal Characteristics of Counsellors

Several years ago, the National Vocational Guidance Association (1949) proposed that general characteristics of counsellors include a *deep interest in people and patience with them, sensitivity to the attitudes and the actions of others, emotional sanity and objectivity, a capacity for being trusted by others, and respect for facts*. Later, the Association for Counsellor Education and Supervision (1964) indicated that the counsellors should have six qualities such as: *belief in each individual, commitment to individual human values, alertness to the world, open-mindedness and understanding of self and professional commitment*.

Combs and his co-workers (1969) concluded from a series of studies that the major differences between effective and ineffective counsellors were their personal beliefs and traits. These findings led Combs to conclude that the major technique of counselling was to follow the principle of self as instrument; the counsellor's self analysis technique became the major facilitator of positive growth for clients. In addition, Combs studied some basic beliefs that counsellors held concerning people and their ability to help themselves. He found that effective counsellors perceived other people as able rather than unable to solve their own problems and manage their own lives. Effective counsellors also perceived people as *dependable, friendly* and *worthy*. They were also more likely to identify with *people* rather than *things*, to see people as having an adequate *capacity to cope* with problems, and to be more *self-revealing* than *self-concealing*.

Combs and Soper (1963) found that effective counsellors perceived their clients as capable, dependable, friendly and worthy, and perceived themselves as altruistic and non-dominating. Rogers (1961) concluded from his experiences and his reviews of research that the counsellor's theory and methods were far less important than the client's perception of the counsellor's attitudes. Rogers was pointing out that an effective counsellor must be an *attractive, friendly person, someone who inspires confidence and trust*.

The research suggests that one approach to determine counsellor effectiveness would be to look for characteristics of personal effectiveness. Allen (1949), found that the effective counsellor is a person who is on relatively good terms with his own emotional experience and that the ineffective counsellor is one who is relatively uneasy in regard to the character of his inner life.

3.6.1 A Composite Model of Human Effectiveness

An analysis of personal characteristics of effective counsellors must begin with an analysis of the characteristics of effective persons. Over the years a number of models of human effectiveness have been presented. A composite model can be drawn on the basis of these models of effectiveness. This is not a perfection model; rather, these are characteristics which should be found in effective counsellors, and which counsellors are continually striving to attain. The list is incomplete and still evolving. The model is proposed as a stimulus for present and prospective counsellors to examine their own ideas of what personal qualities they need to become effective counsellors. These same qualities may also be seen as goals for clients to attain if they opt for the counselling process. Now, let us discuss some of the personal characteristics of effective counsellors in the following section.

3.6.2 Personal Characteristics of Effective Counsellors

Effective counsellor embodies the following qualities:

1. Effective counsellors are open to, and accept their own experiences.
2. They are aware of their own values and beliefs.
3. They are able to develop warm and deep relationship with others.
4. They are able to allow themselves to be seen by others as they actually are.
5. Effective counsellors accept personal responsibility for their own behaviours.
6. Effective counsellors aim for realistic levels of aspiration.

Effective counsellors are open to and ready to accept their own experiences. Such individuals do not try to control their emotional reactions but are able to accept their feelings as they are. *Openness,* as used in this context, means being open to oneself, not necessarily revealing oneself to everyone with whom one comes in contact.

Much of our experience teaches us to deny our feelings. Small boys are told. "There, there, now, big boys don't cry!" Even adults are admonished, "Now, don't cry!" or "Don't be nervous! You have nothing to worry about". Pressures are applied to not to breakdown, not to feel depressed or not to be angry or not to be frustrated. Effective counsellors can accept within themselves feelings of sadness, anger, resentment and other feelings ordinarily considered negative. By accepting these feelings as they are, without denying or distorting them, effective counsellors have greater control over their behaviour. Because they are aware of their emotional reactions, they can choose how they wish to act, rather than permitting their feelings to affect their behaviour without their conscious awareness.

Persons learn to accept their experience (a) if the significant individuals in their lives model such acceptance; and (b) if they are not punished for such acceptance. Counsellors have a positive effect on clients when their clients see them as accepting both their own and the clients' undesired emotional reactions such as boredom, anger, anxiety and depression. Accepting the idea that clients have the right to hold negative feelings is far more effective in promoting positive growth than telling clients that they are foolish to feel the way they do, logical though such arguments may be.

Effective counsellors are aware of their own values and beliefs. Effective counsellors know what is important for them and have determined the standards by which they wish to live. Thus, they can make decisions and choose alternatives that are consistent with their value systems. More important, a clear value system allows individuals to find a meaningful role for their lives and also gives them guidelines regarding how to relate to the people and things around them. They can avoid ineffective and inconsistent patterns of behaviour and instead can engage themselves in more positive, purposeful and rewarding behaviour.

Effective counsellors are able to develop warm and deep relationship with others. They give due regard to other individuals—their feelings, their opinions and their personalities. This regard is caring, but a non-possessive caring with little evaluation or judgment; the other person is accepted with few conditions. Such warmth or caring is not widespread. Most people experience a certain amount of fear in expressing warmth toward another person. They fear that if they let themselves freely experience such positive feelings towards another, they will become trapped and, therefore, vulnerable. Other persons may take advantage of them; they may make demands that they are unable to reject; they may reject their feelings by failing to reciprocate. So they keep their distance, rarely permitting themselves to get close to someone.

Effective counsellors are less vulnerable to such fears because they recognize that the risk involved is worth the value to be gained. They, therefore, respond to other people more freely, developing close relationships with those who share their interests and values. They have wide freedom of choice in developing such relationship because of their ability to take care and their relative lack of fear towards taking care.

Effective counsellors are able to allow themselves to be seen by others as they actually are. This characteristic results in an attitude of realness or genuineness. When individuals gain awareness of and accept the feelings they are experiencing, they need not impose feelings on others nor put up a facade to make people think they are something they are not. Authentic persons are willing to be themselves and to express, in their words and in their behaviour, the various feelings and attitudes they hold. They do not need to present an outward facade of one attitude while holding another attitude at a deeper level. They do not pretend to know the answers when they do not know. They do not act like loving persons at moments when they feel hostile. They do not act as though they are confident and full of assurance when they are actually frightened and unsure. On a simpler level, they do not act well when they feel ill.

Part of the difficulty for most individuals is that energy spent on playing a role or presenting a façade prevents them from using that energy for accomplishing tasks and solving problems. In addition, effective counsellors, by presenting their authentic selves to others, are more able to develop cooperative relationships with others, thus gaining support for problem-solving tasks. They can share the limelight; therefore, they are able to secure the help of others.

Effective counsellors accept personal responsibility for their own behaviours. Rather than denying the way they are and blaming others, effective counsellors can handle their failures and weaknesses. They recognize that, while many situations are largely caused by factors beyond their control, they are responsible for their actions in these situations. Recognizing that they can determine, in large part, their own behaviour gives them the freedom to consciously choose either to conform to external group control or to ignore those controls, with that choice based on well-considered reasons.

This acceptance of personal responsibility also means that these individuals are able to accept criticism in a much more constructive way. Instead of constantly defending themselves, effective counsellors view criticism as a desirable feedback mechanism permitting them to lead more effective, constructive lives. They stand by their behaviours rather than 'passing the buck' or blaming others.

Effective counsellors have developed realistic levels of aspiration. Ordinarily, persons raise their goals slightly as a result of success and lower their goals after failure. In this way they protect themselves from both too easy achievement and continued failure. Sometimes this self-protective mechanism is thrown out of balance, and individuals either set their goals too high, which results in inevitable failure, or too low, which robs them of a sense of achievement, no matter what they do.

Effective counsellors, on the other hand, are able to set obtainable goals and take failure in their stride. Because they are aware of their own skills and abilities, they can accurately estimate what to expect from themselves. Their acceptance of their experiences—both positive and negative—enable them to evaluate previous goals realistically and to use this evaluation to establish future goals.

MAINTAINING EFFECTIVENESS AS A COUNSELLOR

Individuals who have the capabilities to learn both from their mistakes as well as their successes generally lead a healthy personal life. They are able to concentrate on the concerns of the clients with more sensitivity and help them grow therapeutically. The ability to adapt to gains as well as to losses helps them to be relatively free from destructive thought patterns, and makes them an effective counsellor (Gaushell and Lawson, 1994).

Counsellors have to maintain a good physical and psychological health and well-being. They might have to take therapeutic and preventive measures to manage problematic situations, especially like burnout (Grosch and Olsen, 1994). Burnout is a state of physical, mental and psychological exhaustion leading to a state of dysfunctionality. In a state of burnout, an individual enters into a state of negativity, and experiences a situation of loss of concern, compassion and feeling for others (Lambie, 2007). This has been found to be one of the most severe problems to be experienced by the counsellors. A timely correction of the environmental issues, associated with interpersonal and individual concerns will aid in the prevention and cure of burnout (Wilkerson and Bellini, 2006). Counsellors will have to identify and define areas to rejuvenate themselves. Some of the ways by which the counsellor can address these concerns are:

- By associating with physically and psychologically healthy individuals
- Working with organization which has a defined well-meaning mission and committed colleagues
- By believing in the theory of counselling
- Having an ability to identify the stressors in the environment, and using stress-reduction exercises
- By engaging in self-assessment
- Periodically examining and clarifying counselling roles, expectations, and beliefs (i.e., work smarter, not necessarily longer)
- Obtaining personal therapy
- Maintaining healthy work-life balance
- Developing an attitude of detachment especially while working with clients
- Maintaining an optimistic and positive outlook towards others as well as towards life in general

3.7 Values in Counselling

That counselling should stress rational understanding and problem-solving skills is increasingly being questioned. Several studies have shown that a certain amount of anxiety is necessary for achievement. It appears that too much attention is being paid to rationality hence necessitating some rethinking on this vital issue.

The rapid and extensive changes taking place in society create problems for the counsellor. Let us take an example of the basic unit of the society—the family in this context. The joint-family system, known traditionally to provide social and economic security to its individual members, is fast disappearing. The nuclear families are confronted with problems, which they had not bargained for. This has meant for many people an increase in anxiety resulting from uncertainty as to what values to hold and what rules to follow. Consequently this anxiety leads to emotional breakdown.

Social change has affected not only family life but also several other things, for example, the status of women. This issue involves a change in several other types of relationships as well. These include parent-child and husband-wife relations. Many families today are characterized by a lack of understanding even when there is no open conflict between the generations. Sexual relations is another area where it is not easy for the counsellor to advise those families in which the parents have one set of standards and the children another. An interesting phenomenon increasingly becoming apparent is 'ascending education' in which the young become teachers of the old. It is not uncommon to hear from the young that adults do not know about new things and that they have to learn from them.

Another aspect, which is for fundamental importance to us in India, is our concern and anxiety for modernization. We are engaged in a drastic movement from the traditional to the modern form of living, and by 'modern' we tacitly mean westernised technological modes of living. Many aspects of this movement are of considerable concern to the counsellor like, what are the effects of this thrust? Is it true that the effects of rapid industrialization are the disruption of inter-personal relations, an increase in crime, alienation of the youth, disrespect for elders, sharp increase in delinquent behaviour and other maladjustments and how should the counsellor deal with this situation?

With advances in the field of medicine, environmental hygiene and better nutrition, man's longevity has increased. What is the role and status of these older people in society? Retirement from positions of authority and prestige can be a very devastating experience. How can the 'retirement-shock' be assuaged? The counsellor's role should be to assist the senior citizens to make optimum adjustment.

The tremendous technological progress may create problems of obsolescence or unemployment where the government could suggest two approaches—recycle, that is, using adult members for new tasks by putting them through well-planned and designed refresher-courses or encyclage, i.e., providing training to individuals in occupations different from those they are engaged in to enable them to enter new careers, if it becomes necessary. The counsellor will, therefore, have to play the role of a cultural mediator, and help individuals adjust themselves to the new conditions of living. This has implications for value-orientations in counselling. Should the counsellor impose his values on the clients? It is agreed in all circles that he should not, but he inevitably does. He must inculcate the development of healthy and desirable attitudes.

By establishing warm and friendly relations, the counsellor has to help clients overcome their inhibitions about discussing their problems freely and openly with him. The next issue concerns decision-making. In the western culture, this comprises a very important aspect of the counselling of young people. But in oriental cultures in general, and in India particular, decision-making is to a certain extent culturally determined. A young man or a woman is expected to consult the adult members of the family even in matters, such as choosing a course of study, entering a specific occupation or choosing a life partner. Hence, autonomy, independence and the ability to stand on one's own feet and make one's own decisions are not stressed upon. But in western cultures, however, these are considered positive attributes.

In India we are passing through an unenviable phase of transition. There is a tendency to cling to past values and simultaneously crave for things, which are not consonant with the past values. This has resulted in an identity crisis, particularly of the youth. The counsellor has to be mature enough to strike an appropriate balance with his counselees who may be struggling with the new values and trying to cling to the past values. The counselee's value structures are thus of a crucial nature and the counsellor has to work in terms of his own value structure which may not be similar to that of the counselees. In this context the counsellor is concerned with the question of whether or not to impose his own values upon his clients. The basic rule is that the counsellor should not impose his values on the counselee as he inadvertently breaks the rules either unknowingly or unwittingly.

In the contemporary Indian context several basic values, traditionally held sacrosanct, are increasingly being questioned. One of the major values concerns the attitude to authority. Youth is becoming increasingly resentful of authority and the implications of this for counselling are obvious. The closer the counsellor is to administrative authority the farther he will be from his counselee. In the words of Wrenn (1973), the counsellor should "be a person who does not represent authority per se, but who represents the concern for the individual per se".

The generation gap also affects counselling. The importance of past experiences for solving present problems is becoming questionable. The counsellor too must be on his guard not to use his past experience on the counselee for this may not always give him a clue to understanding the counselee's problems as they may not be applicable in this case.

As has been mentioned earlier, the attitude towards women has undergone a considerable change. They are no longer confined to their homes but are taking up careers, which earlier were exclusive only to men. The counsellor, therefore, should not look askance at a female counselee who does not propose to enter into matrimony or one who proposes to enter such fields as mountaineering, forestry and the like. The counsellor would do well to present the facts in full and not try to influence the counselee. The Indian attitude towards sex has been different from that of the Occidental. Sex is looked upon as something intimate, precious and sacred. Sex is not identified with the fulfilment of carnal desire. Women are not expected to freely mix with men and they are expected to maintain a certain distance. In contemporary life when women and men work together in offices and factories side by side it becomes impractical for women to observe the *safe distance* dictum. Questions such as what should be done about pre-marital sex; sex outside marriage; bigamous relations, etc. loom large. The masculine attitudes towards these are obviously biased in their favour. Different standards for men and women create avoidable confusion, conflict and also crisis. There are several other values of equal importance but it is not practical to discuss them here.

The counsellor must of necessity widen his field of work to include the new problems, which are surfacing as a result of rapid changes in society. If the counsellor is understood to be a culture-interpreter, a culture-mediator and an agent for culture-change, he must of necessity move into a wider area (of human life) and make it the canvas for his work.

3.8 The Counsellor's Values

As was previously pointed out, counsellors must understand their own values and the values of others. No *one set* of values is superior to others. Every person has a set of beliefs that determines the decisions he makes, his ability to appreciate the things around him, his consciences, and his perceptions of others. Since the counsellor's values are an integral part of his personality and, therefore, a part of his professional role, we are particularly concerned with how those values contribute to the counselling process (Belkin, 1984).

Values serve as reference points for individuals. They provide a basis for determining which course of action an individual should take. Individuals have always needed these guidelines to provide structures and meaning in their lives and to avoid an existence of 'running around in circles'.

3.8.1 Influence of Counsellor's Values on Client's Values

A key issue is whether or not counsellors should avoid conveying their values to their clients. Some maintain that the counsellors should remain neutral while counselling and communicate no value orientation to the client. In such a situation, counsellors would strive to appear non-moralizing and ethically neutral in their counselling; they would focus on the client's values. Such counsellors would know their own value systems but would avoid introducing these values into the counselling interview. They would not indicate their own position on any of the moral or value areas that arise. The basic belief supporting this position is that in any counselling situation the client must move from a position of outside evaluation by others to a position of internalized self-evaluation. Any value input by the counsellor would work against this objective.

Williamson (1958) called for an abandonment of this position in favour of an open and explicit value orientation in counselling. He suggested that attempts to be neutral in value situations could easily lead the client to believe that the counsellor accepted unlawful behaviour and even condoned it. Such a situation could lead to the client's feeling that the counsellor supported behaviour that is completely unacceptable by any social, moral or legal standards.

In support of Williamson's position, Samler (1960) states that a change in values constitutes a counselling goal and that counsellor intervention in the client's values is an actuality to be accepted as a necessary part of the counselling process. He urges counsellors to develop an awareness of their own values and to clarify how these values might relate to their own counsellor-client interaction.

Patterson (1958) points out that the counsellor's values influence the ethics of the counselling relationships, the goals of counselling and the methods employed in counselling. Patterson cites evidence for the assertion that, no matter how passive and valueless the counsellor appears, the client's value system is influenced and gradually becomes more similar to the counsellor's value system. However, Patterson suggests that the counsellors are not justified in consciously and directly imposing their values on clients, for the following reasons:

1. Each individual's philosophy on life is different, unique and unsuited to adoption by another.
2. All counsellors cannot be expected to have a fully developed, adequate philosophy on life.
3. The appropriate places for instruction in values are the homes, the schools and the religious institutions.
4. An individual develops a code of ethics, not from a single source or in a short period of time, but over a long period of time and from many influences.
5. No one ought to be prevented from developing his or her own unique philosophy since it will be more meaningful to him or her.
6. The client must have the right to refuse to accept any ethics or philosophy of life.

Such disagreements have led to extensive research into the nature and desirability of the influence of counsellor values upon clients. Rosenthal (1955) contended that some types of counsellor values invariably influence the client. He suggested that most counsellors believe that the counsellor's values should be kept out of therapy as much as possible, but his own research results indicated that those clients who improved mostly changed their moral values to conform more closely to the values of their counsellor. In an experiment using the *Study of Values* test, Cook (1966) found that differences in the counsellors' and clients' value systems affected counselling outcome. He found that when the clients were grouped by keeping in mind how similar their values were to the values of the counsellor, clients who were in a medium similarity group improved more than those in either high similarity or low similarity or too different from that of the other.

Counsellors do expose their values to clients. Since counsellors are in an intimate relationship with their clients, their values will be a part of that interaction, either consciously or unconsciously (Rokeach and Regan, 1980). Counsellors cannot pretend that they do not possess a values system or that they are something other than what they really are. The issue is to what degree counsellors should expose those values and influence the client.

3.8.2 Importance of Valuing Human Freedom

Counsellors must be committed to some values in order to maintain meaning and fullness in their lives. Belkin (1984) suggests that the primary value to which counsellors must commit themselves is freedom. Freedom is an ideal that propels the individual to certain types of actions. Freedom allows the individual to determine the direction in which to move. It allows the individual to be creative, to make choices and to be responsible for them. Freedom also commits the client to assume responsibility for his action and its consequences.

A lack of understanding about the counsellor's role has unquestionably reduced the counsellor's effectiveness in our organizations and agencies. Much of this lack of understanding has come about because counsellors fail to define clearly the roles they fulfil, perhaps because of an extreme desire to help others and to meet whatever others needs may bring to them. Yet much of what happens during counselling is a result of what the client expects the counsellors to do. Frequently, clients seek counselling because they expect the counsellors to solve their problems such as to advice them whether to get a divorce, quit organization, change the job or attend the some professional course. But counsellors have generally recognized that they cannot tell others how to live their lives. Thus, at the very beginning conflict arises between the clients' expectations and the counsellors' in terms of the goals of their relationship.

The organization where the counsellor works also has some expectations concerning the role the counsellor will assume. Frequently the organization expects the counsellor to represent that institution and to interact with clients in a way that meets the goals of the institution, even at the expense of neglecting the needs and goals of the individual client. Counsellors in such situations often feel a great deal of frustration and guilt. They complain bitterly about the failure of the administration to permit them to perform their role in the most effective way. However, if counsellors are to be able to operate most effectively, they must recognize the need to clarify their roles and communicate those roles to both the clients and the institution they serve.

In any institution counsellors may attempt to fill varied counselling role. These roles are not mutually exclusive; in fact they are often supportive. However, the counsellor must determine which role or roles seem most plausible in that particular situation. Counsellors in many settings share similar frustrations in defining their role and functions. However, the basic function of all counsellors, regardless of setting, was clearly stated by Wrenn (1973).

The functions of the counsellor in any setting are (a) to provide a relationship between counsellor and counselee, which is that of mutual trust in each other, (b) to provide alternations in self-understanding and in the courses of action open to the client, (c) to provide for some degree of interpretation of the situation in which the client finds himself and with 'important others' in the client's immediate life, (d) to provide leadership in developing a psychologically secure environment for his clients and finally

(e) to provide for importance of the counselling process through constant individual criticism and (for some counsellors) extensive attention to improvement of process through research.

Thus, counsellors must work towards a personally defined role that takes into account the expectations of their clients, the regulations of their institution, and their own personal understanding of their professional role. This role definition can best be facilitated by discussing differences in expectations with appropriate institutional personnel, then providing clear communication of the counsellor's roles to staff and clients alike.

3.9 Summary

The goals of the counselling should be decided both by the counsellor and the client. The major goals of the counselling are: facilitating change in client's behaviour, improving the client's ability to establish and maintain relationships, enhancing the client's effectiveness and ability to cope, the decision-making process and facilitating client potential and development. Some of the personal characteristics of effective counsellor which are required to achieve the goals of counselling are: they are open to, and accept their own experiences, they are aware of their own values and beliefs, they are able to develop warm and deep relationship with other, they are able to allow themselves to be seen by others as they actually are, they accept personal responsibility for their own behaviours and they aim for realistic levels of aspiration.

Chapter 4 explains in detail how the counselling process works and the appropriate attitudes required to make this process work.

Review Questions

1. List and discuss major goals of counselling. Is there a commonality among these goals? Discuss.

2. Identify and discuss the personal characteristics of effective counsellors. What are the positive and the negative motivators of being a counsellor?

3. Highlight and discuss realms of life which may require counselling in the present context of environment.

4. What is the impact of counsellor's values on clients? Is it appropriate for the counsellors to impose their values on the clients? Why or why not?

Chapter 4

The Process of Counselling

The word *process* helps to communicate much about the essence of counselling. A process is an identifiable sequence of events taking place over time. For example, there are identifiable stages in the healing process for a serious physical wound, such as a broken leg. Similarly, there are identifiable stages in the process of human development from birth to death. Although the stages in this process are common to all human beings, what happens within each of these stages is unique for each individual.

Counselling also has a predictable set of stages that occur in a sequence. Initially, the counsellor and client must establish contact to identify client's current difficulties. A deeper understanding of the client's problems follows this. Once the problems have been understood, specific goals for change are defined and then a plan of action for change will be agreed on and carried out. This is generally followed by a follow-up so as to ensure that the goals of the counselling have been achieved. On the basis of this process many models of the counselling process have been devised. One of such models is 5-D model, which has been discussed in the following section.

4.1 5-D Model of the Counselling Process

The 5-D model of counselling describes the process in five phases, which are easy to remember because they all start with the alphabet 'D'. The stages are shown in Figure 4.1.

1. Develop relationship
2. Define problem
3. Determine goals
4. Decide plan of action
5. Do follow-up

The process of counselling is fluid. Phases do not necessarily follow strictly in the order given in the model. The counsellor will sometimes go back and forth between stages, and he might jump around.

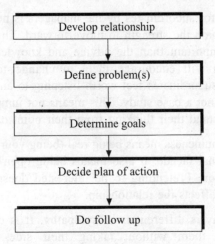

Figure 4.1 5-D Model of Counselling.

Not all the phases are always necessary. Counselling could stop after any phase. Sometimes the first one or two phases are all that are required. The client having expressed the problem and then examining it more clearly with the help of the counsellor might make a decision immediately regarding the goals to follow or come to a realization, and might not require any help at all.

Counselling could also start anywhere in the process, although earlier phases will either already have been established or will have been quickly reconfirmed. For example, a subordinate in an organization might see the problem clearly and know what needs to be done, and yet be unable to act. In this situation the counsellor can start at Phase 4.

Let us examine different phases of counselling in detail.

4.2 The Phases of Counselling

4.2.1 PHASE 1: Developing the Relationship

During this initial stage the counsellor manager must create an appropriate atmosphere and try to establish a special rapport with subordinates in the organization. This safe environment encourages them to open up more, to take a closer and more objective look at them, and ideally to challenge themselves in a way they might not otherwise do. The ability to self-criticize is a prerequisite to change and improvement. The conditions, which induce people to open up in such a way, are referred to as the proper counselling attitudes. Carl Rogers, renowned for his client-centred counselling, emphasized the importance of the relationship between the counsellor and the client in fostering client's growth, and what he called the counsellor's unconditional positive regard for the client.

In order to build an appropriate relationship there are attitudes which have to be adopted in order for the counselling process to work:

Respect: Respect for subordinates by the managers is necessary for them to feel confident and gain the strength to move forward. The counsellor's belief in them is more important than the advice and knowledge in setting up a relationship, which will encourage them to change for the better. It is important to make subordinates feel worth listening to and to treat them as a unique individuals, not a case study. This means not jumping to conclusions, but trying to understand their thinking from their point of view.

Genuineness: Genuineness means being real (being yourself) and not putting on a fake professional façade. It also means being open and showing a real interest in the person. Pretending to be interested doesn't work. Falseness shows through and affects the relationship.

Empathy: Empathy is different from sympathy. It is caring about people and understanding them without taking their side, or agreeing with them completely, or becoming too involved. Responding to people in an empathetic way will encourage them to shift from talking about the problem in a general detached manner to talking in a more personal and emotional manner.

Sometimes it can be difficult to remain distant enough from the problem if the counsellor relate to the problem personally. On the other hand, he can be too distant if he cannot relate to the problem at all. It is important to be aware of both extremes and maintain the right balance. Communicating empathy entails showing that the counsellor has heard, understood and accepted (not necessarily agreed with) what the other person has communicated.

Equality: An equal relationship is necessary for the process to work. A counselling session is a meeting between equal individuals instead of a meeting between a superior manager and an inferior subordinate. This *meeting of equals* needs to be established early and even more explicitly when using counselling skills in a work situation, since a manager does at other times behave more directively.

Listening: The counsellor should establish in the beginning that he or she is there to listen to their subordinates. The subordinates should be doing most of the talking, especially in the early stages of the process. They should be leading the conversation. This does not mean that the counsellor has no input or control whatsoever, or that he or she can sit back and take it easy. The kind of listening he or she will be doing is hard work and involves much more. It has been referred to as *active listening*.

The counsellor needs to avoid changing the topic or taking the conversation in a new direction, except in cases when it is definitely necessary, such as when the subordinates are waffling, talking in circles, or not talking about what is really significant. In these cases, it is best to point out to them what is happening and why they are changing the topic or the direction of the conversation. But generally the counsellor needs to keep the focus on what is important to the client, and let them lead the conversation.

Confidentiality: It is very important to set clear boundaries on what will be kept confidential and what cannot. The subordinates will trust the counsellor more if they are clear regarding his or her confidentiality boundaries. Ideally, all employees should have some awareness of this before coming to the counsellor. It should be stated as part of company policy. If the counsellor wants or needs to break confidentiality for some reason (for example, if he or she has obtained information which indicates that someone else may be in danger), this needs to be explained to the subordinate.

The effects of the relationship created by adopting the attitudes discussed earlier are that the subordinates not only gain confidence and independence, but it also enables them to tackle the problem successfully. During this initial phase, they are often unloading, simply getting things off their chest. Talking about their feelings, thoughts and behaviours is a great relief. It clears their thinking and relieves tension and anxiety. When people think or worry about problems, their thoughts are vague. Amorphous, partially formed ideas, fears, hopes and images float around in their heads, often not in any logical or sensible order. Having to put them into words in a way, which will make sense to someone else, helps the person to begin to see the problem much more clearly.

4.2.2 PHASE 2: Defining the Problem(s)

During this phase, the problem is first of all defined by the subordinate from their point of view. The problem often then needs to be redefined more objectively before moving on towards finding a solution. It is important to show that the counsellor understands the problem from the subordinate's point of view before challenging them to look at the problem more objectively. The following steps should be taken in this direction:

Examining the problems: The counsellor should seek to define and understand the problem clearly from subordinate's frame of reference, and also to show acceptance of their view, even if he or she doesn't agree with it. Demonstration of understanding is achieved by using a skill called **reflecting**.

Prioritising the relevant issues: The counsellor may need to encourage the person to talk about the most significant concerns, i.e., the ones having deep influence on their lives. This may mean helping them to organize the issues. Often distressed people will throw a lot of confused talk at you, some related and some unrelated. In these cases, the counsellor needs to help them to sort out the issues.

Focusing on the perspective: The subordinate will frequently need to gain a more objective view of the problem situation before they can move on to finding productive ways of managing the problem. Often people will initially describe a problem as being insoluble, or as being someone else's problem or the result of someone else's actions as depicted in Examples 4.1 and 4.2:

EXAMPLE 4.1

There is nothing I can do about the situation. I am stuck. I have no control over company policy or management decisions so there is nothing I can do to remedy the situation.

EXAMPLE 4.2

She just doesn't like me. She is always trying to make my life difficult. She needs to learn to be more responsible.

Acceptance of the problem: The subordinates need to come to the point of accepting that the problem does indeed exist before they will be motivated to do something about it. There is no point in using counselling skills with someone to help them to solve a problem, which they do not understand to be a problem.

Emphasizing on self-responsibility: After acceptance of the problem's existence, the next step for the counsellor is to make the client realize that it is his or her own problem and not some one else's. Ownership is a key concept in counselling because it leads to self-responsibility. Ownership means acknowledging that the problem is affecting them, and is therefore theirs, so they need to decide what to do about it.

Analyzing and solving problems: For providing effective counselling, the problem of the subordinate or the client should be analysed minutely, and then corrective steps should be taken to make them understand why the problem occurred and how it needs to be tackled. A subordinate's dependency on the counsellor may have to be continuously but gently fought off, especially at first. Subordinates are likely to try to get the counsellor to give them answers to all their queries. It is a good idea to talk about the dependency/self-responsibility issue openly. Keeping the problem analysis and solution generation in the hands of problems-owners is the basic force behind effective counselling. They need to accept responsibility both for the problem and for doing something about it, which means they recognize that the counsellor is not going to take over the problem for them but it is them who have to work on the problem themselves. When using counselling skills, one should not allow oneself to be forced or tempted into producing quick and easy answers.

Consider the difference between the following two interactions:

INTERACTION 4.1

Manager/Counsellor:	"Right, that's the problem. What now"?
Subordinate/Client:	"Well, uh, what do you think I should do about it?"
Manager/Counsellor:	"This is what you do. First you ... Then you... And finally you...."
Subordinate/Client:	"All right. Thank you."

After this interchange, the subordinate or the client may leave feeling delighted that the problem is solved. However, the subordinate could possibly have other feelings about being told what to do. He or she could leave thinking "that was a lot of use; I knew all that before I went in", or "that might be what they want, but I am going to do it my way."

In the following version of the interchange, the problem is put back where it belongs, with the problem-owner, so that they themselves work through from the problem to the solution as much as possible.

INTERACTION 4.2

Manager/Counsellor:	"Right, that's the problem. What now?"
Subordinate//Client:	"Well, uh, what do you think I should do?"
Manager/ Counsellor:	"You must have given some thought to the possible solutions. Have you any ideas your-self?'
Subordinate/Client:	"I'm not sure, but one thing we might be able to do is...."
Manager/Counsellor:	"OK, that's one solution. Is that the only one or are there any other possible approaches?"
Subordinate/Client:	"Well, I did think that perhaps...."
Manager/Counsellor:	"Good. Any others?"
Subordinate/Client:	"No. I can't think of any more."
Manager/Counsellor:	"We could always have a look at...."

Examples adapted from: *The Skills of Interviewing* (1988) by Leslie Rae.

4.2.3 PHASE 3: Determining Goal(s)

During this phase the subordinates or the clients will establish their goals. They need to decide what they want to change, and they need to consider what can be *solved* vs. what can only be *managed* differently.

Choosing and prioritising goals and objectives: Now, the subordinates or the clients have to finally choose and prioritise their goals. The general goals need to be determined and then broken down into workable objectives. Objectives must be prioritised, and realistic time frames for meeting them considered. Some problems (such as an immediate difficulty with a subordinate or client) are short term: the problems which can be solved in shorter time frame and others (such as a desired change in career direction, etc.) are long term: which might require longer time frame to be solved.

Making commitment: The subordinate or the client must be committed to the goal(s); otherwise, they are unlikely to carry out the plans decided on. The level of commitment and the need for it may need to be discussed rather than taken for granted.

4.2.4 PHASE 4: Deciding the Plan of Action

For each objective, a specific and workable plan of action needs to be devised. To be workable, the plan must fit in with the subordinate or client's life plan, goals, values, and the time that is available.

Generating and exploring alternatives: The subordinates or clients may need encouragement or even help in exploring the range of options open to them. The manager or the counsellor might even need to remind them about the other options available. For example, consider the following interaction:

INTERACTION 4.3

Manager/Counsellor: "You have expressed concern about your relationship with the manufacturing department managers. What do you think can be done about it?"

Subordinate/Client: "Want to consider options, but don't know what options are available for me. Can you please help?

Then the counsellor or manager may decide how to help and how much to assist. He can make suggestions or the subordinate can be offered a resource for finding alternatives like consulting literature or seeking any other knowledgeable person's opinions or the counsellor can continue to probe the subordinate or client for his own suggestions.

The manger or the counsellor may further encourage the subordinate or the client to consider all options, even ones they would rule out immediately, in order to examine why each is being dismissed. The reasons for ignoring or dismissing options can be significant. An alternative, which is ruled out initially sometimes, turns out to be the one eventually chosen. There is another reason for considering all the practical options available: it is useful to have fallback plans if the first option chosen does not work out.

Decision-making: Reluctance or difficulty in making a decision can be a barrier to moving forward. Different methods for arriving at the decisions can be used with the help of decision-making skills.

Specific steps: Once a decision has been made regarding the choice of option then the strategy to be pursued needs to broken down into specific steps. The subordinate or the client may be tempted to jump into action with only a broad strategy to guide him, but it should always be kept in mind that the action is much more likely to be effective if each step is planned and considered carefully beforehand.

4.2.5 PHASE 5: Doing the Follow-up

The phase of counselling which is easiest to overlook is making sure that the action plan is implemented. The subordinates or the clients will need to be taught, encouraged and reminded to manage monitoring (looking at indicators of progress), support provision and incentive provision for themselves. However, the manager or the counsellor can check with them at regular intervals to see how it's going, and can be available for back-up support, especially to help them to work through any blocks. In a work situation, depending on how directly the change is related to the objectives, as a manager one may want to arrange regular follow-up meetings in any case.

All talk and no action: In some situations some of the subordinates may be a bit too comfortable in self-pity mode, complaining about a situation, but not doing anything about it. Throughout the counselling process, even during the first phase of empathetic listening, the manager or the counsellor must adopt such attitudes that the meetings are for working on problems rather than just talking about problems. Exceptions to this are serious personal problems such as the death of a spouse, where the manager is not qualified to help with the problem and can only offer an empathetic ear and/or referrals.

Several precautions can be taken in order to facilitate action and to avoid the 'all talk no action' syndrome. Opening the meeting with statements, which set the expectations and time limits, will assist in focusing the meeting. While the subordinate is determining the steps of their action plans, the manager or the counsellor should encourage them to think ahead regarding what resources will be needed, and what is going to impede the implement-ation of the action plans, and ways of lessening these impediments. Have them plan ahead for the provision of motivating incentives. Another source (or sources) of support may be necessary in cases where change is not going to be an easy process.

Emotional block: The manager or the counsellor may be tempted to encourage the subordinate or client to take actions by pushing them. Unfortunately, this is likely to make subordinate or the client more anxious and even less likely to take action. If the above procedures have been used and still the subordinate or the client is not taking action, then it might be an emotional block, which is preventing him from acting. The manager or the counsellor can use the counselling process to help them to recognize and overcome these blocks.

Following is a simplified example of a subordinate working through the five phases:

PHASE 1: DEVELOPING THE RELATIONSHIP

    (a) The manager or counsellor tries to develop friendly relation with the client. The client may be afflicted by bout of anger, depression and anxiety and wants to be left alone. The counsellor may like to talk about it.

    (b) Discussion leads to stating of the problems like colleagues don't involve him in decision-making and also keep him out of the grapevine so the client finds the behaviour of the colleagues hostile.

PHASE 2: DEFINING THE PROBLEM

(a) As the client sees it initially, others are excluding him.
(b) Continued discussion reveals that his workstation is physically isolated relative to his colleagues.
(c) It emerges that he may be contributing to the problem by not listening well and by being forgetful.
(d) Problem is redefined as general communication difficulties.

PHASE 3: DETERMINING GOALS

(a) After realizing the problem the counsellor or the manager may suggest to the client to find new ways to receive information, which is being disseminated around the office.
(b) The counsellor instructs the client to improve his listening capabilities and remembering skills.
(c) The counsellor also suggests the client to change the workstation, i.e., get a transfer.

PHASE 4: DECIDING PLAN OF ACTION

(a) After listening to the suggestions the client determines specific steps involved in devising and proposing a new system for memo distribution.
(b) He decides to request now a change of workstation next time someone leaves.
(c) He determines steps, which need to be taken in order to obtain communication skills training for himself.

PHASE 5: DOING FOLLOW-UP

(a) The client meets again with his manager a week later to discuss progress so far.
(b) Two weeks later, his manager approaches him to see whether his situation has improved.

4.3 Summary

The process of counselling can be easily described with the help of 5-D Model comprising five stages. The first 'D' corresponds to Developing relation-ships and requires acquisition of certain attitudes in the counsellor like respect, genuineness, empathy, equality, listening and confidentiality. The second 'D' pertains to Defining the problems and includes an understanding of the problems of the client from his perspective. The third 'D' involves Determining the goals. During this stage, the counsellor helps the client determine the goals of counselling. The fourth 'D' corresponds to Deciding the plan of action. After the goals have been determined the client and the counsellor together generate and explore alternatives and take the action. The fifth 'D' is Doing the follow up to ensure that the action plan is implemented effectively. The distinct feature of this model is that the stages are fluid and need not necessarily be followed in the same order.

There is an understanding of how the process works and the appropriate attitudes required to create an atmosphere conducive to using counselling skills. It is the combination of the attitudes and skills, which makes the counselling style of management work. Attitude alone is not enough; but applying the skills without the counselling attitudes won't work either. Chapter 5 describes in details the procedure of counselling in business organizations.

Review Questions

1. What is 5-D Model of counselling? Discuss with examples.

2. What are the set of attitudes required during the first stage of counselling process to help build the confidence levels of clients?

3. List and discuss the steps of the second phase of the counselling process. What is the relevance of these steps in the process?

4. How does the third phase of the counselling model help the client during counselling?

5. What role does the counsellor play in the fourth phase of counselling?

6. Why is the fifth phase of counselling often overlooked? What are the responsibilities of the counsellor during this stage?

Chapter 5

Counselling Procedures

In this chapter, we will explore the counselling environment and the initial interview and review skills that are basic to the beginning stages of the counselling process. At the outset of the counselling experience, attention must be given to the specifics of organizing the first interview. Seating arrangements, intake procedures, opening the first session, structuring the interview, setting goals for the process, termination, and referrals are all fairly simple procedures that must be dealt with regardless of the theoretical orientation of the counsellor.

As counselling begins, the counsellor's primary goal is to establish rapport with the client so that the therapeutic climate will develop. In large measure, the establishment of the therapeutic climate will depend on the personality of the counsellor and the extent to which the core conditions are communicated. There are some basic skills, however, such as observing non-verbal behaviours, and using attending behaviours, open-ended leads, silent listening and summarization that facilitate the initial stages of communication, which would be discussed in Chapter 6.

5.1 The Counselling Environment

Several investigations have focused on the importance of the setting and the relationship of such factors as chair arrangements and room size to the client's response to counselling. Haase and Mattia (1976) studied affected changes in the verbal behaviour of the client. Their most significant finding was that room size does, in fact, affect the counselling process.

In this particular investigation, a small room diminished the number of positive self-referent statements made by the client. In another study, Chaikin, Derlega, and Miller (1976) found that client self-disclosure is significantly more intimate in a soft room environment than in a hard one. Client preference for seating arrangements was that submissive and dependent clients tended to prefer greater distance between chairs; subjects who were dominant, self-assured, and independent preferred the closer seating arrangements.

While these investigations lend support to the theory that the environ-ment does affect the counselling interview, the counsellor cannot always control environmental conditions. Some organizations, for example, may not provide the counsellor with an office, and interviews may have to be conducted wherever space is available.

In arranging an environment conducive to counselling, the privacy and soundproofness of the room are possibly the most significant factors to consider. Counselling interviews can be anxiety producing, the clients should be able to discuss their concerns without fear that people walking by will hear their personal self-disclosures. Frequently, counsellors prefer a casual environment as conducive to relaxation. Comfortable chairs, indirect lighting, and warm colours help develop a relaxed mood. Seating should be arranged in such a manner so that the client is not threatened by the counsellor's physical proximity. The counsellor's freedom of movement toward the client is also important. Some counsellors have found swivel chairs useful for keeping spatial distance directly under their control. Clients with high levels of anxiety may prefer the security of a desk between themselves and the counsellor, but generally a desk is felt to be a barrier to communication.

The secretary plays a significant role in the counselling environment. Often the first person to greet the client, the secretary sets the tone and therefore should be a warm and friendly individual who relates well to others. The secretary needs to be hospitable, but should not assume the role of therapist by becoming emotionally involved in the clients' lives. Likewise, a secretary who has access to client's records and files must understand that these are strictly confidential. The secretary should also insure that the counsellor is not interrupted during the session.

5.2 Intake Procedures

In private settings or community agencies the intake procedure includes clients filling out personal data sheets and often also taking a battery of psychological test. In some settings an intake interview may be required. Such interviews are conducted either by the counsellor assigned to the case or by a paraprofessional who acts as an intake worker. Counsellors in some setting may not follow formal intake procedures.

The purpose of the intake interview is to obtain a case history on the client. This case history is a collection of facts about the client's current and past life and may take many forms depending upon the style and preference of the counsellor or therapist and the type of problem situation (Brammer and Shostrom, 1982). A career counsellor, for example, would focus on factors influencing career choices; a psychoanalytically oriented therapist would want a detailed description of the client's early childhood experiences and affective development.

5.2.1 Confidentiality and Counsellor Dependability

All that transpires in an interview is private, and counsellors are obligated not to discuss client relationships with outside parties unless the client has given the counsellor written permission to do so. The counselling relationship may be the only relationship in which the client can freely share the anxieties, fears and feelings that have been harbored in many instances for a lifetime. As the client becomes confident that the counsellor respects the privacy of the relationship, trust in the counsellor grows. Because of the relationship between trust and confidentiality, counsellors must respect at all times the client's right not to have information divulged to parties outside the relationship.

The dependability of the counsellor affects the client's perception of trust in the relationship. As Benjamin has noted, it is more than a matter of courtesy for the counsellor to meet scheduled appointments and to be on time. Counsellors who are late or miss appointments can cause clients to wonder "whether we have forgotten him, whether he is of importance to us, whether we are keeping him waiting for some dark purpose unknown to him, whether we are being fair with him" (Benjamin, 1974).

5.2.2 Physical Set-up

The room set-up and seating arrangement can greatly contribute to but also detract from the creation of the right environment. Both communicate the counsellor's attitudes in a subtle but significant way.

Chairs placed at a slight angle to one another generally make people much more comfortable than chairs placed straight across from one another. Figure 5.1 shows that by sitting directly opposite someone (Position A), it is

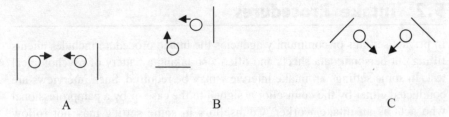

A   B   C

Figure 5.1 Sitting Positions.

easy to feel confrontational. Sitting at a 90 degree angle (Position B) is better, but not ideal because this angle can take away too much of the eye contact. Sitting at an angle slightly off head-on (Position C) is the ideal arrangement for counselling. This way it is easy to observe the other person and make direct eye contact, but also easy to break eye contact at times when it is uncomfortable.

It is best to use either no table or a low coffee table so that physical barriers will be limited and body language can be observed. If a table is necessary for papers and writing then considerations should be made. Figure 5.2 illustrates that a small round table is more flexible than a square or rectangular table or desk because there is a range of angles at which he can get the chairs placed. If the counsellor must use a table with sides then sit at right angles on one corner rather than straight across, and turn the chairs slightly towards one another. Comfortable soft chairs are a nice touch, but if they are too low and soft they are not conducive to a serious atmosphere.

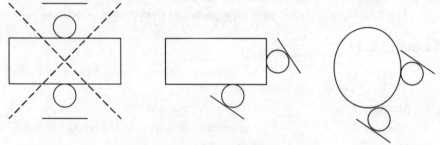

Figure 5.2 Table Arrangement.

The counsellor should give some thought to the room chosen for the interview ahead of time. Rather than arranging the meeting in his office or the subordinate's office, a neutral meeting room, such as a small conference room, will help to take away distractions and power differentials. Whatever room is chosen try to prepare it ahead of time. It is best to have it as tidy and as empty as possible, at least with a clear desk. The counsellor should put a clock from where he will be able to see it without looking at it and not making it obvious to the subordinate, for example, on a wall or shelf behind them. Remember to close the door to ensure privacy and plan for someone to take the calls to avoid interruptions. This gives the subordinate the impression that his issue is important, and that they are the total focus of counsellor's attention.

5.3 The Initial Counselling Interview

Counselling is a process that moves through predictable phases and stages. The process has a beginning, middle and an end, and counsellors must be familiar with the appropriate procedures for opening the interview, for continuing the interview, and for terminating it.

5.3.1 How to Open the Session

At the beginning of a counselling session, it is essential to establish an appropriate atmosphere. An invitation to the subordinate to talk is conveyed by the counsellor's posture, manner, gestures, tone of voice and words.

Equality in the relationship also needs to be confirmed. As a manager there will be many times when he will be required to take the position of authority and lead, and the subordinate may expect that from him. So it is all the more important to establish that this discussion is going to operate in a counselling style and, therefore, will be a meeting of equals. Do this early on by setting up the room appropriately, displaying listening responses, and by encouraging subordinates to take responsibility to help themselves.

When your subordinate enters the room, greet him warmly using his name, and offer him a seat. Then say something which makes him feel welcome and acknowledged, and communicates that it is up to him to define the problem as he sees it, and that you are ready to listen.

The following are examples of appropriate conversation openers:

EXAMPLE 5.1

Manager 1:	"Good morning, Suman. Please have a seat. How can I help you?"
Manager 2:	"…What is on your mind?"
Manager 3:	"…I understand you want to talk about…"
Manager 4:	"…Tell me about the situation."

If the counsellor, not the client, has initiated the conversation, then:

Manager 1:	"You don't seem yourself. Is anything going on? I've got some time if you'd like to talk."

Not seeming rushed is important, but clear time boundaries should be set at the start, along with limitations on confidentiality (if appropriate). If the meeting is only going to be partially conducted in a counselling style then it is a good idea to let the subordinate know which part this applies to and which parts will be otherwise.

After the client has been introduced to the counsellor by name, the counsellor may want to spend a few minutes in social conversation to relieve the tension and anxiety the client is probably experiencing; however, the counsellor must be careful not to spend too much time in this fashion. Whether the client is self-referred or has been referred to counselling by another party will influence how the counsellor opens the session. With a self-referred client, the counsellor could begin the session by saying to the client any of the following:

EXAMPLE 5.2

Manager 1:	"We have about half an hour to talk and I'm wondering what brings you to counselling."
Manager 2:	"Asha, We have an hour and I'd be interested in listening to anything you would like to share."
Manager 3:	"Raj, I thought we might begin today by your telling me about your expectations for counselling. We have an hour to talk."
Manager 4:	"Sonam, How would you like to spend our time today? We have about forty-five minutes."

In these examples, note that some structure is given in terms of time limits. Also, each statement communicates that the responsibility for the interview is the client's and that the client is to use the time in the most meaningful way.

Some clients come to counselling at the insistence of a third party. Teachers, parents and some managers often require an individual to see a therapist for psychological counsellors. Clients referred under such circumstances are frequently more anxious and resistant to the process. This situation requires careful thought and planning on the counsellor's part. Regardless of the reason for the referral, the counsellor must come across as warm and accepting. The counsellor may want to discuss the reasons for the referral, but the client should not feel judged and the client should be allowed to choose the topic for the interview. Although the client may have been referred to the counsellor for drinking habits in the office, the client may need to discuss other personal concerns, such as his/her impending divorce. Counsellors must be careful not to allow their preconceived notions of the problems to interfere with their response to the client's immediate needs.

5.3.2 Structuring the Session

The counsellor must give attention both to structuring the initial session and to establishing the long-term counselling relationship. Structuring the interview is essential because it clarifies for the client what can be expected of the counselling process. Clients frequently come to counselling with misconceptions. Some perceive counselling as a magical cure, as quick help, as problem solving or advice giving. Others often assume that the responsibility for success lies on the counsellor's shoulders. These unrealistic expectations need to be clarified at the outset of the counselling process.

The counsellor should open the first session by addressing the specific issues relating to client and counsellor roles, client goals and the confidentiality of the relationship. Such a statement should be as brief as possible. As noted earlier, the counsellor could choose to begin by asking the client what made her opt for counselling and what is expected of the process. After listening carefully to the client, the counsellor reacts to the expectations expressed. Time permitting; the interview can then proceed with a topic of the client's choosing.

In this initial interview, the counsellor must also deal with time limits as part of the structuring process. The length of the interview will vary, depending on the age of the client and the setting. For example, an interview with a child between the age group of five and seven years would be approximately twenty minutes long; between eight and twelve, approximately half an hour long; and for twelve and above, approximately an hour. In an office, the duration of the interaction would depend upon the time available with the client and the intensity of the problems. Obviously, these are guidelines only and cannot always be strictly adhered to.

The counsellor should state at the beginning of the session how long the interview will be. This is important; clients need to understand how much time is available so that they can pace themselves accordingly and can bring up personally relevant material early enough in the session to allow discussion. Counsellors who do not specify time limits frequently find that clients will hold on to a particularly painful concern until just before the end of the interview. This behaviour can be very manipulative. To help prevent this situation, the counsellor tells the client towards the end of the session how much time is left, giving the client an opportunity to raise any unfinished business before time runs out. A typical counsellor statement might be, "Harish, we have about ten minutes left today; is there anything else you would like to discuss?" Clients are often so involved in their concern that they often lose track of the time and need a reminder from the counsellor.

The duration of the counselling relationship can also be discussed in the initial interview, although the counsellor will probably want to have one or two sessions with the client before estimating the duration. Most counselling will continue for at least a month and not longer than a year; the duration will depend on the severity of the problem and the effectiveness of the counselling.

5.3.3 Goals for the First Session

The initial counselling session is in some ways the most important. The client begins to build trust in the counsellor during this session, and many of the counsellor's behaviours are being carefully scrutinized. The primary goal of the first session is establishing rapport. Eisenberg and Delaney (1977) have listed the following as appropriate process goals for the first session:

(a) Stimulate open, honest and full communication about the concerns needing to be discussed and the factors and background related to those concerns.

(b) Work toward progressively deeper levels of understanding, respect and trust between self and client.

(c) Provide the client with the view that something useful can be gained from the counselling sessions.

(d) Identify a problem or concern for the subsequent attention and work.

(e) Establish the "Gestalt" that counselling is a process in which both parties must work hard at exploring and understanding the client and his or her concerns.

(f) Acquire information about the client that relates to his or her concerns and effective problem solution.

5.3.4 Termination of the Initial Interview

The counsellor will need to prepare his client for the end of the counselling session. About ten minutes before time runs out, he should tell him how much time is left. It is useful for both of them to be aware of the limitation on the remaining time so that they can decide how they want to use it. They may want to go into an area not covered yet, or to go deeper into an area previously only touched upon.

Then, two or three minutes from the end, summarise the main points covered during the meeting. If the manager or counsellor and the client plan to meet again, arrange the time and summarise action to be taken by either of them before the next meeting. If they will not be meeting again then leave the subordinate with some positive feedback (for example, courage in raising a difficult issue) or something constructive to think about. Following example explains how an initial interview can be terminated in the work setting (refer to Interaction 5.1).

INTERACTION 5.1

Area Manager to Retail Store Manager:

"I see we're running out of time. Let's see if we can pull together what we've covered. You began by explaining why you are becoming dissatisfied in your current position as you approach retirement age. You feel more and more removed from your staff, both by age and style, and you would like to move to the IT department at central office, where you can make use of your favourite hobby and pastime, computing, during your last five years. You are aware that this has only been a whim up to now, but that you are feeling more and more discontented as time goes on. During the course of our conversation, you have determined that it is time to do something. Maybe between now and next time you could do the networking you suggested, in order to see if your skills could be used in that department."

At the close of the initial counselling session, the client and the counsellor must make a decision regarding the continuation of their relationship. If the client and the counsellor both agree that another session is required then the next appointment must be scheduled. It should be reiterated that the client should be notified that the session is drawing to a close before the time period ends. The counsellor may do this or may instruct the secretary to knock on the door or buzz the intercom at the appropriate time.

At the end of the initial interview, the counsellor must decide whether or not to refer the client to another counsellor or agency. The referral procedure requires some skills, which are being discussed in Section 5.4.

5.4 Referral Procedures

A manager who is proficient in counselling skills will tend to attract people to come to him or her with their problems, and will run into situations where it is not appropriate to help with the problem. Instead the subordinate needs to be referred elsewhere. But how should the counsellor or manager decide where to refer the person seeking help. He should refer the client when he feels that he is out of depth, i.e., he does not feel himself to be qualified to deal with the issues or when he feels uncomfortable in handling the task or does not have the resources to deal with the problems. Also he should refer the client to someone else when time constraints do not allow him to help. He should try to follow the axiom: "Do not try to take on everything yourself. Be aware of when professional help is needed and what sorts of professional help are available".

A manager should stick to dealing with 'here and now' problems, not deeply ingrained or long-term emotional problems which require a more permanent and professional nurturing relationship to heal. If he does not refer when he is out of his depth he could make matters worse. If he encounters a situation where phases of developing the trust required for openness and defining the problem, are going to take a long time, then it is likely that the subordinate would be better off referred to a professional.

In many instances, counsellors cannot provide the counselling service needed by the client and must send the client elsewhere. Although some may view referring a client as a sign of inadequacy, a great deal of competency is needed to identify situations that require specialized services. It is unrealistic for counsellors to assume that they can be of service to every person seeking assistance.

5.4.1 When to Refer

To make a good referral, the counsellor must have information about the client and the nature of the client's concern. A brief interview may be conducted to gather this information, or as noted earlier, the referral can be made at the close of the initial interview.

It is appropriate to refer a client to a professional counsellor under the following conditions:

(a) When the client presents a concern that is beyond the counsellor's level of competency.

(b) When the counsellor feels that personality differences between him and the client cannot be resolved and will interfere with the counselling process.

(c) Also in case the client is a personal friend or relative, and the concern is going to require an ongoing relationship. Because of their basic skills in human relations, counsellors are often the first persons sought out by friends and relatives in need of assistance, and it would be inhumane not to respond. However, it is difficult and in fact undesirable to maintain a counselling relationship over a period of time with a friend or relative. When it becomes obvious that the concern requires an ongoing therapeutic relationship, the individual should be referred to another counsellor.

(d) The client is reluctant to discuss his problem with the counsellor for some reason.

(e) After several sessions, the counsellor does not feel your relationship with the client is effective.

5.4.2 How to Refer

Following points should be borne in mind while referring a client to some other professional counsellor agency:

(a) Rather than referring a client to an agency, whenever possible the counselling manager should refer the client to a specific person in the agency. Become familiar with the services provided by local agencies and with the staff of each agency, so that he can match the client's needs with a specific counsellor's competencies.

(b) The counselling manager should provide the client with accurate and specific information, including the names, addresses and phone numbers of the persons or agencies to which he is referring him. The client may wish to place a call for an appointment from the office, but the counsellor should not make the appointment for the client. The client must assume responsibility for getting further help, and making the appointment reflect some commitment to the process.

(c) The client may ask the counselling manager to share information about his concern with the person to whom he has been referred. It is recommended that this information not be given in front of the client. Often this kind of contact relieves some of the client's anxiety about seeing a new counsellor. It is preferable to get written permission from the client for this consultation.

(d) Do not expect to be informed regarding the confidence shared by the client with the next counsellor without the client's permission. If the counselling manager continues to have a working relationship of a different nature with the client, he can request information regarding how to relate to the client in future interactions if such information is necessary.

(e) Whenever possible, follow up the referral by checking with the client to see if the new relationship is satisfactorily meeting the client's needs. But avoid pressuring the client for information and accept whatever the client wishes to share.

Like the counselling process, referrals procedures must be based on trust and respect for the individual seeking assistance. Counsellors can only make clients aware of the alternatives that will provide the best means of assistance on the client's terms. The client may choose to ignore or accept the help available. The counsellor's role is to create an awareness of the alternatives and to see that the client has the maximum opportunities to utilize them. Counsellors should be aware of the legal issues surrounding the referral process and should be careful to take appropriate steps to prevent the possibility of legal action.

5.5 Guidelines for Effective Counselling

Once the initial process has begun, there are some guidelines that need to be followed for effective counselling. These are as follows:

5.5.1 Keeping the Focus on the Other Person

When the subordinate focuses excessively on another person (or people), it is important to redirect the conversation towards his focusing on himself, and make them take responsibility for his own actions. Often people will talk about difficulties in the third person—"he said ..., she said ..., he did ..., she did ..." Valuable time will be wasted if the focus is not kept on the subordinate and his own feelings and actions. Discussing others over extensively is not going to help the subordinate to decide what action to take for themselves. Consider the following interactions:

INTERACTION 5.2

Subordinate: "My assistant has frequently been absent recently. He is going through a divorce, and I think he is finding it very stressful. I am finding it difficult to cope without him, especially since his absences are sporadic and unpredictable."

Manager 1: "So your assistant is going through a difficult divorce."

Subordinate: "My assistant has frequently been absent recently. He is going through a divorce, and I think he is finding it very stressful. I am finding it difficult to cope without him, especially since his absences are sporadic and unpredictable."

Manager 2: "You are frustrated at not knowing when he will be out of the office."

Manager 2 was able to keep the focus on the subordinate, whereas Manager 1 was directing the conversation towards externals—the assistant, the difficult divorce.

The manager should encourage his subordinate to focus on themselves by using 'I' statements rather than outwardly focused 'he', 'she' or 'they' statements. This will promote acknowledgement of their feelings, thoughts and actions, and ownership of his problems.

Focusing on externals is very common, especially since those who come to seek counselling advice often really believe that the problem belongs to another person and not to them. There is nothing wrong with the question that Manager 1 asks in the Interaction 5.3. It is simply too early to consider someone else's point of view when the subordinate's point of view has not been fully examined. In the beginning, the focus is best kept on the subordinate. Once the counsellor has fully explored the problem as it exists for him and have explored his feelings about it and are ready to move on to changing the way he perceives and deals with the problem, then this question would be appropriate.

INTERACTION 5.3

Subordinate: "My secretary is always irritable. She is difficult every time I ask her to do something."

Manager 1:   "Why do you think she is irritable?"

Subordinate: "Maybe she's having problems at home. She is irritable with other people as well."

Subordinate: "My secretary is always irritable. She is difficult every time I ask her to do something."

Manager 2:   "What effect is this having on you?"

Subordinate: "It's making me avoid her."

Manager 2:   "You now prefer not to have contact with her."

Subordinate: "Yes, and this is now affecting our work!"

Manager 2's response focuses on the subordinate and the effects the situation is having on him. Talking in this manner will help the subordinate to see that the situation is causing a problem for him and the work is suffering and that action needs to be taken by him to get over the problem.

Not only the counselling manager should encourage subordinate to acknowledge that he has a problem of his own on his hands, but he should take this a stage further and encourage him to acknowledge that some of his own actions (or inaction) may be supporting or continuing his problem.

5.5.2 Silence is Golden

If counselling skills are used appropriately, there will be silent periods in the conversation. At first, this might make the client uncomfortable. Many people are uncomfortable with silence, and feel as if they need to fill it by saying something. When counselling, however, silence actually improves the conversation remarkably. It allows time to consider what has been said, and to gather thoughts and clarify them. Silence also gives time and space to get in tough with thoughts and feelings, which are not so immediate and close to the surface. If a manager talks too much, he blocks his subordinates from feeling, thinking and talking. Using silence effectively is another way of encouraging them to take responsibility for talking about the real problem. This silent time is not wasted; it is very productive.

Their silence can mean one of many things such as: thinking about what has been said, or where to go next; sorting out feelings, or just feeling the feelings; wanting you to speak; conveying anger, refusal to engage; not having words to express, blockage or blankness; respect; fear; embarrassment; boredom; sadness; or contempt. If subordinates are silent for a very long time, the manager can talk to them and try to find out what the silence means.

5.5.3 Managing Emotions

In order to use counselling skills effectively, the manager needs to understand emotions. When subordinates bring problems to the manager, there are two ways in which emotions can have an effect on the conversation: the subordinate might be in an emotional state to start with, or suddenly have an emotional outburst during the course of the conversation; or they might be repressing emotions in a detrimental way. In the first case, the manager needs to know how to respond to their emotional behaviour, and in the second case the manager needs to address the repressed emotions.

Outbursts and ventilation: When the subordinates are already in or get into an emotional state, the manager should be aware that they will need a period of time to discharge the emotions (in Phase 1) before moving on either to define or resolve the problem. The manager has to allow this discharge, often referred to by psychologists as ventilation, to happen. See it as positive because discharging emotion will allow them to move on. The manager's encouragement of their accepting, expressing and releasing (rather than suppressing) emotions is extremely important and healthy. If emotions are not dealt with, feelings will bubble beneath the surface, and affect the subordinate in detrimental ways, blocking them from proceeding or showing up as unwanted behaviours.

How should the manager deal with strong emotions? Allow subordinates to cry rather even encourage it. Let them continue crying until the tears subside naturally. Crying is a healthy release of the build-up of tension and stress. Interrupting the crying process is interrupting the restoring process of emotional release. Acknowledge verbally what the person is feeling and let them experience the painful emotions fully. This is what is needed in order for them to move on.

One problem in our society is shame about showing emotion. Managers tend to think that they are doing the proper and polite thing by ignoring emotions—by behaving in a professional manner and saving face for people who might be embarrassed about a display of emotion. This well-intentioned attitude causes a lot of damage because it means that problems are not fully worked through and resolved. Time and time again it has been seen that managers get stuck to the logical and matter-of-fact problem solving and do not show acknowledgement and understanding of the feelings communicated, then the feelings are repeatedly brought up by the subordinates, sometimes verbally, other times non-verbally, stopping the process from continuing until the feelings are acknowledged.

The same is true of other emotions, such as anger. So long as subordinates are not threatening the manager or company property, allow them to express their anger. While they are expressing strong emotions the manager may even feel at a loss for what to do. The best is to do as little as possible while waiting patiently. Anything the manager tries to discuss while they are in a highly emotional state will not be heard anyway. The only useful comments are reflections of what the subordinates are feeling, and reassurances that their feelings are normal and natural, which show them that the manager understands and accepts their emotions.

Sometimes this discharge of emotions in the presence of an empathetic human being is all that is needed. After the release of emotions is over, the person's mind may be clearer, their will and confidence may be stronger, and they may be ready to resolve matters on their own.

At other times, seeing subordinates through an initial emotional phase will lead to their being able to express their thoughts in a rational enough manner to begin determining specifically what the problem is and what can be done about it. This is one of the reasons why it is not appropriate for managers to help subordinates with long-term, deep-seated emotional problems. The initial phase of recognizing and releasing pent-up emotions will take much more specialist skill and time than a manager has to offer.

Repression: Figure 5.3 shows the interaction between feelings (emotions), thoughts and behaviours. The inner arrow demonstrates the cycle in one direction: feelings affect thoughts, which affect behaviours.

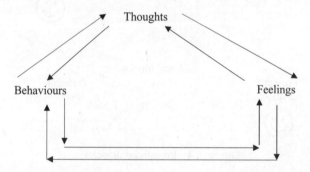

Figure 5.3 Interaction Between Feelings, Thoughts and Behaviours.

Thoughts are often expression of feelings at various levels of awareness. If your subordinate is exhibiting strange or inexplicable behaviours, it may be due to a repressed feeling. For example, belligerent behaviour towards authority figures could be due to a fear of them. The person may not be aware of the feeling (fear), and may not even be conscious of the resulting behaviour (belligerence). Another example is a supervisor's compulsive perfectionism, which causes him or her continually to watch over employees' shoulders. The underlying feelings could be inadequacy. Feelings are often displaced onto a safer and easier target. For example, anger towards a dominating partner can be taken out on subordinates. Once the feeling is revealed, acknowledged, expressed and accepted then the behaviour is likely to lessen. Behind poor performance is often an unexpressed feeling.

When subordinates are avoiding discussing emotions—refusing to acknowledge emotions and talking only on a logical level when the counsellor suspect there are indeed emotions involved—then encourage them to talk about the repressed feelings. The counsellor can either reflect only the emotional content of their communication, or ask direct questions about what they are feeling.

Positive thinking: The emotions/thoughts/behaviours cycle works in both directions. The outer cycle of arrows illustrates that thoughts also affect feelings, which in turn manifest themselves in behaviours. This cycle in the diagram is very useful for explaining to subordinates the power of positive thinking. People can feel more positive if they change their thoughts. Note that positive thinking tends to work only after negative feelings have been validated; otherwise, it just becomes another way of repressing them.

Emotional blocks to taking action: Emotional blocks can impede people from taking action, even when, on a logical level, they want to do so. If there is no apparent reason why the subordinate is not implementing his action plan then there is likely to be an emotional block, which is preventing them from progressing. Try to help them to recognize and work through the block (Refer Figure 5.4).

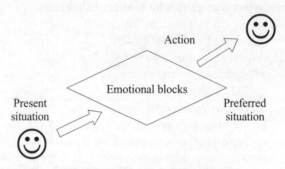

Figure 5.4 Emotional Blocks.

The counsellor manager should ask them about what thoughts and feelings may be blocking them. For example, he could ask, "what are you feeling when you consider doing X?", or "What thoughts are going through your mind when you imagine trying this option?" Becoming aware of and talking about the blocks will help them to overcome them.

Some common emotional blocks, which prevent the necessary action being taken to bring about the desired change, include:

1. Fear of failure or of their efforts being wasted.
2. Fear of other people's reactions to their changes.
3. Fear of higher expectations from others—not being able to cope with the new situation.
4. Uncertainty about choice like, 'Am I making the right decision?'
5. Difficulty visualizing self in new position.
6. Fear of the unknown and risk—known pain (in their present situation) is comfortable because it is predictable.

The change itself can be what is frightening them. People are creatures of habit and somehow comfortable in their present situation, even if they don't like it. People get used to being unhappy, and the fear of trying to change (which leads to a new, unknown situation) can be greater than the fear or remaining unhappy in the present situation. If they do begin to change, they can become frightened of their own strange new feelings, which result in distressing them more.

One note of caution, i.e., occasionally people get stuck in a rut, remaining in an emotional mode for too long. Once the feelings have been adequately expressed and released, the counsellor should encourage them to move on.

Symptom or cause: The manager or counsellor should be aware that the original problem as presented by the subordinate is often not a full explanation of the real problem. It could be a symptom of the underlying problem, or it could be totally unrelated, especially if the subordinate feels too uncomfortable to jump straight into talking about the real problem. Sometimes a smaller sub-problem of the bigger, deeper problem is brought up. The counsellor or manager should be prepared either to probe or to offer plenty of time/space (silence) to let things emerge so that he is sure that he has a full picture of the situation before moving on to problem solving. The subordinate is likely to need encouragement, rapport and trust building to go deeper.

Probing carefully will also help to determine what is the best method of problem solving. It is all too easy just to send someone who is struggling on a training course, which sounds as if it will cover the general area of the problem. Sending subordinates for training is a very typical attempt to solve their problems. If the training does not address the real issues, however, it can be an expensive error. Using counselling skills can sometimes be more effective (and cost-effective) than a training course. At other times the subordinate's problem is part of a larger organizational problem. Try to uncover and face the real feelings and issues underlying superficial problems. Example 5.3 depicts how to solve a problem, how best to manage a real problem rather than focusing on the symptoms only.

EXAMPLE 5.3

Neha was a young applications administrator within a large insurance firm. She had been with the company in this position for eight months and her supervisor, Sharad, was concerned because she was not performing as well as he had expected her to. She did not seem to remember procedures, and was always asking him and colleagues for help with simple tasks. Sharad was puzzled because the work was not difficult, and Neha had performed well during her induction training.

When Sharad met Neha to chat about how things were going, he was surprised to find out that she expressed no concern or dissatisfaction with her performance. When Sharad mentioned that she seemed to need a lot of help, Neha replied in an unconcerned manner that she tended to be a bit forgetful, but that people were always very helpful.

Sharad, feeling annoyed by her requests for help, was tempted to say that he was very concerned about whether Neha was appropriate for a role which required efficiency and organization and that she needed to pull her socks up. Instead he asked her whether she thought she was happy in the position. She responded that yes she was, but she would prefer to have an assistant to help her. Sharad questioned Neha at length regarding why she required an assistant when no one working in that position before had ever needed one, but got nowhere until Neha finally gave an emotional reason instead of trying to rationalize: 'I suppose it would just be nicer to have someone to work with.' Sharad asked whether Neha had ever worked alone before and it turned out that her previous jobs had all been very social, Neha then realized that Sharad was questioning her regarding her poor work performance so she admitted that owing to her social nature and previous job experience, she was deliberately trying to find out excuses to intercept with people which not only distracted and annoyed them but also impeded her work performance.

Sharad's patient and determined questioning got to the underlying problem (loneliness) behind the surface problem (ineffectiveness). He and Neha could then work together to decide how best to manage the real problem (the cause), rather than focusing superficially only on one result (symptom) of that problem.

5.6 A Word of Advice

Do not try to become proficient at all the counselling skills at once. The counsellor manager will be setting himself up for discouragement and failure. Focus on one skill at a time. Wait until one feels natural, comfortable and effective before moving on to the next. He is likely to get worse before you get better! Concentrate on one thing at a time: things will improve. There are four stages following that people go through when working on interpersonal skills:

Unconsciously incompetent: The counsellor manager is blissfully unaware of his lack of skill.

Consciously incompetent: He receives some feedback about his incompetence; reads a book, takes a course, and somehow realizes that he can improve his skills.

Consciously competent: Things get worse for a while before they get better. The counsellor manager self-consciously struggles to apply what he has learned.

Unconsciously competent: As his new skills become more automatic, they become part of his natural style.

Moving through stages 2 and 3 is the most difficult transition, but don't give up!

5.7 Advanced Skills in Counselling

Once the counselling process has begun and the therapeutic climate has been established, the counsellor's task is to facilitate client self-exploration and to increase the level of client self-understanding so that effective and desired changes in behaviour can occur. The counsellor must employ more advanced skills to help clients reach this level of self-exploration and self-understanding. Such skills include advanced empathy, theme identification, self-disclosure, perception check, interpretation, clarification, confrontation and immediacy. While these advanced skills will facilitate action in terms of behaviour change in some clients, it is necessary for counsellors to be prepared to implement action programs in the advanced stages of the counselling process with those clients who need specific help.

5.7.1 Advanced Empathy

Empathy is defined as the ability to tune in to the client's feelings and to be able to see the client's world as it truly seems to the client. Empathy, then, can be viewed as a skill as well as an attitude, and it can be employed at different levels. At its primary level, an empathic response communicates an understanding of the client's frame of reference and accurately identifies the client's feelings. In contrast, advanced empathy takes the client a step further into self-exploration by adding deeper feeling and meaning to the client's expression. Egan (1975) has illustrated the difference between the primary and the advanced accurate empathy in the following interaction:

INTERACTION 5.4

Client: "I don't know what's going on. I study hard, but I just don't get good marks. I think I study as hard as anyone else, but all of my efforts seem to go down the drain. I don't know what else I can do."

Counsellor A: "You feel frustrated because even when you try hard, you fail."

Counsellor B: "It's depressing to put in as much effort as those who pass and still fail. It gets you down and maybe even makes you feel a little sorry for yourself."

Counsellor A tries to understand the client from the client's frame of reference. He deals with the client's feelings and the experience underlying these feelings. Counsellor B, however, probes a bit further. From the context, from past interchanges, from the client's manner and tone of voice, he picks up something that the client does not express overtly, that the client feels sorry for himself. The client is looking at himself as a victim, as the one who has failed, as the one who is depressed. This is his frame of reference, but in reality he is also beginning to say, "Poor me, I feel sorry for myself." This is a different perspective, but one that is also based on the data of the self-exploration process.

In Interaction 5.4, the advances empathy of counsellor B takes the client to a new level of self-understanding. Because this counsellor not only sees the situation from the client's perspective, but also sees it more clearly and more fully, that he can share the implication of the client's perspective for effective or ineffective living.

5.7.2 Theme Identification

The advanced empathic response also helps the counsellor identify themes in the counselling session. Typically, clients express a variety of concerns during a session. At the outset these concerns may seem unrelated. The counsellor who listens carefully and with a trained ear can begin to hear the relationship among various incidents, situations, problems and feelings. For example, a client may bring up a concern such as his wife making most of the household decisions and then may express a concern that he doesn't feel very competent at work. As the session develops, the counsellor may respond with the following statement: "It sounds to me like your inability to make decisions is beginning to have an impact on how you see yourself both at home and at the office."

Themes that might arise in a counselling situation could include the following:

1. The client's self-concept—a poor self-image
2. The client's as a dependent person
3. The client's need for approval
4. The client's need to be loved and accepted by everyone
5. The client's lack of assertiveness
6. The client's need for control
7. The client's rebellion against authority
8. The client's insecurity with women (men)
9. The client's manipulative nature
10. The client's need for security
11. The client's inability to experience feelings in the here and now

As Egan (1975) has noted, by identifying themes the counsellor takes clients beyond their expressed concerns and facilitates the self-exploration process by helping clients confront their interpersonal style. A counselling session may consist of several themes, but the central theme underlying the client's interpersonal style will be repeated throughout the interview. Often a theme will be signalled by what might be called a **red flag**—a word or a phrase that stands out from the rest either through the voice tone used or the significance the word or phrase seems to have in the context of the discussion. Themes that are repeated throughout the session appear and reappear like a red thread woven into a cloth.

Consider the client who begins the session complaining about her teacher who caught her cheating, and progresses to talking of her difficulty relating to her father, and ends by complaining about how you confront her about the inconsistencies she has stated. The red thread is the client's difficulty relating to authority figures in her world.

This example illustrates the importance of theme identification in helping clients come to new awareness regarding their interpersonal style. In this sense the identification of a central theme communicates an understanding of the client's frame of reference beyond the present level of self-awareness and thus is related to the advanced accurate empathic response.

5.7.3 Self-disclosure

Self-disclosure involves revealing your feelings and reactions to events and people as they occur. Within the counselling relationship, the counsellor may choose to reveal himself to the client to facilitate the client's openness. In one method of self-disclosure, the counsellor might use immediacy to share his reactions to the client or to their relationship openly in the here and now. In another method the counsellor might respond to a client statement that is closely related to the counsellor's own experience by sharing the similar experience in feeling terms. This, however, can prove to be difficult, for two reasons: first, because the counsellor's experience must in fact closely resemble that of the client; and secondly, the counsellor must make the self-disclosure long enough to draw the similarity and brief enough so as not to take the focus of the session off the client.

Self-disclosure, when properly implemented, can promote a client's feeling of being understood. It can also enable the counsellor to identify the client's feelings at a deeper level than might otherwise be achieved. In this respect, self-disclosure can facilitate an advanced empathic response. The following interaction illustrates how this skill might be used in the counselling session:

INTERACTION 5.5

Client: "I am having difficulty with my father. He is getting older and he is very lonely. He comes over and stays all day and I feel like I have to entertain him. I get behind on all of my chores, and my children are neglected. I want to be helpful to him, but it is becoming more and more difficult."

Counsellor: "I think I can understand how angry and resentful and yet guilty you must feel. My mother-in-law is widowed and is lonely and bored. She keeps showing up at the most inconvenient times and stays for hours. I can hardly be pleasant anymore, and I feel for being so selfish."

In this statement the counsellor bridges the gap between herself and the client first by letting the client know something about her personal life and second by communicating an accepting and understanding attitude toward the client's guilt. In essence, such a self-disclosure communicates to the client that the counsellor is a real person with problems and concerns too.

Timing is very important in the success of self-disclosure. It cannot be over emphasized and the self-disclosure must be brief so as not to take the focus off the client.

Giannandrea and Murphy (1973) conducted an investigation using college males as subjects. They found that when the counsellor employed an intermediate number of self-disclosures, significantly more students returned for a second interview than when the counsellor used fewer or more self-disclosures. Self-disclosure may increase the counsellor's attractiveness as well as encourage the client to respond to the counsellor.

Jourard and Jaffee (1970) found that when counsellors increased the length of their self-disclosures before discussing a topic, the client responded with lengthier self-disclosures.

Drag (1969) found that counsellors who themselves use self-disclosure elicit more self-disclosures from their clients, and are also perceived as more trustworthy.

5.7.4 Perception Check

Counsellor's statements made in response to a client's feelings should be stated tentatively. The counsellor must avoid coming across in as "I think I understood how you feel." Another alternative is for the counsellor to use a perception check, which is an interpretation of the other's feelings stated in a tentative form. A perception check communicates to the client the counsellor's interest in understanding exactly what the client is experiencing, especially when the client may not be expressing feelings directly. A counsellor could check his or her perception with a tentative statement: "You seem to be really irritated with me for being late", or "Shalini, you seem rather removed from the discussion today, and I'm not sure if you're feeling bored or just tired." Still another example might be, "Shobha, if I were you I might be feeling hurt that my feelings were not responded to. Is that what you're experiencing?"

5.7.5 Interpretation

Interpretive statements cover a broad range of counsellor responses; their purpose is to add meaning to client's attitudes, feelings and behaviour. Interpretive responses draw causal relationships among these three areas. Because interpretations are a process of imposing meaning on behaviours, the interpretation will vary depending on one's theoretical orientation (Brammer and Shostrom, 1982).

Timing is important in making interpretive responses. In the early stages of the relationship, the counsellor typically stays with the client and responds to the client's concerns from the client's frame of reference. As the relationship progresses, the counsellor gains increasingly greater insight into the client's dynamics and is in a more able position to suggest or infer relationships, perceive patterns of behaviour and motives, and is able to help the client integrate these understandings. It is of utmost importance that the client is at a point of readiness that will allow the counsellor's response to facilitate growth and behaviour change. If inappropriately timed, an interpretive response can cause the client to become defensive and resist the process. Because of the nature of the interpretive response, it should always be phrased tentatively, allowing the client to reject the comment if it is inaccurate or if the client is not ready to hear it.

Interpreting too Quickly / Over interpreting: Common mistakes, which an amateur counsellor makes when beginning to use counselling skills often, involve over interpreting, or interpreting too quickly. Reading between the lines and following hunches can usually only be carried out successfully by the professional counsellors. Amateur or lay counsellors should only interpret very tentatively, putting forward their interpretation as a question, and only when there are definite indicators (body language, tone of voice) as evidence.

The following is an interaction of interpreting too quickly, and therefore focusing on the wrong topic.

INTERACTION 5.6

Security Department Head:	"Our security system is extremely out of date. I can't get the guy in charge of purchasing to listen to me. He's hopeless! The cost of investing in a new one is a lot less than the cost of theft. People go unchecked in and out of this building as they please."
Manager:	"So we are having a problem with theft then."

The real concern of the security head may be communication with the purchasing department and the process for making purchasing decisions, or it may be a personality conflict with the guy in charge of purchasing. But the manager probably interpreted that theft was the reason issue because he or she jumped to conclusions too soon. More open questions (which don't lead the conversation yet) and/or listening are needed at this stage to discover which issue is of real concern to the security department head.

Interaction 5.7 is a situation where the manager is over interpreting.

INTERACTION 5.7

Regional Sales Manager:	"One member of my sales team, Renu, is cleverer than I am. She often wants to rewrite bits of my proposals."
Product Manager:	"You feel threatened by Renu's intelligence."

Unless there were previous indications, or telling body language or tone of voice along with the sales manager's statement, this would be over interpretation. The regional sales manager did not mention feeling threatened. Maybe he or she feels proud of Renu and her intelligence, and is excited about what she can contribute to the sales team.

The product manager's interpretation may or may not be correct. Other people may have a different and legitimate interpretation or explanation.

Therefore, interpretations need to be put forward very tentatively, allowing the subordinate plenty of opportunity to modify them. If the regional sales manager in the last interaction sounded angry and was physically tense then a better response to him would be: "You seem a bit anxious. Is it possible that Renu's intelligence is worrying you?"

If there were no indications from the regional sales manager's voice or body language regarding feelings about Renu's cleverness then asking a simple question such as "How do you feel about that?" would be more appropriate.

How the counsellor uses interpretive techniques will depend on his or her theoretical orientation. Traditionally, client-centred counsellors have cautioned against the use of interpretive responses (Rogers, 1942). However, by the classic client-centred technique, reflection of feeling can be viewed as an interpretation.

To make the concept clear a discussion on the three interpretive techniques: clarification, confrontation and immediacy follows:

5.7.6 Clarification

In clarification, the counsellor's response attempts to make a client's verbalization clearer to both the counsellor and the client. A clarification can focus on cognitive information, or it can seek to highlight a client's meanings that are not initially clear. Clarification is related to both skill of interpretation and the core condition of concreteness. Some examples of clarification are: "I'm not sure if you got into a fight before or after you got to the school playground"; "Are you feeling angry or resentful?" and "Is the issue whether or not you can afford to quit your job or are you concerned about how others might respond to your unemployment?"

5.7.7 Confrontation

Confrontation holds the potential for promoting growth and change or for devastating the client. Because it is so powerful, counsellors must implement a confrontive response with great skill. Here let us examine the various uses of confrontation, some guidelines in practicing the skill, and some cautions.

Confronting another's behaviour is a delicate procedure which requires both a sense of timing and a sensitivity and awareness of the client's receptivity. When properly done, confrontation can help clients become more integrated and consistent in their behaviour and in their relationships with others. A confrontive response should only be made in the context of trust and caring for the client and should not be used as a means of venting anger and frustration.

A confrontation may take several forms. It can be used to point to discrepancies between what they think and feel, and what they say and what they do, their views of themselves and others' views of them, what they are and what they wish to be, what they really are and what they experience themselves to be, their verbal and non-verbal expressions of themselves.

Some specific examples of these discrepancies adapted from Egan (1975) would be the following:

INTERACTION 5.8

Client 1: "I'm depressed and lonely, but I say that everything's okay."

Client 2: "I believe that people need to make their own decisions, but I constantly give my children advice about their lives."

Client 3: "I see myself as witty and others perceive me to be sarcastic."

Client 4: "I would like to be a good student, but I'm a slow learner, yet I party every night and don't study."

Client 5: "I experience myself as overweight when in fact others see me as having a good build."

Client 6: "I say 'yes' with my behaviour and dress, and yet hold others at a distance and am fearful of physical intimacy."

Client 7: "I say that I want to listen and be helpful to others, but I consistently dominate conversations."

Confrontation can also be used to help clients see things as they are rather than perceiving situations on the basis of their needs. In other words, counsellors can help clients attain an alternative frame of reference, enabling them to clear up distortions in experience. An example of a distorted perception would be, "My husband has taken a job that requires him to travel because he doesn't love me." In a marriage counselling situation, the counsellor could confront this message by responding to observations that indicate that the husband does love her, but that their financial situation requires that he take this better paying position, although it will require him to be away from home.

Still another use of confrontation is to help clients understand when they may be evading issues or ignoring feedback from others. When a client is evading an issue, the counsellor might confront him with a statement such as: "We've been meeting for two sessions, and you haven't raised the one issue you mentioned as a major concern—your relationship with your wife. Every time we get close to the topic, you change the subject. I'm wondering what's going on."

When a client is ignoring feedback, the counsellor might say: "I heard Aditi saying that she has difficulty feeling close to you because you speak so cognitively about your experience, yet I haven't heard you even acknowledge her comment. What is your reaction to her statement?"

Because the question of when to confront so often arises, the following guidelines are offered:

1. The counsellor should confront the client when he is willing to become more involved with the client.
2. He should confront more when the relationship has been built and the client's level of trust in counsellor is high.

3. The confrontation should be done out of a genuine caring for the client's growth and change.

Confrontation should not be used as a way to meet the counsellor's needs.

Little research has been done on confrontation. Kaul, Kaul and Bedner (1973) examined the relationship between client's self-exploration and counsellor's confrontation. They found that confrontive counsellors did not elicit more client's self-exploration than speculative counsellors, whether judged by raters or clients. When Berenson and Mitchell (1974) investigated confrontation they found it to be useful and concluded that confrontations help clients to see and experience problems rather than just understanding them. The research on confrontation is rather inconclusive, and it is recommended that confrontation be used discreetly and with care rather than as a modus operandi.

5.7.8 Immediacy

Of the myriad difficulties, which clients bring to counsellors, most involve interpersonal relationships. The counsellor-client relationship mirrors the client's behaviour in the outside world, which makes it an ideal situation in which to explore the client's interpersonal skills. If counsellors can be sensitive to the dynamics of their relationships with clients, they can help their clients explore interpersonal issues ranging from trust and dependency to manipulation. The skill of immediacy involves counsellors' being sensitively turned into their interactions with and reactions to clients as they occur. They can respond to these feelings about either the client or the relationship in the here and now. Immediacy is closely related to the skills of self-disclosure and confrontation, as well as to counsellor genuineness.

Immediacy requires that counsellors should trust their gut-level reactions and that they respect the client. The following interaction may help to illustrate this point.

INTERACTION 5.9

Counsellor: "I'm having difficulty staying tuned in today. It seems that we're rehashing old stuff, and I suppose that I'm getting tired of hearing the same things over again. How are you feeling about being here and what's transpired between us?"

Client: "Well, I suppose I'm avoiding talking about some issues that are very painful and that I'd like to ignore."

In this dialogue the counsellor was able to share quite candidly her lack of involvement in the process, and this exchange led the client to explore more personally relevant material.

5.8 Action Strategies

Since the purpose of all counselling is to facilitate a change in client, counsellors should be familiar with the basic principles underlying behaviour change. As noted in the discussion later on goal setting, internal processes and behaviour are not viewed as separate entities; rather, they are intimately related to each other. Many clients are able to act on the insights and new under-standings they gain through the therapeutic climate and through the various advanced skills employed by the counsellor. However, at times counsellors must facilitate the behaviour change process by implementing specific action strategies or programmes. The timing for implementation of these programmes will depend on the theoretical orientation of the counsellor and on the nature of the client's concern.

5.8.1 Behavioural Techniques

Systematic Desensitization: Desensitization is appropriate when the client has a high level of anxiety associated with problem behaviour. Examples of such problems would include anxiety about test taking, fear of heights and fear of speaking to groups, and so on. Counter conditioning coupled with muscle relaxation procedures are used to desensitize the client to anxiety-producing situations.

Behaviour Contracts: A behaviour contract is an agreement between two parties aimed at changing the behaviour of one of the persons involved. The agreement specifies the reinforcement contingent on reaching the goal. The behaviour contract obviously has many applications in facilitating client action and has been used with behaviours ranging from smoking and weight reduction to disruptive behaviour and speech problems.

Social Modelling: When the present concern of the client involves a problematic relationship with another person, it is often useful for the client to practice new ways of relating to the other party with the counsellor. The client is given instructions regarding how to act so that the situation will resemble real life, and then the client and counsellor act out the situation. This gives the client the opportunity to get feedback from the counsellor regarding the effectiveness of the client's behaviour. This technique is similar to the "empty chair" technique from the Gestalt approach.

Assertion Training: Used in conjunction with a therapeutic relationship, assertion training may supplement client growth and change when clients have difficulty saying no or expressing both their positive and negative feelings.

The above behavioural techniques, though typically associated with behavioural counselling, may be used in conjunction with the therapeutic relationship to facilitate client action.

In addition to the behavioural techniques described earlier, counsellors should be familiar with two other approaches that facilitate client action: decision-making methodologies and problem-solving strategies.

5.8.2 Decision-making Methodologies

The ability to make good decisions is an integral part of healthy personal functioning. We are constantly faced with situations that require effective decision-making skills. Many problems, which clients bring to counsellors, involve the inability to make good decisions. Counsellors are not interested in solving client's concerns for them; rather, they aim to give clients the skills to solve their own problems. This approach facilitates client's independence.

Many authors have proposed that the decision-making process involves sequential steps. Stewart et al. (1978) list the following steps in their decision-making model:

Identify the Problem: This step should include answers to problems such as—What is the problem? What prevents a solution? When and under what circumstances does the problem occur? And so on.

Identification of Values and Goals: During this phase the clients' values are examined so that the solution will be consistent with the clients' values and long-range goals.

Identify Alternatives: A list of possible alternatives is formulated.

Examine Alternatives: At this stage the advantages and disadvantages of each proposal are weighed, based on factual information such as amount of time and money involved.

Make a Tentative Decision: At this stage a tentative decision is taken regarding how to solve the problem.

Take Action on the Decision: If the decision is critical and the client is unsure about the choice, the decision may be tested at this stage, then further information can be gained and fed back into the decision-making process.

Evaluate Outcomes: Evaluation should be a continual part of the process.

It should again be emphasized that the role of the counsellor is not to make decisions for the client but to give them the skills not only to deal with the present concern but also to deal effectively with future problems. Krumboltz's (1966) model emphasizes this important point by adding the step of generalizing the decision-making process to future problems. The steps of the generic model to deal effectively with the present problems as well as the future problems are:

1. Generating a list of all possible courses of action.
2. Gathering relevant information about each feasible alternative course of action.
3. Estimating the probability of success in each alternative on the basis of the experience of others and projections of current trends.
4. Considering the personal values, which may be enhanced or diminished under each course of action.

5. Deliberating and weighing the facts, probable outcomes and values for each alternative.
6. Eliminating from consideration the least favourable courses of the action.
7. Formulating a tentative plan of action subject to new development and opportunities.
8. Generalizing the decision-making process to future problems.

5.8.3 Problem-solving Strategies

Egan (1975) proposes a systematic problem-solving methodology that includes his approach to the decision-making process and incorporates force-field analysis. The steps of the model are briefly summarized here.

Identify and Clarify the Problem: Clients often present counsellors with rather vague problems that, as stated, are insolvable. Therefore, as a first step the problem must be stated in a solvable manner. Instead of accepting vague descriptions of feelings, such as "I am so depressed", the counsellor seeks the stimulus for the client's feelings, "I am feeling sad and lonely as I have just moved into this new city and I don't have any friends." The counsellor emphasizes that problems cannot be solved when stated vaguely, when they are not dealing with the present and when they are attributing to the outside forces.

Establish Priorities in Choosing Problems for Attention: After clients have a grasp for their problems and their resources, they must decide which problem to tackle first. Some criteria would include (a) problems directly under client's control, (b) situation that can cause crisis in client's life, (c) a problem that is easily handled, (d) a problem which when solved will bring about some improvement or (e) move from lesser to greater severity (other than crisis).

Establish Workable Goals: Problems reflect the ways things are and goals represent the future. In other words, problems equal restraining forces; goals equal facilitating forces. Goals should be workable and concrete and should be owned by the client.

Take a Census of Available Means for Reaching the Goals: List restraining and facilitating forces related to goal achievement. List action steps that could reduce restraining forces and enhance facilitating forces.

Choose the Means that will most Effectively Achieve Established Goals: The means must be consistent with the client values, should have a high probability for success, and should help the client move systematically towards the goal.

Establish Criteria for the Effectiveness of the Action Programmes: Some criteria need to be established which will become the basis for measuring the effectiveness of the action programmes.

Implementation: The chosen mean has to be implemented to achieve the established goals in a right manner.

5.8.4 Goal-setting

Whether or not to set goals for the counselling process and the type of goals considered acceptable will largely be determined by the counsellor's theoretical orientation. Traditionally, behaviourists have been concerned with identification of specific counselling goals, stated as behaviours that can be easily identified and measured. Counsellors with a humanistic orientation, on the other hand, would be inclined to identify a few broad goals, such as improved self-concept or increased self-understanding, rather than to focus on behaviours. The difference here may be attributed to the value placed on observable behaviours, which can be measured vs. the value of unobservable feelings, attitudes and values, which can only be inferred from clients' behaviour and clients' self-report of their internal experiencing.

The broad goal of all counselling is one of change, whether in attitudes, values, beliefs, feelings or behaviour. Since internal processes and behaviour walk hand in hand, many counsellors feel it is appropriate to focus on both areas, if at different points in the process. Behavioural goals give the humanistic counsellor a focus for action either during the session or between sessions. These action goals can be formulated throughout the process as they coincide with changes in the client's awareness. The basic difference between these approaches, then, becomes one of emphasis and the formality of the goal-setting procedure.

Most counsellors' find it useful to formulate both process and outcome goals for each client for each counselling session. Process goals refer to the goals that counsellors set for their own behaviour in the relationship. These goals will obviously change throughout the duration of the relationship. Examples of appropriate goals for a counselling session midway through the process would be such as, to confront the client's unwillingness to be assertive with his or her boss; to disclose instances when the counsellor has experienced a similar difficulty; and to use advanced accurate emphatic responses. Some outcome goals might be to work on assertive responses through behaviour rehearsal and to work on having the client become more direct and honest in the session.

5.9 TERMINATION AND FOLLOW-UP

Ending counselling on a positive note is the final task of the counselling process. The process of termination is characterized by an understanding between the counsellor and the client that the purpose for which this engagement was being carried out has been achieved successfully. There is a definite sign of mental and emotional growth of the client with enhanced self-understanding and broadening of the coping skills. In other words, the client will be now better able to transfer learning from this situation to other problems. A positive termination process can provide another important kind of learning for the client—it can instruct clients on how to leave relationships with a sense of 'mastery and fulfillment' (Kleinke, 1994). Another issue that needs attention at the stage of termination is the issue of loss that is generally felt by the client as he or she has been in this relationship for long and some degree of attachment has taken place between the client and the counsellor (Ward, 1984).

5.9.1 Readiness for Termination

A client seems to be ready for termination when he or she has achieved whatever was desired, and the expected changes have been sufficiently internalized to be maintained independently. There are different signs of readiness which include:

- Positive changes in the client's mood
- Consistent reports of improved .ability to cope with stress
- Clear expressions of commitment to verbalized plans for the future
- Sense of relief and
- An increase in energy

The amount of preparation required for termination would depend on the intensity and length of the counselling relationship. For long-term clients, termination should be discussed weeks in advance of the last session. For example, Shulman (1984) recommends that termination from long-term counselling should constitute about one-sixth of the counselling process, and Ward (1984) suggests that termination from counselling takes on special importance when the issues the client brought to counselling deal with dependency and separation from significant others.

With some clients, the process of termination is very smooth. As the client expresses the desire to leave the situation when he or she feels better, and counsellor observes the same, it may be the time to look back, look forward and say good bye (Marx and Gelso, 1987; Ward 1984). With other clients, readiness for termination may not be so easy to determine. The client wanting to overcome depression may be depressed less often, but may still get mildly depressed occasionally, or the client wanting to behave more assertively may be able to respond assertively to some situations, but may still have difficulty under more challenging conditions. If the client expresses the lack of desire to maintain the suggested changes or feels insecure the process of termination should be done with lots of caution. In fact, it is then advisable to postpone the process. In such instances, the client may need a second or a third stage of discussion and analysis. Generally, the counsellors then start with a less frequent schedule of counselling sessions to help the client become more self-reliant and self-confident. The apprehensions of the clients may be more related to difficulty handling the loss of the counselling relationship (i.e., saying goodbye). When this pattern emerges, it is important to frame the end of counselling as a step forward in client's growth rather than a trauma. It may help relieve some of the client's fears about handling the world independently.

5.9.2 Client Responses to Termination

Research by Marx and Gelso (1987) suggested that the positive feeling associated with termination is more than the negative feelings. The positive feelings include calmness, better health and an overall sense of satisfaction. But in situations where the client and the counsellor have become too close to each other as a result of continuous interaction or when the client has a fear of loss of dependency, intimacy issues or traumatic loss, he or she may not be able to terminate the counselling relationship with a positive note. In this circumstance, the experience of separation may be a reminder of past experiences (Hackney and Cormier, 2001; Weinberg, 1984). Client in these situations start identifying the counsellors as anchors which provide them with a sense of security. They feel cared for and develop strong attachment bonds with the counsellor (Lowenstein, 1979; Weiss, 1973). Letting go under these conditions may cause the client to feel a sense of loss.

To make the stage of termination smoother and easier for the client, it is essential that the counsellor discusses this topic in advance stages of counselling itself, and not encourage too much dependency on the counsellor. Counsellors should be cognizant of their role as anchor, and work to help clients establish close friendships and support systems before counselling is ended, as these will ease the sense of loss of contact with the counsellor.

5.9.3 Counsellor Responses to Termination

The ultimate goal in counselling is for counsellors to become obsolete and unnecessary to their clients (Nystul, 2003). But it has been observed that the resistance to separate also comes from the counsellors. Ward (1984) observes that ending is often a difficult issue for counsellors to talk about. Goodyear (1981) suggests different conditions under which termination becomes challenging for the counsellor:

1. When the relationship was very significant for the counsellor
2. When the abilities of the clients to function independently are doubted by the counsellor
3. A feeling of guilt generated in the counsellor for not being effective with the client in resolving the issues
4. When the relationship ends with client leaving the scene with anger and protest
5. When the counsellor had been trying to live his or her life through the experiences of the client and suddenly feels anxious
6. When the counsellor begins to view termination as one of the another farewells in his or her life
7. When counsellor starts questioning his or her own personality

It is not ethical on the part of the counsellor to keep on avoiding termination for the sake of their unmet needs. They are then violating the basic professional ethics of doing well without intending harm. Counsellors who make their clients dependent, and do not let them function independently and are pained at the time of termination may be required to see another counsellor to help them overcome their own personality related issues.

5.9.4 Ending in a Positive Way

As mentioned earlier, in an intensive and long-range counselling, preparation for termination begins well-before the last counselling session. The issue of termination should emerge automatically as the positive changes in the client become evident. As the signs of completion become apparent, counsellors should schedule one or two more sessions that concentrate on follow-up work and help the client apply what he or she has learned. Welfel and Patterson (2005) have suggested important guidelines, which are essential for ending this counselling relationship in a positive way. These are:

Be aware of the client's needs and desires: Client should be given time to express them. Client expressions of gratitude for the counsellor's help should be graciously accepted and not minimized, but the ultimate credit for change belongs to the client.

Review the major events of the counselling experience: This helps the client affirm that growth and change are part of life and gain greater perspective on his or her changes. Seeing self over time helps create closure. Review process has to be made more personalized by reflecting on the experiences of the first few meetings and comparing them with the later improved stages.

Supportively acknowledge the changes the client has made: Any kind of change is difficult to accept. It is likely to invoke resistance and dis-contentment. This has to be dealt with lots of encouragement and affirmations. The counsellor can also discuss the option of future counselling if the client ever wants it.

Request follow-up contact: This can be done through telephone, corres-pondence or in person. The knowledge that follow-up will occur also acts as an additional incentive for the client to maintain the changes that counselling has produced. It also helps the counsellor to have direct assessment of counselling on the client so as to enhance his or her capability to indulge in future counselling projects. It also depicts the counsellor's care and concern for the client.

5.10 Summary

In this chapter, the counselling environment and the basic procedures followed to counsel are explored. The counselling environment has both the physical and the emotional component, which should be kept in mind by the counsellor to provide a conducive and relaxed environment to the client.

The intake procedures are required to obtain the case history of the client, which require both confidentiality and dependability on the part of the counsellor. The physical set-up of the room where the session is to be conducted is very crucial to the success of counselling. The process of opening the session, structuring the session and terminating the session has to be given importance. The procedure of referral is important when the counsellor feels that he will not be able to help the client with his problems. Some guidelines for effective counselling like keeping the focus on the other person, maintaining silence and managing emotions are vital for its successful implementation. Certain advanced skills in counselling like advanced empathy, theme clarification, self-disclosure, perception check and interpretation help to enhance the quality of counselling procedure. Certain action strategies in the form of behavioural techniques, decision making methodologies, problem solving strategies and goal setting are used to continue the procedure effectively. And finally the termination and follow up involves summarization of main themes, feelings and issues of the session.

Chapter 6 explores the distinct counselling skills that are used in counselling procedures by the effective counsellors.

Review Questions

1. What is the role of counselling environment in leading to effective counselling? How does the physical set up add to this effectiveness?

2. The initial interview stage in the counselling sets the tone of the entire counselling process. How would you, as a counsellor, take this forward? Discuss with examples.

3. When and why should a manager-counsellor use a referral? How should referral be done?

4. After the initial rapport formation the counsellor can take the process of counselling forward by using some effective guidelines. List these and discuss how they help in enhancing the process of counselling.

5. List and discuss the advanced skills in counselling to help the client reach the level of self-exploration and self-understanding.

6. What are some of the specific strategies or programs to facilitate behavioural changes among clients?

7. Discuss the importance of termination and follow-up stage of counselling process. What are the specific requirements of this stage?

8. As a counsellor, which signs would you consider to ensure that the client is ready for termination?

9. What are the responses of the clients and the counsellor towards termination of counselling relationship?

Chapter 6

Counselling Skills

The present chapter will focus on specific counselling skills that are basic to the therapeutic process and are used by most counsellors and therapists regardless of their particular theoretical orientation. We will define each skill, explore how it is practised, and attempt to assess the impact of the skill on the client.

Counselling has been described as a person-to-person interaction process to stimulate change in affect, thought and behaviour of the client. Changes are regarded as desirable if they help the client make an important life decision, cope more effectively with incumbent developmental issues and life stresses, achieve a sense of personal effectiveness or learn to use freedom responsibly. This chapter is devoted to understanding the important properties and related skills of the first stage.

Effective counselling procedures in the initial disclosure stage lead to sustained self-disclosure by the client for the following purpose:

1. To let the counsellor know what has been occurring in the client's life and how the client thinks and feels about those events.
2. To encourage the client to gain some feeling of relief through the process of talking about his or her problems.
3. To encourage the client to develop a clearer definition of his or her concerns and greater understanding about exactly what is disturbing.
4. To help the client begin to connect components of his or her story that may lead to new insight.

The first of the purposes is obvious because the counsellor has nothing to work with until the client does some sharing. It is important for the counsellor to try to understand the client's experience thoroughly and to perceive how the client thinks and feels about what has occurred. At the outset of the counselling session, counsellors often overlook the importance of the other three purposes. Reflecting on your own personal experience, try to recall a time when you talked about an important problem with someone else. Did you feel better after sharing the concern with someone else, even if no new solution was evident? This process is known as **catharsis**, and it is explained by the emotional release that comes from getting the problem out. In telling your story to someone else, did you discover that you understood more precisely just what was bothering you? And, finally, did you discover that through the telling of your story you reached new understanding of how things fit together? Clients frequently gain such new insights, too, through the process of sharing their personal experiences.

Relationship building is the first important step in the counselling process. If the total counselling experience is to be of benefit to the client, the counsellor's time and energy must be devoted to developing a relationship that can be characterized by mutual trust, openness, comfort and optimism about the value of continued counselling sessions. These supportive conditions provide the necessary basis for counselling to evolve into an experience of deeper exploration, which characterizes the second stage of counselling.

In describing the initial stage of counselling, we will first discuss the problems that clients bring with them to the first counselling session. Next, the counsellor's characteristics and skills that facilitate the relationship and lead to initial disclosure will be described. The effects of initial disclosure for the client will be examined. Finally, behaviours that are often thought to be helpful by well-intentioned but untrained people are shown to detract from relationship building and to block exploration in the early phases of counselling.

6.1 What Clients Bring to the Counselling Experience

Many clients enter the counselling experience voluntarily. They become aware of tension, anxiety, dissonance, confusion or lack of closure in their lives, and they realize that they need assistance. The degree of felt tension may vary from **mild**, as in the case of a high school student who wants to know what elective courses will be available the next semester, to **intense**, as in the case of person who has just learned that he or she has a terminal illness. Voluntary or self-referred clients have several characteristics in common: they experience tension and conflict in their life, the tension motivates an effort to seek help and to initiate at least some disclosure about themselves and their concerns, and they are willing to do some serious thinking. For such clients, a counsellor's initial question, such as "How can I help?" is usually sufficient to initiate relevant communication.

Other clients are reluctant to participate in counselling. They may be experiencing tension but do not acknowledge the need for help. Examples of reluctant clients may include individuals abusing drugs or alcohol, victims of domestic violence, people whose behaviours are aggressive and disruptive to others at work or otherwise (and may have led to arrest and legal problems), or students who are unmotivated and unsuccessful in school. Because such clients are generally pressured (or required) by a third party to make initial contact with the counsellor, they often put up strong barriers to genuine participation. They may avoid offering relevant disclosures and doing the work that can lead to growth.

Even clients who seek counselling voluntarily usually experience some anxiety about the process and resistance to facing their difficult issues. Some of the anxiety stems from the inherent condition of the counselling process that requires the client to share information about one's self and one's personal life with a person who is initially a relative stranger. Critical questions that clients ask themselves include "What will this person do with the information I share with him or her?" and "What impressions of me will the counsellor develop if I honestly describe my concerns, stresses and doubts?" Some of the anxiety comes from the unknown, i.e., "What will happen to me during this experience?"

Hesitation also results from a variety of cultural messages that suggest caution about seeking help with problems. Some believe that people should be able to manage their own affairs and that seeking help is a sign of weakness. Some people may even believe that only crazy people need to see counsellors. And certain individuals from some ethnic groups, though in need for help, are reluctant to talk with a counsellor outside their ethnic group. Similarly, certain minorities are also very cautious about discussing their personal problems outside the family.

Because caution and anxiety are usual, the objectives during the initial stage are to help the client feel comfortable about the process of communicating and feel less anxious about exploring fully, honestly, and in depth those concerns requiring attention. Counsellors initiate disclosure with three interconnected patterns: by inviting communication, by responding to client concerns in a caring and understanding way, and by avoiding doing and saying things that block communication.

6.2 Ways to Invite Communication and Build the Counselling Relationship

The entire process of counselling depends on the open and honest interaction between the counsellor and client. Both should avoid things that block communication and also things that send out wrong signals. When they discuss a specific problem they interact not only verbally, but also non-verbally. To interact in a more comfortable zone, they both should try to keep an open and should also do a lot of self-analysis. The following section will discuss both types of communication in details.

According to communication specialists, people communicate far more through posture, gesture and expressions (body language) and with the way the voice sounds than through the actual words.

Most people are not aware of how much they communicate to others through body language and tone of voice. Nor are they aware how much they are, often subconsciously, picking up from others non-verbal communication.

For example, if a person is asked whether he is excited about his new job, and he responds by looking at the ground, shifting his feet, and saying in a dull tone, 'Oh yes, I am looking forward to it', which action should be believed—his words or his voice and body language? Most people would interpret the person as not being thrilled about his new job, but not really wanting to say so.

In order to understand people best, we need to pay attention to all three components of their communication, i.e., their body language, words and sound of voice. Because of its enormous impact, body language is very important. The counsellor will be able to communicate what he wants to much more effectively if he is conscious of his own body language, and he will be able to increase his understanding of others (what they really think and feel) if he learns to interpret their body language. Through research studies (Mehrabian, 1972) it has been found that the three components of communication get expressed in the following manner as shown in Table 6.1.

Table 6.1 Components of Communication

Communication component	Percentage expressed
Gestures/expressions	55%
Tone of the voice	38%
Words	07%
Total communication	100%

6.3 Non-verbal Communication

Mehrabian (1972) has stated that individuals are continuously transmitting information about themselves through their facial expressions, body movements and proxemic behaviour. In many ways, we cannot avoid communication. We send many messages about how we feel, what we think, and how we react to people and situations without uttering a word. Hence, non-verbal communication plays a significant role in communication process, and non-verbal channels are frequently less distorted (Hall 1966).

The importance of non-verbal communication in the counselling process has been acknowledged by counselling theorists and practitioners who assert that the complex interplay of verbal and non-verbal messages is an integral part of the counselling process. Counsellors must be skilful at observing and responding to the non-verbal messages of clients, and they must be aware of the impact of their non-verbal behaviour on the client during the counselling interview.

6.3.1 Modalities of Non-verbal Communication

This section will begin by examining non-verbal communication and its modalities in general terms, and then explore specific client's and counsellor's non-verbal behaviour and its impact on the counselling interview.

Gazda et al. (1991) have categorized non-verbal communication into three modalities, as discussed in Tables 6.2 to 6.4 as an aid in developing awareness and observation of non-verbal communication. It should be emphasized that non-verbal communication is highly idiosyncratic; interpretation of these clues must be tentative and based on the context in which they are made.

Table 6.2 Non-verbal Communication Using Time

Sl. no.	Non-verbal behaviour	Indicates the following
1.	Promptness or delay in recognizing the presence of another or in responding to his/her communication.	*Ignorance:* No expressions on the face while the client is expressing his or her concerns. *Recognition:* Responsive face breaking into a smile.
2.	Amount of time another is willing to spend communicating with a person.	*Willingness:* Warm smile and calm expressions. *Unwillingness:* Stiff/rigid/stern facial expressions.
3.	Relative amounts of time spent on various topics.	*Interest:* If more time spent by the counsellor in discussing the concerns of the client. *Lack of interest:* If the counsellor seems to be in hurry or is busy with his own tasks.

Table 6.3 Non-verbal Communication Using the Body

Sl. no.	Non-verbal behaviour	Indicates the following
I	**Non-verbal behaviour using eye contact**	
1.	Looking at a specific object	Observation/concentration
2.	Looking down	Embarrassment
3.	Steady gaze	Firmness and attention
4.	Hard eyes glaring	Anger or outrage
5.	Shifting eyes from object to object	Observation or disturbance
6.	Looking at helper but looking away when looked at	Shyness or embarrassment
7.	Covering eyes with hands	Avoidance
8.	Frequently looking towards the helpers	Attention
II	**Using Eyes**	
9	Sparkling eyes	Excitement
10.	Tears	Sadness
11.	Wide eyes	Amazement
III	**Using skin**	
12.	Pallor	Fear or sickness
13.	Perspiration	Impatience or anger
14.	Blushing	Embarrassment
15.	Goose bumps	Fear
IV	**Using Posture**	
16.	The body poised on chair	Eager as if ready for activity

Continued

Table 6.3 Non-verbal Communication Using the Body (*Continued*)		
Sl. no.	*Non-verbal behaviour*	*Indicates the following*
17.	The body slumped on the chair in the state of inertia	Tired
18.	Arms crossed in front as if to protect self	Ready to face the situation
19.	Crossed legs	Impatience or withdrawal
20.	Sits facing the other person rather than side-ways or away from	Ready to listen
21.	Hanging head, looking at floor, head down	Shyness or embarrassment
22.	Body positioned to exclude others from joining a group	Avoidance
V	**Using Facial Expression**	
23.	No change in facial expression	Unconcerned and not paying attention
24.	Wrinkled forehead (lines of worry), frown	Worry or tension
25.	Wrinkled nose	Disgust
26.	Smiling, laughing	Willingness and consent
27.	Sad mouth	Dejection
28.	Biting lip	Nervousness
VI	**Using Hand and Arm Gestures**	
29.	Symbolic hand and arm gestures (abstraction in place of realism)	Depicts ideas, emotions
30.	Literal hand and arm gesture	Depict size or shape
31.	Wide movements on hands and arms	Demonstrates action
VII	**Self-inflicting Behaviour**	
32.	Nail biting	Nervousness or anxiety
33.	Scratching	Irritation or restlessness
34.	Cracking knuckles	Restlessness
35.	Tugging at hair	Frustration
36.	Rubbing or stroking	Pain or affection
37.	Repetitive behaviours	Restlessness or attention
38.	Tapping foot, drumming or thumping with restlessness	Impatience, restlessness
39.	Fidgeting, squirming	Nervousness
40.	Trembling	Fear
41.	Playing with button, hair or clothing	Lack of attention, restlessness
VIII	**Using Signals or Commands**	
42.	Snapping fingers	Impatience
43.	Holding fingers	Ready to face the challenge
44.	Pointing	Accusation
45.	Nodding head from left to right	Disapproval
46.	Shrugging shoulder	Not bothered
47.	Waving	Taking leave
48.	Nodding in recognition	Acknowledging the presence
49.	Nodding and shaking in agreement	Showing approval
50.	Sweet smile and tender eyes	Affection
51.	Eyes full of lust	Sexual attraction

Table 6.4	Non-verbal Behaviour Using the Environment	

Sl. no.	*Non-verbal behaviour*	*Indicates the following*
I	**Distance**	
	1. Moves away when the other moves toward	Avoidance
	2. Moves toward when the other moves away	Tries to follow
	3. Takes initiative in moving toward or away from	Quick to respond
	4. Distance widens gradually	Want to move away from each other
	5. Distance narrows gradually	Want to come closer
II	**Arrangement of the Physical Setting**	
	6. Neat, well-ordered	Well organized
	7. Untidy, haphazard	Careless
	8. Casual vs. formal	Personal vs. professional
	9. Warm vs. cold colour	Involvement vs. distance
	10. Soft vs. hard materials	Caring vs. coldness
	11. Cheerful and lively vs. dull and drab	Welcoming vs. unwelcoming
	12. Discriminating taste vs. tawdry	Choosy vs. no taste
	13. Expensive or luxurious vs. shabby or Spartan	Rich vs. poor
III	**Clothing**	
	14. Bold vs. unobtrusive	Confidant vs. easy-going
	15. Stylish vs. non-descript	Extravagant vs. ordinary

6.3.2 Interpretation of Non-verbal Communication

As Gazda and his associates (1991) have noted, non-verbal communication must be viewed simply as clues to the individual's underlying feelings and motives rather than as proof of them. The counsellor must interpret non-verbal messages tentatively and must realize that a given behaviour may have opposite meanings for two individuals or even for the same person on two different occasions (Gazda et al., 1991). The meaning of non-verbal communication also varies among societies and cultures, and counsellors should be sensitive to these differences.

The client's non-verbal communication within the counselling interview is obviously important. It provides the counsellor with additional information about the client's thoughts and feelings. Often an individual will communicate one message verbally and an entirely different message through voice tone, facial expression or body posture (refer Interaction 6.1).

INTERACTION 6.1

Counsellor: "How are you feeling today?"

Client: "Oh, fine. Everything's just fine."

Counsellor: "You didn't look as though you felt good as you walked into the office. You were holding your head down and staring at the floor and now you seem to be avoiding my eye contact."

Client: "Well, I guess it's difficult for me to talk about how depressed I feel."

A common goal of the counselling process is to help the client openly express emotions; therefore, the counsellor must be sensitive to non-verbal cues and, as illustrated in the example, skilful at responding to discrepancies between the client's underlying feelings and verbal expressions of those feelings. The counsellor's ability to be empathic is directly related to his or her ability to observe and respond to non-verbal communication.

In many instances it is sufficient for the counsellor to bring the client's attention to the non-verbal communication (refer to Interaction 6.2).

INTERACTION 6.2

Counsellor: "Are you aware that you break out in a rash each time we discuss your relationship with your husband?"

Client: "I suppose I just get terribly anxious when we discuss my marriage because I feel guilty that I have wanted a relationship with another man."

By bringing the non-verbal communication to the client's awareness, the counsellor encouraged the client to share more important and personally relevant unspoken feelings.

Frequently the ability to observe non-verbal communication and to respond on same level to the message being sent enables the counsellor to project unusual warmth, sensitivity and perceptiveness that enhance the intimacy of the relationship. Responding to client's frown before the concern has been verbalized makes the client feel that the counsellor is tuned into him or her at a level that perhaps he or she is not yet aware of experiencing. This type of interaction is possibly the source of the idea that counsellors have a sixth sense and an almost mystical perceptiveness.

6.3.3 The Counsellor's Non-verbal Messages

There are people whose body language invites communication, and there are others whose body language indicated disinterest and perhaps even anxiety about communicating. The active, interested listener faces and leans toward the speaker in a posture of interest and even excitement. Eyes are focused in the general direction of the person's face. Arms are in an open mode in relation to the client, as if to say, "I am very interested in receiving, with all my sensory processes, what it is you want to say to me." The attentive listener maintains an interested facial expression and makes encouraging gestures (nods, smiles, friendly gestures, and so forth). The energy for offering these cues seems to come naturally and without contrived effort; it is a bodily representation of a strongly held belief about how to receive and welcome another human being.

These skills of reception are referred to as attending skills, and quite literally they communicate the counsellor's undivided attention to the client's concerns. Egan (1998) defines attending as the way helpers can be with their clients both physically and psychologically that demand's a certain intensity of presence. Attending behaviour encourages client to talk and, therefore, it reduces the need for the counsellor to talk (Ivey, 1994), placing the content of the session more in the client's control.

In contrast, the listener who is disinterested and uncomfortable does not use his or her body to invite communication. Facial focus may be forty-five degrees or more away from the client's face, arms folded in a self-protective position, eyes on the desktop. Body cues such as these communicate messages such as "I'm not interested, "I don't care", "I don't have the energy to be available to you", or "I'm afraid to be open with you." Cues that indicate the listener is closed can be subtle, often outside the person's awareness.

Habits of attending vary somewhat from one culture to another. For example, the patterns of eye contact that have been described are typical for whites in a North American Culture. Ivey (1994) indicates that African American often show a pattern of greater eye contact when speaking than when listening and that native Americans may avoid eye contact altogether when speaking of important matters. The skilled counsellor will learn to respect these cultural differences and will interpret the meaning of client's behaviours in the context of their culture.

Ivey (1994) also suggests that the counsellor can shape what the client talks about by intentionally showing greater attentiveness when the client is discussing pertinent material and less attentiveness to non-productive talk. In the initial stages of a relationship, however, intentional withholding of attention might easily be misinterpreted by the client as a lack of caring. Furthermore, a counsellor may inadvertently limit talk about material that is important to the client but that makes the counsellor feel uncomfortable. Ivey uses the example of how furtive eye contact may be interpreted by the client as permission to talk about or avoid certain topics, such as sex.

In addition to the non-verbal messages of body language, the counsellor also communicates attending or caring by means of voice characteristics and manner of speaking. These qualities are sometimes referred to as paralinguistic because they are communicated by voice but have nothing to do with verbal content. For example, rapid speech, stumbling over words, loud tone, and tightness of voice all may signal stress. Slow, quiet, listless speech may indicate inattentiveness. Vocal tone and emphasis can highlight certain material as important. Comfort may be communicated by a pleasant tone, purposeful but easeful pacing, and other qualities of voice.

Finally, it is important to realize that just as counsellors communicate comfort and attention by their non-verbal communication, the clients also give many cues to their emotional state by non-verbal communication. Brammer, Abrego and Shostrum (1993) suggest that counsellor non-verbal behaviour match the non-verbal behaviour of the client, called as **mirroring**, for example, in the case of body posture, position, breathing, voice volume, rate of speech and other qualities.

Though many of the attending skills seem commonsensical, it is nevertheless true that persons in positions to be helpful frequently do not exhibit these behaviours. Can you think of examples of persons who were deficient in attending skills and thus made necessary communication difficult? Gilliland and James (1997) state that attending is both an attitude and a skill, and that practice leads to improved performance.

The non-verbal communication of the counsellor, as discussed hereinafter also communicates unspoken feelings and thus has an impact on the client's perception of the relationship.

Attending Behaviours: The non-verbal communication of counsellors that has received the most attention in the literature are referred to as physical attending behaviours. The physical presence of the counsellor helps communicate to the client that the counsellor is involved in what the client is sharing. The concept of physical attending may seem basic, yet in daily interactions we often fail to exhibit or experience basic attending.

How many times has someone said to you? "You're not even listening to what I'm saying!" Or someone has read magazine while you are talking to him, or it becomes obvious that the person at the other end of the telephone conversation is eating lunch, reading or engaged in some clandestine activity that prevents him from giving his complete attention to you (Egan, 1975).

These examples from daily interactions illustrate that, simple though the principles of basic attending are, yet we frequently find it difficult to apply them. Among the physical attending behaviours, Egan (1975) lists eye contact, adopting an open posture, facing the person squarely, leaning slightly forward, and assuming a natural and relaxed position.

Eye contact: It is important that the counsellor should maintain good eye contact with the client. This does not imply that the eye contact should be uninterrupted. Rather, it should be as natural as possible.

Adopting an open posture: As discussed previously, non-verbal communication is idiosyncratic. The same behaviour by an individual can mean different things at different times. Crossed legs and arms are generally interpreted as signs of withdrawal. Although such an interpretation may not always be valid, the counsellor should avoid communicating a lack of involvement through crossed leg and arm positions.

Facing the person squarely: The physical environment should allow counsellor and client to face each other without a table or desk between them. A posture directly facing the client promotes involvement.

Leaning slightly forward: Physical proximity to the client is an important indicator of involvement. Some counsellors begin an interview leaning back on their chairs, then lean forward as the level of interaction becomes more intense.

Assuming a natural and relaxed position: Since many clients are anxious as they enter a counselling session, it is important that the counsellor act as normal and relaxed as possible. As the counsellor becomes more and more comfortable with the basic attending posture, it will seem natural without losing the sense of involvement.

6.3.4 Non-verbal Listening

It would be advisable for the counsellor to stop and think about how he would like someone to behave towards him if he approached him or her for help with a problem. How would he like to be treated? Think about what a difference it makes when someone listens really attentively and encourages a person, rather than someone who seems preoccupied, bored or in a hurry.

A useful exercise for the counsellor for practicing non-verbal listening is letting someone else speak for a few minutes without saying anything, but showing his attentiveness through body language. The second part of the exercise consists of doing the opposite, showing non-listening through body language while they are speaking. Tables 6.5 and 6.6 tabulate a list of the feelings and consequences, which have been described by people occurring as a result of being listened to attentively and inattentively, respectively.

Table 6.5 Feelings and Consequences as a Result of being Listened Attentively

Sl. No.	Feelings	Consequences
1.	Reassured	Builds trust
2.	Important	Encourages talking more
3.	Validated	Leads to opening up
4.	Worthwhile	Makes a person more receptive to listener's comments
5.	Special	Builds honesty
6.	Cared about	Builds hope for future
7.	Relaxed	Relaxes a person
8.	Respected	Builds respect .
9.	At ease	Increases the mutual comfort levels
10.	Confident	Boosts a person's confidence

Table 6.6 Feelings and Consequences as a Result of not being Listened Attentively

Sl. No.	Feelings	Consequences
1.	Small	Loses train of thought
2.	Unimportant	Speaks incoherently
3.	Stupid	Goes blank
4.	Upset	Stops talking
5.	Annoyed	Uses defensive body language
6.	Angry	Aggression
7.	Depressed	Energy and thoughts diverted to getting back their
8.	Demotivated	attention
9.	Confused	
10.	Rejected	
11.	Irritated	
12.	Defensive	
13.	Frustrated	
14.	More fearful about talking	

Because of the strong impact of attentive or inattentive body language, when using counselling techniques the counsellor must be sure that his body language displays full attentiveness.

6.4 Verbal Communication

Communicating with people is an art, which should be developed in such a way that it helps a person not only to interact amiably but without creating problems. It should also help him to explain his viewpoints clearly. To develop communication one should follow open-leads and also should be a good listener, which will help in building trust; encourage talking and help in creating a healthy atmosphere. Some of the processes, which can help a counsellor communicate effectively with the clients, include:

Open-Ended Leads: An open-ended lead essentially says to the client, "tell me about it." Unlike a closed question, the open-ended lead requires more than a yes or no; typically, it opens the door to a discussion of feelings rather than facts. Some examples of open and closed questions are as follows:

EXAMPLE 6.1

Open Questions   "Where would you like to begin today?"

"How are you feeling about that?"

"What kinds of things make you feel sad?"

Closed Questions   "What time did you leave the room?"

"Where did you go after that?"

"Which way did you go?"

"How many times did that happen?"

Open-ended leads encourage clients to share their concerns with the counsellor. They place the responsibility for the interview on the client and allow the client to explore attitudes, feelings, values and behaviours without being forced into the counsellor's frame of reference. Closed questions, by comparison, elicit factual information that rarely has actual relevance to the client's concern and are asked out of the counsellor's curiosity (Ivey, 1971).

Ivey (1971) has noted that open-ended leads are used in several different counselling situations (refer Example 6.1). The following table describes the purpose served by open-ended leads in structuring the counselling process (refer to Table 6.7)

Despite the value of good, open questions in the counselling process, most beginning counsellor trainees rely too heavily on questions simply because they have not mastered other, more productive responses. Excessive reliance on questions may lead to the following problems: (a) the interview digresses to a question-and-answer interrogation in which the client waits for the counsellor to come up with the next topic, (b) the responsibility for the

Sl. no.	Purpose served	Open-ended leads
	Table 6.7 Purpose Served by Open-ended Leads	
1.	They help begin an interview.	"What would you like to talk about today? How have things been since the last time we talked together?"
2.	They help get the interviewee to elaborate on a point.	"Could you tell me more about that? How did you feel when that happened?"
3.	They help elicit examples of specific behaviour so that the interviewer is better able to understand what the interviewee is describing.	"Will you give me a specific example? What do you do when you get depressed? What do you mean when you say your father is out of his mind?"
4.	They help focus the client's attention on his feelings.	"What are you feelings as you're telling me this? How did you feel then?"

interview and the material to be discussed reverts to the counsellor, (c) the discussion moves from affectively oriented topics to cognitively oriented topics and (d) the interview loses a sense of flow and movement. For these reasons beginning counselling trainees are often instructed to avoid questions except as a way to open the counselling session.

Listening: The process of tuning in carefully to the client's messages and responding accurately to the meaning behind the message has been referred to simply as *listening*. Yet this type of listening moves a social conversation to different levels of communication, and it is the core of effective counselling. Listening at its simplest level calls on the counsellor to feedback the content and feelings that the client has communicated. This decoding process is necessary because human communication is often indirect. When we speak, we have a tendency to encode our message rather than communicating clearly and directly what we are thinking and feeling.

Listening, then, is a synthesis of the skills of restatement of content and reflection of feeling. It promotes within the client the feeling of being understood. It must be emphasized, however, that listening, as critical as it is to the counselling process, is not sufficient to produce the desired client growth and change. It must be implemented in conjunction with other counselling skills.

Listening is the most important skill for effective counselling. There are four basic types of things, which you need to listen for when counselling subordinates (Egan, 1994):

1. Their experiences—What do they see as happening to them?
2. Their behaviours—What do they do or fail to do?
3. Their sentiments—What are their feelings and emotions?
4. Their points of view—What are their opinions?

The special kind of active (as opposed to passive) listening, which is exhibited by a counsellor, has many positive effects:

1. It builds rapport.
2. It helps the subordinates to express themselves even regarding issues not so welcome in the ordinary business environment, such as emotions.
3. The subordinate feels that the manager is there for them.
4. The subordinate feels heard, understood and accepted.
5. The manager will be more influential—listening builds trust. If the subordinate feels heard, they will in turn listen to their managers.
6. It helps the subordinates to resolve their own problems.

In a counselling situation, the manager must focus on making sure that he has really heard what the subordinate has said, even when it is annoying or uncomfortable, and however much he disagrees. He must also concentrate on the emotions involved and encourage the discussion of feelings—attempting to acknowledge the feelings rather than driving them away. This can be very difficult for managers who are not comfortable discussing feelings or listening attentively to attitudes and opinions with which they disagree.

Most of us are not really very good listeners at all. Even though as adults we spend the largest percentage of our time listening, as school children we are taught a tremendous amount about reading and writing, a bit about speaking, and very little about listening. Given the lack of training, it is not surprising that our listening skills as a society are not very well-developed.

The concept of active rather than passive listening is important because most people consider listening to be a passive, receiving activity. Real active listening is hard work and is very tiring because it requires an extremely high level of concentration. Unlike with reading, where a person can go over a passage again and again, with listening you have only one chance.

Listening can be broken down into a variety of component skills:

1. Reading body language
2. Listening to the way things are said (the sound of the voice and the words chosen)
3. Being able to look through the conversational style and vocabulary in order to follow the thoughts that lie behind the words.
4. Trying to understand values and way of thinking.
5. Noticing what is not being said (due to hurt, embarrassment or guilt)
6. Listening to the parts and the whole at the same time—learning to highlight the important things in one's own mind as the other person speaks, to think about how these might relate to one another, and to try to put them together to form a meaningful whole, or concept.
7. Becoming familiar with the person's normal speech pattern so that you can discern anomalies, which may indicate areas of importance?
8. Practicing self-discipline in order to eliminate distractions, overcome boredom, and concentrate on what is being said all the way through to the ends of the sentences?
9. Demonstrating verbally and non-verbally that you are listening.

6.4.1 Counsellor's Verbal Messages

Vocal messages also give away a tremendous clue about true feelings. Often a change in the sound of someone's voice is telling, so knowing their typical voice and noticing when they change from the norm can be useful. Some of the variations in voice include:

1. Volume, which could be loud or quiet.
2. Pace, which could be, slow or fast.
3. Clarity, which means pronunciation of words (affected or perfectionist, slurred or mumbled).
4. Pitch could be high or low, intense or relaxed.

Tables 6.8 and 6.9 depict some of the verbal and non-verbal cues as expressed in different emotional states.

Table 6.8 Verbal Communication using Vocal Media

Verbal communication	Indicates
Tone of Voice	
Flat, monotonous, absence of feelings	Absence of feelings
Bright, vivid changes of inflection	Happy state
Strong, firm	Confident
Weak, shaky	Hesitant
Broken, faltering	Lack of confidence
Rate of Voice	
Fast	Nervousness
Medium	Normal
Slow	Sad or depressed
Pitch of Voice	
Loud	Anger or excitement
Medium	Normal
Soft	Well mannered and sophisticated
Diction	
Precise vs. careless	Careful/careless
Regional (colloquial) differences	Normal
Consistency of diction	Well read

Table 6.9 Verbal and Non-verbal Cues Expressed in Different Emotional States

Verbal and non-verbal cue	Anger	Happiness	Sadness	Anxiety
Tone of voice	Harsh	Warm, excited	Soft	Timid hesitant
Voice volume	Loud	Easy to hear, Shouting for joy	Quiet	Quiet
Eye contact	Direct	Direct	Averted	Averted, very intermittent
Facial expression	Clenched teeth	Grinning open	Tearful mouth turned down	Forced smile
Posture	Rigid	Relaxed	Slouched	Tense
Gestures	Fist clenched Finger pointing	Arms raised, Jumping for joy	Holds head in hands	Finger tapping

Source: (Nelson-Jones, 2005)

Sometimes people's speech is totally muddled and incomprehensible, and therefore, difficult to follow. However, the fact that the speech is muddled can, in itself, be valuable and telling information.

6.4.2 Verbal Listening

By now the manager will be convinced of the importance of body language. It is also necessary to indicate verbally that he is listening to his subordinate. This section discusses several ways in which this can be done e.g., by using encouragers, echoing and key word repetition and reflecting.

Encouragers: The most common way to verbally respond to someone in order to demonstrate listening is by the use of encouragers. Encouragers are the short phrases and noises that we make to tell people that we are listening, that we are interested, and that we want them to continue. Encouragers are minimal responses—enough to show that we are paying attention and not daydreaming, yet minimal so that we will only encourage, and not distract, the speaker.

If encouragers are too infrequent, the speaker will question our attention level. While using encouragers frequently is, of course, encouraging, over-doing it becomes artificial and distracting, and actually demonstrates non-listening. It sounds better to the speaker if the counsellor varies the encouragers he uses, rather than repeating the same one over and over again, which becomes monotonous.

As with nodding (which is actually a non-verbal encourager), the timing of encouragers makes a difference as well. It is best to encourage at the end of a speaker's phrases, in response, rather than during or speaking over them, which then would be an interruption.

Following are some commonly used encouragers:

1. Uh-huh
2. Mmm
3. I see
4. Right
5. That's interesting
6. Yes

Echoing and Key Word Repetition: To demonstrate listening, echoing and repeating key words are gentle ways of asking probing questions and directing the conversation. Echoing is simply repeating the last few words spoken, and key word repetition is picking out important words from statements and repeating them. For example, if a subordinate says, "Last year's Chennai conference was not worth the trouble. The hotel was uncomfortable, the conference planners were disorganized, and we sent several sales-people leaving our office short-staffed. However, Shravan doesn't agree with me."

An example of echoing would be, "Shravan doesn't agree with you?" An example of key wording would be, "The planners were disorganized?"

These examples indicate listening; they both encourage the subordinate to continue speaking, yet they both subtly direct the conversation as well.

Reflecting: Encouraging motivates the speakers to continue; verbal listening can communicate to them the understanding of what has been said. Reflecting is a way of showing understanding, without agreeing or disagreeing.

The counsellor without becoming emotionally involved in the problem shows that reflecting is a way of showing non-judgmental understanding and acceptance. Reflecting demonstrates empathy and unconditional positive regard as well as listening.

So what exactly is reflecting? It is playing back to someone in your own words what they have communicated to you. The difference between reflecting and paraphrasing is that reflecting plays back the total message communicated to you (reflecting what you have learned from their words, the sound of their voice and their body language), whereas paraphrasing plays back just the verbal part of their message. In Interaction 6.3, Manager 1 is playing back the verbal content of what the subordinate has said, and Manager 2 is playing back the total communication.

INTERACTION 6.3

Subordinate:	(Looking downward) "I have been asked to apply for that next grade position which was advertised. It looks interesting. (Sounding unconvinced) Apparently I have all the qualifications necessary. I ought to apply." (Annoyed tone of voice)
Paraphrasing by Manager 1:	"You think you should apply for a position for which you have been specifically asked to apply due to your qualifications."
Subordinate:	(Looking downward) "I have been asked to apply for that next grade position which was advertised. It looks interesting. (Sounding unconvinced) Apparently I have all the qualifications necessary. I ought to apply." (Annoyed tone of voice)
Reflecting by Manager 2:	"You sound as if you are some-what reluctant about applying for this position, but I feel you ought to because it was requested."

Reflecting total communication is often more helpful than reflecting only verbal communication. Manager 1 has understood what the subordinate said, but Manager 2 has given the subordinate some feedback, and offered an opportunity to explore the situation more deeply as well as showing understanding of what was said. The subordinate is more likely better understood by Manager 2.

By choosing carefully which bits of subordinate's speech to reflect, the manager can direct conversations. This must be done with care because the subordinates generally lead counselling conversations. The manager can direct the conversation when it will help the subordinates to go in a direction, which is important to them. This is different from taking control of the conversation for his own purposes. Manager 2 in Interaction 6.3 focused on the subordinate's reluctance because the subordinate's total communication indicated that may be important. Manager 2 is not manipulating the conversation in this case. Instead the subordinate is being encouraged to elaborate on an emotion, which is obviously significant.

The manager can reflect emotion, thinking and/or behaviour. It is best to try to reflect as many of these as possible in a reflective statement when trying to communicate full understanding as depicted in Interaction 6.4.

INTERACTION 6.4

Supervisor: "My head technician, Sikander, has been doing steadily excellent work for some time now. He also trains the new staff in a very positive manner, which boosts their morale at a critical time. In order to keep him motivated, I need to do something more than just giving him praise, yet there is not another position between his and mine for him to aspire to."

Manager: "You have been rewarding Sikander with good reviews, but you are concerned because you think something more may be needed to motivate him."

The manager reflected the feeling (concern), the thinking (need for more motivation) and the behaviour (praise).

Sometimes it is useful to reflect back only the emotions, which are not being communicated verbally, especially when the subordinate is avoiding discussing feelings. Thinking and behaviours are more often readily communicated verbally whereas emotions are more often implied or communicated non-verbally. For example, the statement, "I think I am being taken advantage of" implies anger, and an accompanying angry tone of voice or table thumping communicate anger. Reflection of feelings and emotions is a very important counselling skill because emotions are often a block to progress. Reflecting is a way of bringing emotions out into the open and discussing them, so that progress can then occur. Simple statements such as, "You seem upset by this", "You don't look so happy", or "You seem quite worried" can help to get people talking about their emotions.

Benefits of reflecting for manager (Listener). The benefits of reflecting emotions and thoughts for managers are:

1. Reflecting demonstrates that manager is listening to the subordinate.
2. It helps for checking the understanding and helps to build clearer mental picture.
3. Reflecting thoughts helps to build rapport.
4. It helps to pace conversation as well as gives the manager and his subordinates time to think about where to go next.
5. It contributes to the conversation without leading it.
6. It also helps in equalizing the conversation, which is very useful for

putting the problem back to them (avoiding taking on the problem and fixing it).

7. Reflecting emotions forces concentrated listening.
8. Reflecting also encourages opening up and probing deeper to get to the hidden emotions.

Benefits of reflecting for the speaker or subordinate

1. Reflecting helps to 'hear oneself'—therefore, keep on track.
2. Reflecting helps to gain feedback about oneself—leading to better self-understanding.
3. Reflecting gives a feeling of being listened to, validated, reassured and accepted.
4. Reflecting makes one feel understood, or have opportunity to correct listener if misunderstood.
5. Hearing oneself more objectively through someone else helps to put one's thinking in perspective.
6. Reflecting clears and focuses thinking.
7. Reflecting helps one to tell one's story.
8. It allows one to set pace.
9. Reflecting allows one to come up with own realizations/solutions.

If the manager tends to give reflective/understanding responses in day-to-day conversation you will find it easiest to adapt to giving reflective responses when operating in a counselling style. If he tends to give evaluative or probing responses he may find it difficult to add reflecting to his repertoire of responses. Expect reflecting to be awkward, slow and hesitant at first. The manager will need to concentrate very hard in order to reflect accurately. Then he needs to think about how to rephrase what he has just heard. Keep practicing because it will become easier, quicker and more natural in time. The manager should gradually include it in his style. He could try it out with friends and family before trying it out at work. He should practice reflecting initially in a role-play situation if it is very uncomfortable to him. Remember, if it seems difficult, it is because his mind is thinking about many things at once.

A few words of caution regarding reflecting: First, avoid starting all the reflective statements with the same few words. This is a frequent mistake amongst beginning reflectors: 'So, you ...' is the most common. Used too many times in a row, the same initial phrase sounds very repetitive and superficial. Vary the ways that you reflect. Reflective responses can also be questions or statements. Some line openers, which can be useful for reflecting and checking understanding, are given in Example 6.2:

EXAMPLE 6.2

Manager: "If I understand you correctly…"
Manager: "It seems as if you feel…"
Manager: "Do you feel…"

Manager: "What I am hearing is that you..."
Manager: "Am I correct in saying..."
Manager: "So, you think that..."

Secondly, the manager should compose his reflective statements carefully so that they are not leading, manipulating or patronizing. For example, a reflective statement, which over interprets and says, "So what you are really saying is..." can be very irritating. The manager should not mandate how the subordinates are feeling or what they are saying. Instead he should suggest how he thinks they might to feeling based on his interpretation of what they have communicated. Therefore, "Do you feel..." is better than "You must feel ..."

And thirdly, do not use phrases such as "I understand, but ...", "I hear what you are saying", "I know what you mean", in place of reflecting. These phrases may not convince subordinates that they have been understood properly because the manager has not shown that he has been understood by him.

6.4.3 Silence or Passive Listening

Possibly the most basic of all skills is using silence within the counselling interview. Clients need opportunities to explore their feelings, attitudes, values and behaviours; initially they need someone to listen, even passively, to what they wish to share. New counsellors are typically uncomfortable with time lapses during the interview but if the counsellor can become sensitive to the various meanings of silence and skilful at handling these pauses, these silences can prove very useful. First, silence lets clients know that the responsibility for the interview lies on their shoulders. Too often counsellors rush in to fill up the space, thus assuming inappropriate responsibility for the session. Second, silence allows clients to delve further into thoughts and feelings and to ponder the implications of what has transpired during the session. Clients need this time to reflect and process without feeling pressured to verbalize every thought and every emotion.

As Brammer and Shostrom (1982) have noted, silence during the interview can have other meanings. It can mean that the client feels uncomfortable and is anxious or embarrassed at having been sent to the counsellor. It may also indicate client resistance to the process. In this instance the client may attempt to use it to manipulate the counsellor. Silence can mean that the counsellor and client have reached an impasse in the session and both are searching for direction. In each of these instances the question raised is whether or not the counsellor should interrupt the pause. Counsellors must learn to trust their own feelings in particular situations, which require great sensitivity to the client's non-verbal communication. Often the most appropriate response a counsellor can make to client-initiated silence is an accurate empathic statement, such as, "You look very thoughtful; would you like to share what you're feeling?" or "You seem pretty quiet, and I'm wondering if you really are angry that you are here." As a rule of thumb it is wise to let the client assume responsibility for breaking the silence when the silence is client-initiated.

In summary, the therapeutic value of silence cannot be overstated. Silence communicates to the client a sincere and deep acceptance. It demonstrates the counsellor's deep concern and willingness to let the client experience the relationship without sensing pressure to be verbal. Rogers (1951) has cited an excellent example of the therapeutic value of silence:

> *I have just completed the strangest counselling case I've ever had. I think you might be interested in it.*
>
> *Joan was one of my very first clients when I started counselling one half-day each week at the local high school. She told the girl's adviser, "I feel so shy I couldn't even tell her what my problem is. Will you tell her for me?" So the adviser told me before I saw Joan that she worried about having no friends. The adviser added that she had noticed that Joan seemed always to be so alone.*
>
> *The first time I saw Joan she talked a little about her problem and quite a bit about her parents, of whom she seemed to be quite fond. There were, however, long pauses. The next four interviews could be recorded verbatim on this small piece of paper. By the middle of November Joan remarked, "things are going pretty good." No elaboration on that. Meanwhile, the adviser commented that the teachers had noticed that Joan was now smiling a friendly greeting when they met her in the halls. This was unheard of before. However, the adviser had seen little of Joan and could say nothing of her contact with other students. In December there was one interview during which Joan talked freely; the others were characterized by silence while she sat, apparently in deep thought, occasionally looking up with a grin. More silence through the next two and one-half months. Then I received word that the girls of the high school had elected her 'woman of the month'! The basis for that election is always sportsmanship and popularity with other girls. At the same time I got a message from Joan, "I don't think I need to see you any more." No, apparently she doesn't, but why? What happened in those hours of silence? My faith in the capacity of the client was sorely tested. I'm glad it did not waver."*

This example demonstrates Rogers's unfailing trust in clients' ability to help themselves if the therapeutic relationship is available.

6.4.4 Restatement of Content

The ability to restate the content of the client's message or to paraphrase a client's statement is a beginning in the process of learning to listen. In restating the content of the client's message, the counsellor feeds back to the client the content of the statement using different words. In paraphrasing a client's statement, the counsellor may respond to a feeling, but the focus of the restatement is on content. Some interactions of paraphrasing are as follows:

INTERACTION 6.5

Client 1:   "I am so sick of this company I can hardly get up in the morning to go to office."

Counsellor: "You've just about reached your limits as far as your job is concerned."

Client 2:   "I don't know what to do with my life. Sometimes I think I should just go out and get a job for the experience, and then again sometimes I think I should just go on to graduate school, but I'm not sure what to major in."

Counsellor: "You're struggling with a big decision about where to go from here with your life, and you're not sure which of the two choices makes the most sense."

In each of the above examples, the counsellor responds to the content of the client's statement by paraphrasing the message in different words.

Paraphrasing is appropriate at the beginning of a counselling interview because it encourages the client to open up and elaborate upon the concern. However, paraphrasing does not lead to in-depth exploration and can result in circular discussion if the counsellor does not bring in other skills as the interview proceeds.

6.4.5   Reflection of Feeling

The basic difference between restatement of content and reflection of feeling is one of emphasis. In reflecting a client's feeling, the counsellor listens carefully to the client's statement and responds by paraphrasing the content of the message, but he places the emphasis on the feeling the client expressed. By responding to the client's feelings, the counsellor is telling the client that she is trying to perceive and understand the client accurately from the client's internal frame of reference. The counsellor tries to identify the feeling accurately by listening not only to what the client says but also to how the client says it. For example see Interaction 6.6.

INTERACTION 6.6

Client 1:   "I was happy to hear I've been selected for a scholarship to the university I want to attend."

Counsellor: "What a thrill for you. You must be very excited and proud to know that you were selected for such an honour."

Client 2:   "My mom and dad fight constantly. I never know what to expect when dad comes home from work."

Counsellor: "It must be pretty scary for you to live with such uncertainty."

In both instances, the counsellor's gives response to the basic feeling state of the client and thus communicates to the client the counsellor's acceptance of his or her world.

6.4.6 Summarization of Content

Summarization enables the counsellor to condense and crystallize the essence of the client's statements. It can further client's exploration and can also serve as a perception check for the counsellor. The summary of content differs from paraphrasing in that the summary typically responds to a greater amount of material. A paraphrase normally responds to the client's preceding statement; a summary can cover an entire phase of the session or even a total interview (Ivey, 1971).

Ivey has noted that a summarization of content is most frequently used in the following situations:

1. When the interviewer wishes to structure the beginning of a session by recalling the high points of a previous interview.
2. When the interviewee's presentation of a topic has been either very confusing or just plain lengthy and rambling.
3. When an interviewee has seemingly expressed everything of importance to him on a particular topic.
4. When plans for the next steps to be taken require mutual assessment and agreement on what has been learned so far.
5. When, at the end of the session, the interviewer wishes to emphasize what has been learnt within it, perhaps in order to give an assignment for the interval until the next session.

6.4.7 Summarization of Feeling and Emotions

In the summarization of feeling and emotions the counsellor attempts to identify and respond to the overriding feelings/emotions of the client, not only the expressed feelings/emotions but also the general feeling tone of the phase of the interview being summarized. Summarizing a client's feelings/emotions forces the counsellor to synthesize the emotional aspects of the client's experience; as such it requires that the counsellor respond in a deep and perceptive way to the emotional component of the client's experience (Ivey, 1971).

Ivey has suggested that the counsellor should make use of the following rules while imparting counselling:

1. Use reflections of feeling to indicate to the client that the counsellor is with him. Selective attention to feelings will assist the counsellor in exploring the client's emotional states.
2. Note consistent patterns of emotion as the client progresses through the interview. Also note his inconsistencies or polarities of feelings.

Most clients have mixed feelings toward important love objects or situations and showing the client how he has expressed his mixed feelings may be especially valuable to him.

3. At two or three points during the session and at the close of the session the counsellor should restate in his own words the feelings and perceptions that the client has been communicating.

In looking at the aspect of genuineness in a counsellor's style note that it could not mean exactly the same for a manager as it would for a professional counsellor, though its essential nature could not be compromised.

The same caution may come in handy when we look at the rest of the qualities said to be necessary for a professional counsellor. Taken together these qualities seem more like a preparation for sainthood than for a job; and make one wonder how such people could actually demand money for their services.

6.4.8 The Counsellor's Verbal Encouragement to Disclose

Encouraging communication usually begins with the counsellor offering an open invitation to communicate. A statement such as one of the following is usually sufficient to offer an invitation: "How can I help?" "What would you like to discuss today?" "How would you like to begin?"

Most voluntary clients will respond to such invitations with the expression of a concern along with an implied need for help. Following are examples (refer Interactions 6.7 to 6.11) of initial client statements and of counsellor responses that encourage further clarification and/or development of the initial statement.

INTERACTION 6.7

Client: "My husband is an alcoholic and has been that way since before we were married. I can't get him to stop and I'm scared and I don't know what to do."

Counsellor: "You're worried about your husband's drinking. Can you tell me more specifically what has been happening that led to your decision to seek help now?"

INTERACTION 6.8

Client: "I don't feel like seeing my boss. Every time I go to meet him, he starts shouting at me."

Counsellor: "It sounds as though you do not have a good rapport with your boss and this has been troubling you."

INTERACTION 6.9

Client: "Salil keeps bothering me on the playground. He pushed me off the jungle gym again and yesterday he punched me."

Counsellor: "You say Salil keeps bothering you. Sounds like this has been going on for a while."

INTERACTION 6.10

Client: "It's just two weeks until graduation and I don't have any idea what I'm going to do next."

Counsellor: "It sounds like you're feeling some pressure about this. Help me understand what you have been thinking about doing up till now."

INTERACTION 6.11

Client: "Well, my daughter really seems to be out of control. She stays out till late hours of the night and refuses to talk about what she's doing."

Counsellor: "It sounds like you're worried about your daughter. Why don't you fill me in on exactly what has been happening?"

In each example, the counsellor first acknowledges the content and/or feeling in the client's statement of an initial concern. Further development and clarifications are always necessary. Follow-up invitations that encourage further development take the following general forms (refer to Interaction 6.12):

INTERACTION 6.12

Counsellor: "Tell me more about..."

Counsellor: "Help me understand more fully..."

Counsellor: "Tell me what happened when..."

Counsellor: "Help me understand what you are thinking about..."

6.5 Listening Barriers

The counsellor should be aware of what is going on in his own head while he is listening. The following are some barriers to listening to look out for:

6.5.1 Fear of Listening too Well

Are you afraid to really listen? Do you fear losing your own train of thoughts if you listen too well? You may worry that if you do not jump in to disagree you will be seen to be agreeing. All these fears are unfounded. If the counsellor loses his train of thought, it will be temporary. If the opinion is changed, maybe the other person's ideas are better. And there will always be time later on, after listening to disagree.

6.5.2 Listening for What One Wants to Hear

If the counsellor is a very poor listener he hears what he wants to hear rather than what is being said. This has a disastrous effect on relationships with subordinates.

6.5.3 Personal Limitations, Which Affect Interpretation

The counsellor's basic assumptions can affect what he hears. These assumptions are based on his personal experiences and memories, perceptions, values, biases, attitudes, expectations and feelings.

6.5.4 Emotional Reactions

Sometimes people react strongly to certain words or phrases, which happen to evoke emotional responses. This interferes with their ability to hear what is being said after the emotive words.

6.5.5 Lack of Self-awareness

The counsellor's lack of awareness of his own feelings and struggles makes it difficult to listen to other people.

6.5.6 Thinking Ahead

Words are spoken at a rate of approximately 150 per minute, but the brain can process information about three times as fast. When counselling it is inappropriate for the counsellor to use this spare thinking time for planning his own next words or thinking about something else, as he might during ordinary conversation. Concentrated listening means listening all the way to the ends of sentences and using spare time to think about what the other person is communicating.

6.5.7 Self-consciousness

If you are worried about how he appear or is nervous about what he is going to say next, his listening will be distracted.

6.6 Tips to Enhance Listening

1. *Patience:* The counsellor should give the space and time to be really there for his subordinate.
2. *Concentration:* He should focus on what is happening and try not to be distracted.
3. *Reflection:* He should check for understanding frequently by reflecting.
4. *Watchfulness:* The counsellor should watch the subordinate's body language.
5. *Good Listener:* He should listen to how things are said.
6. *Attention:* He should also be able to listen for what is not said—what is being avoided?
7. *Analytical ability:* The counsellor should recognize his responses and try to put his own feelings aside. He should be able to analyze whether he is switching off? Mentally arguing? Over identifying? Or stereotyping?
8. *Self Analysis:* He should be aware of his own body language (The SOLER acronym can be used to help him remember):

    (a) Sit squarely
    (b) Open gestures
    (c) Lean slightly forward
    (d) Eye contact
    (e) Relax.

6.7 Counsellor's Qualities

Nevertheless a random sampling might give the practicing manager enough of a flavour of useful/ideal qualities in counselling to calculate his or her own chances of successfully transplanting them into local management style. Table 6.10 highlights some of the ingredients required or recommended by employers and trainers of counsellors:

	Table 6.10 Qualities of a Counsellor	
1.	Analytical ability	To sift, track and control the flow of information
2.	Judgment	To know when to suspend it
3.	Patience	To control one's immediate reactions
4.	Warmth	To create a safe atmosphere
5.	Alertness	To note non-verbal signals and discrepancies
6.	Resilience	To tolerate ambiguity and seeming contradictions
7.	Plainness	To say what one means
8.	Trustworthiness	To refuse to gossip
9.	Restraint	To control the urge to talk about oneself
10.	Concentration	To hear what is implied as well as what is said openly

Continued

	Table 6.10	Qualities of a Counsellor (*Continued*)
11.	Experience	Of life, to allow an element of compassion for people
12.	Training	To supplement commonsense
13.	Self-confidence	To allow the client to be in charge sometimes
14.	Courage	To confront when necessary
15.	Coolness	To know when to reassure or sympathize and when not
16.	Firmness	To stop the client focusing responsibility on outside sources
17.	Prudence	To stay clear of organizational conflicts
18.	Integrity	To refrain from abusing authority
19.	Creativity	To shift the focus of solutions
20.	Realism	To understand organizational, cultural and political factors
21.	Sensitivity	To connect with others' feelings

Having looked at what our celestial counterparts are doing, let us turn to a rather shorter list of personal qualities the mundane manager, colleague or friend may need in order to get started.

6.7.1 Tolerance

A practising counsellor may well get started with the lack of a need for perfection suggested above. Counsellors need tolerance and a measure of self-acceptance if they are ever going to show it to others. Counsellors who like things to be neat and tidy are in for a hard time. People and their personal problems are not generally neat and tidy.

Secondly, clients and their behaviour often do not fit into the counsellor's own patterns of thoughts or beliefs or judgments as much as one might like; and the perfectionist counsellor will be easily tempted into evaluative comments rather than understanding ones.

Thirdly, such a person will find it difficult to deal with the lack of clarity and precision in many counselling situations. It may not be clear what the client really needs or if this is the same as what he says he wants? It may not be clear what the counsellor's obligations are towards him or towards others. Again, in retrospect, it may not be clear that the counsellor did the right thing. The client may be delighted but the counsellor may not be at all sure if what he did was for the best. On the other hand he may be sure that he did the right thing, but the client is telling him it is not what he wanted.

Engineers, artists, carpenters, gardeners and many others have the satisfaction of seeing the results of their work in a form, which allows them to assess and take pleasure in it. Not so for counsellors. Counselling is full of ambiguity and the perfectionist who likes matters to be unambiguous will be wasting a lot of energy.

From a very practical point of view such a counsellor will be unable to listen properly because the chatter in his own head will drown out half of what the client is saying.

Lastly, the need for perfection usually means making, as few mistakes as possible—better still, none at all—and this inhibits naturalness, which can be rated more highly than perfection in a counsellor. Counsellors, who are not afraid to make mistakes but are quick to realize when they have, and can then rectify the situation, perhaps with an apology if it is appropriate, are preferred over the other type?

Counsellors need to be fairly balanced individuals, sufficiently relaxed in themselves to allow other people to be different; not to be too disturbed by their contradictions, ambivalences and seemingly odd ways of thinking, talking and doing. To be just that secure in oneself means, of course, knowing something about oneself.

6.7.2 Self-knowledge

By self-knowledge is not meant being endlessly self-analytical. That is a separate career in itself, and would not be recommended for most counsellors, let alone the average manager or colleague. People sometimes imagine that to embark on counselling they need to know a lot more about people in general. But it is desirable to begin with, by knowing, a bit more about yourself.

The learning curve should take beginners first through listening skills. In the process they should begin to be aware of their own reactions, to listen to themselves; and then gradually to a greater knowledge of people in general. Counselling is in itself a tremendous education in living. Nobody benefits more from counselling than counsellors. This education, however, will come gradually and naturally in its own time. Learning more about various personality theories may advance it but this is not the first priority. Knowing about oneself is.

The best starting-point for counsellors is to become involved in counselling, to learn to use themselves as the main tool and then to be aware of how the process is affecting them, and how they can improve. They need to aware of three facts that:

Counselling can be taxing: This much awareness of oneself is necessary because counselling can be quite a drain on the coun-sellor's own emotional and mental resources.

Counsellors, whether they be full-time or those whose leadership or colleague position brings them into the role from time to time, need enough self-awareness to know when they themselves need help. Experience seems to show that they are not necessarily the best at seeking help for themselves.

Poor counselling can be dangerous: To be safe, counsellors need to understand something of their own motivation. They need to know why they enjoy counselling, if they do, and if not, why not. They need to know when they may be indulging themselves. Counsellors are in a powerful position. The more effective they are the more they are a force for good—or ill.

Research seems to indicate that the most of the damage is done to clients through counsellors who are perceived as emotionally distant and, at the other extreme, those who are (usually unconsciously) serving their own needs—for love, for closeness, for a sense of being needed. With organizations and companies there is also the danger of the client being manipulated or wronged through the counsellor's privileged knowledge. Consider the following Examples 6.3 and 6.4.

EXAMPLE 6.3

Woman executive, attractive and competent, at least on the surface. But her husband has just left her and gone to live with relatives. Her two daughters are giving more than average trouble for their age. And perhaps she has financial problems. Her insight is good but her self-esteem is at rock bottom and she has next to no support.

Where does she get help? What help does she need? Perhaps if she could develop a bit of backache she could go and see the medical officer or the nurse and talk to them? But would they get to the real problem? Would they have the time?

Any sympathetic listener, even one with personal problems, may quickly, without any conscious malice, seize on her vulnerability. In fact this example belongs to the next, and interlocks menacingly with it.

EXAMPLE 6.4

A middle manager is helping a female colleague who is going through a separation. The manager is smart enough to know he is emotionally involved, that there must be rumours flying around, that he is probably not helping her, that he is suppressing his true feelings for her, etc. But he's always been a real nice guy. He can't just leave her to get on with it, can he? It would tear both of them to shreds, wouldn't it? So what should he do?

He's asking you—what should he do? You are a colleague though not in the same reporting line. It all came out suddenly over a lunchtime drink. How can you help him? Can you walk away from him? Perhaps you ought to walk away from him? Or perhaps you could best help by dealing with the woman directly—you know her, she would probably listen to you?

Enough to show how the counsellor's motivation can be muddled when he or she has some personal investment in the client.

The power of the counsellor: This is overstating the case for most counselling situations, either because the counsellor is not effective enough to generate such a level of trust or because most professionals have been schooled to be aware of such pitfalls and to subscribe to a code of ethics. In any case, most clients still manage to protect themselves to some extent.

All professionals in training have to face at some stage the highly personal question of how to deal with the power which some patients will give them, whether they want it or not. Some trainees thrive on it and need to get the power-hunger out of their systems. Others run a mile at the sight of the power they have in their hands.

6.7.3 Discretion

Thus arises the question of counsellor discretion, which is a topic in itself. Blabbermouths do not make good counsellors, although oddly enough blabbermouths tend to receive more than their share of confidence. There is the ironic little twist that some people (half-) knowingly confine in a blabbermouth ("Promise you won't tell a soul!") because they (half-) know it will be all over the place in ten minutes. Meanwhile, they are virtuously telling themselves they would never have revealed it had they realized.

The good listener, the good counsellor, the good helper, every bit as much as the blabbermouth, cannot help finding out more than they would really like to know.

EXAMPLE 6.5

> [Naveen:] I'm going in to see the manager tomorrow morning and I'm going to let it all hang out. They may think I'm not pulling my weight but there are a few things they don't know. I don't care if I burst into tears in the process. I may bleed all over his carpet but everybody's going to know I've been in there.

Naveen's counsellor-colleague, in this case, was quite excited by such revelations though not in any way worried, since he was not himself involved. Shekhar (the general manager, and two or three echelons higher) was known to shoot from the hip. The fallout from an explosive meeting between him and the notoriously excitable Naveen could keep the place buzzing for days.

What does the counsellor-colleague do? Confidentiality is not the issue here. It is already late evening and the balloon is due to go up first thing in the morning. The problem is what to do with Naveen, and, broadly, should he be calmed down or allowed to go ahead?

This is where the counsellor-colleague needs to understand his own motivation. He can easily persuade himself that it is time anyway for Naveen and Shekhar to have their 'High Noon' confrontation. Simplest is to say nothing, leave Naveen nicely wound up and hope for a good seat at the next day's performance.

There are, even in the counselling profession itself, those who find it stimulating to send clients through interesting minefields ("Why don't you just walk out on him? You know, give him the old heave-ho! Note pinned to the kitchen table—'By the Time I Get to Phoenix He'll Be Sleeping' sort of routine") and then watch to see where they blow up.

In the event, Naveen's colleague was wise enough to mistrust his own motivation, and to talk things through with him. The net result was that Naveen blew out his storm the night before, and went in to see Shekhar in a quiet frame of mind. As it happened, Shekhar was relatively relaxed that morning and the two had a useful and in the end very productive session.

But Naveen's confidant could easily have been less self-aware, could have persuaded himself that a shootout would be good for them both, and left Naveen to get on with a self-destruct.

The counsellor needs to keep in the forefront of his mind the question such as "is this really in the other person's interest, or am I indulging myself, serving my own end?"

6.7.4 Interest

One aspect of the counsellor's own needs may be curiosity. In practice, this is more an asset than a handicap. Someone who is to help others needs some curiosity, some interest in people. And most counsellors, professional or just those whom everyone likes talking to, soon have their general curiosity satisfied. There is a sort of 'paid barrier' which most counsellors go through, when they cry "Enough! I don't want to hear about anybody else's problem ever again. I just don't want to know."

6.7.5 Liking

Does a counsellor need to like people? Consider the following Example 6.6:

EXAMPLE 6.6

An admin manager in his late thirties always wanted to get into sales and has now completed a very successful launch of a new outlet, tripling expected first-year sales. The snag? He has just been fired because the company can no longer afford him. He is on his way to see you, the personnel manager.

In your opinion it is all rather harsh. His appraisal (you have seen it) is bland, too bland, it reflects neither positive nor negative in any concrete way. It also seems strange to say he doesn't have sharp-end sales ability, although you can see that a static, maintenance type of sales manager is all that is needed now, more like an order-taker than a salesman.

Keep him on ice till the next launch? But that is two years away and the people involved say they wouldn't work with him again anyway, though he himself is convinced they would. Is it all a matter of personality clash? That is certainly the case with the man's own manager. So do you go and see his manager? Too late, the man is knocking on the door. What are you going to say? You can soon see what puts people off. He has some quite grotesque gestures and facial expressions, his voice is grating and he appears when sitting to be about to take off like a rocketing pheasant.

But you have been trained in counselling skills, so you know what to do. Right?

Liking people (or perhaps better the ability to come to like people) is useful for a counsellor. Some warmth and some instinctive sympathy is a great asset. Not the constant quest for the down-trodden, the sharp nose for every bird with a broken wing, but a combination of interest in and natural respect for others.

One comes back again and again to respect and tolerance as basic to counselling skills. One does not have to like the client but one does have to have enough respect to see things as he sees them and take that into account. Liking may help but it is not strictly necessary. What sometimes happens is that a client, whom one immediately and instinctively dislikes, if treated with enough empathy and respect, may gradually come to be more likeable.

Liking, of course, is different from being emotionally involved with someone. That inevitably makes counselling more difficult, and usually inadvisable.

6.8 The Core Conditions of Counselling

In the previous section we described some specific counsellor behaviours and skills, both non-verbal and verbal, that invite a client to begin talking about his or her concerns. Many beginning counsellors are able to accomplish these first steps with ease but then have difficulty knowing what to say when the client begins to disclose. It is helpful to remember the purposes of disclosure. The effort is to get the client to describe his or her experience, to release pent-up feelings in the process of telling the story, and to begin to clarify the true nature of the problem or problems presented. The counsellor's goal is to come to understand the client's experience as clearly and as personally as possible. New counsellors are often so predisposed to find a solution to the problem(s) that they forget that it is ultimately the client's responsibility to solve the problem(s). Suggestions made by counsellors for the resolution of client's concerns prior to careful disclosure short-circuit the counselling process, demean the client's own ability to be self-directing, and often provide solutions that don't fit the situations.

To support the clients' disclosure of meaningful issues during the initial stage of counselling, the counsellor maintains an attitude of receiving the client, often referred to as the core conditions of counselling. Three of these conditions—empathy, positive regard, and genuineness—were described by Carl Rogers (1957) as the necessary and sufficient conditions of therapeutic personality change. The fourth condition, concreteness, is the counsellor's skill in focusing the client's discussion on specific events, thoughts, and feelings that matter, while discouraging a lot of intellectualized storytelling. Concreteness is a precaution against the rambling that can occur when the other three conditions are employed without sufficient attention to identifying the client's themes. Concreteness will be evident to the degree that the counsellor identifies and responds to important client themes, while choosing not to respond to small talk, excessive storytelling, and other client material of a social or diversionary nature.

6.8.1 Empathy

Rogers (1961) defined empathy as the counsellor's ability "to enter the client's phenomenal world—to experience the client's world as if it were your own without ever losing the 'as if quality'." Bohart and Greenberg (1997) describe a resurgent interest in empathy in psychotherapy, detailing how it is perceived in client-centered, psychoanalytic, behavioural and cognitive, postmodernist, and eclectic approaches. They describe three categories of empathy:

1. Empathic rapport—"primarily kindness, global understanding, and tolerant acceptance of the client's feelings and frame of reference."
2. Experience near-understanding of the client's world—"what it is like to have the problems the client has, to live in the life situation the client lives in, what it is like to be him." This perspective includes conscious as well as some unconscious elements of the client's experience.
3. Communicative attunement—"The therapist tries to put himself or herself in the client's [sic] shoes at the moment, to grasp what they are trying to consciously communicate at the moment, and what they are experiencing at the moment."

Some authors (Carkhuff, 1969; Egan, 1998; Ivey, 1994; Patterson and Eisenberg, 1983) have reasoned that there are different levels of empathy—meaning that the counsellor may vary in the depth of understanding of the client's experience and may make choices about how much of that understanding is communicated in responding to the client. Sometimes the counsellor will perceive attitudes and motives in the client's statements that he or she is not yet ready to discuss directly. To stimulate client exploration, the level of empathy communicated should be matched to the client's level of readiness. Primary empathy is the level that is usually facilitative in the initial disclosure stage of counselling and advanced level empathy is often more appropriate for the in-depth exploration stage.

Empathy involves the following two major skills:

Perceiving: Perceiving involves an intense process of actively listening for themes, issues, personal constructs, and emotions. Themes may be thought of as recurring patterns—for example, views of oneself, attitudes toward others, consistent interpersonal relationship patterns, fear of failure, and search for personal power. Issues are questions of conflict with which the client is struggling such as "What do I want for my future?" "Why can't I ever do my job properly at any time?" "Why does every event in my family turn into a disaster?" "Why do I still feel that I am fat, when I have lost a lot of weight and am in fact thin?" Relative to each theme or issue a client will have emotions of elation, joy, anger, anxiety, sadness, confusion, and so forth. Understanding the emotional investments is a critical part of the perceptual element of empathy.

George Kelly (1955) described the perceptual element of empathy as understanding the client's personal constructs. He defined personal constructs as the unique set of thoughts a person uses to process information, give meaning to life events, order one's world, explain cause-and-effect relationships, and make decisions. They include beliefs about oneself and others, assumptions about how and why events happen in the world, and private logic and moral premises that guide one's world. The counsellor can detect a client's personal constructs from his or her cognitive structure that has led to interpretation of the events and to consequent feelings.

As the client discloses information about himself or herself, some of the client's themes form very quickly in the counsellor's perceptual foreground whereas others remain in the background. Some personal constructs (for example, "The world is not a safe place", "People are phoney") may emerge quickly, although others remain unavailable. Often as the counsellor listens to the client's story, the counsellor will see errors in the client's logic, construct different cause-and-effect relationships from the client's account, and identify the basis of the client's distressed feelings. This diagnostic thinking will guide treatment planning and serve as a basis for counsellor responding later in the counselling process.

Communicating: In the communication component of empathy, the counsellor says something that tells the client that his or her meanings and feelings have been understood. If a counsellor listens carefully and understands well but says nothing, the client has no way of knowing what is in the counsellor's mind. Sometimes the client may even misinterpret a counsellor's lack of response as a negative judgment about what they have said. It is often through hearing his or her meanings and feelings repeated that the client takes another look at life events and begins to perceive them differently.

Primary empathy is most often communicated through an interchange-able verbal response (though facial expressions and other non-verbal responses can also be used). Interchangeable responses are statements that capture the essential themes in a client's statement but do not go deeper than the transparent material. A paraphrase such as "You felt degraded and angry because your boss criticized you in front of your colleagues and friends" is a fairly typical response of this type. It captures both the feeling and the meaning of the client's previous disclosure in simple language the client can understand. Feeling understood, the client will very likely continue to elaborate on the meaning of that or related experiences. It is important to realize that statements such as "I know just how you felt" do not communicate empathy because they contain nothing of what the client have shared. Advanced empathy is communicated through additive verbal responses, in which the counsellor adds perceptions that were implied but not directly stated by the client. Ability to hear these implied meanings grow with experience and with the quality of the counsellor's diagnostic thinking. The following stages will explain the counsellor's diagnostic techniques:

STAGE I: In the first stage of counselling, primary empathy is used most because it demonstrates to the client that the counsellor is listening effectively, without the threat that can occur if the counsellor seems to be seeing through client's defenses too quickly. The client's sense of progress and of comfort is both served at this relationship-building stage if the counsellor is seen as perceptive, but not too perceptive.

Cultural sensitivity and the knowledge of cultures different from the counsellor's own are important to effective use of empathy. Okun (1997) cautions, "While there are some basic skills and strategies that cut across class, race, and culture, helpers must adapt their counselling style to achieve congruence with value systems of culturally diverse clients." Cultural background will influence not only the personal constructs through which an individual interprets the world but also the style of expression that is experienced as empathic. For example, verbal responses that move too quickly to meanings and feelings are often considered to be rude in Asian cultures.

Effectively communicated empathy has a number of desired effects in the initial disclosure stage of counselling. First, the energy required to listen actively expresses caring and affirmation to the client. The counsellor is saying, "I care enough for you that I want to invest energy into understanding clearly."

STAGE II: Second, the feedback that comes from the counsellor's contact with significant themes helps the client see his or her own themes more clearly. This helps the client understand himself or herself more deeply and re-examine relevant perceptions, attitudes, and beliefs.

STAGE III: Thirdly, such responding establishes expectations about the nature of the counselling experience. Counselling is conveyed to the client as a process that involves attending to oneself, exploring, searching, and perceiving oneself more clearly. Counselling is established as an experience involving work, not simply conversation. Indeed, the counsellor's work is to stimulate the client's work of self-discovery.

STAGE IV: A fourth effect is that if the counsellor is careful to offer a level of empathy that is consistent with the client's level of readiness, the client will feel safe to continue the counselling experience. The client learns that nothing bad will happen as a result of communicating and that something helpful is likely to occur.

STAGE V: A fifth effect is that empathy communicates to the client that the counsellor has special expertise to offer. Empathy is not routinely experienced in the events of daily life. A counsellor who can make empathic contact established himself or herself as having some special skill, which in turn, helps the client experience a sense of optimism about future sessions.

Bohart and Greenberg (1997) report that research over the years has continued to show correlations between therapist empathy and counselling outcomes. This has proven to be true whether the clients themselves rated the empathy or by expert raters watching the counselling—and it has been shown to be true across a variety of clients.

6.8.2 Positive Regard

Positive regard is caring for your client for no other reason than the fact that he or she is human and therefore worthy. Caring is expressed by the enthusiasm one person shows for being in the presence of another and by the amount of time and energy one is willing to devote to another's well-being. The experience of being cared about helps develop and restore a sense of caring for oneself. It creates energy and encourages a person to respond to the demands of life. A counsellor's caring can increase the client's enthusiasm for work and growth.

Rogers (1957) developed the concept that the counsellor's caring for the client can be unconditional. Because the counsellor does not have a role in the client's life outside the counselling situation, he or she can become the client's instrument for change without a lot of preconceived ideas about what behaviours the client should exhibit. The counsellor's respect for the dignity and worth of the individual remains intact regardless of client's behaviour. Parental love—which is probably the most important support a growing human ever experiences—is very much like unconditional regard, but parents can never fully achieve unconditionality because they have a vested interest in what their children do. They believe their children's behaviour reflects on their effectiveness as parents and by extension on their worth as individuals. As a professional helper, the counsellor does not have comparable ego investment in the client. It is, of course, an ideal that the counsellor can care for (love) each client equally. All counsellors, being human, meet clients who are hard for us to like. It is important when this occurs for the counsellor to examine and work through his or her feeling of disregard or to refer the client to another counsellor. If the counsellor does not have a feeling of positive regard for the client, one of the necessary conditions for therapeutic change is missing.

To work through feelings of disregard for a client, the counsellor must first acknowledge him and take responsibility for his existence. After recognition, the counsellor's task is to identify specific characteristics of the client that he or she does not like. For many counsellors, lying, defensiveness, manipulation, destructiveness to oneself and others, unwillingness to conform to reasonable social rules, and irresponsibility to others are traits that often trigger dislike. For example, some counsellors might have difficulty working with a client who is known to have been a wife basher. After taking whatever steps are necessary to secure the safety of the victim, the counsellor's task is to become committed to helping the client get beyond a very serious problem in his life. Though the client's behaviour may have been repugnant if judged through the moral imperatives by which the counsellor lives his or her own life, the counsellor tries to understand the meaning of the behaviour in the client's life without judgment so that strategies for change can be devised.

Several parameters of human behaviour may help counsellors to work through their own emotions. One is that the counsellor may be tempted to impose 'should' statements on the client. But the counsellor attempting to impose these 'shoulds' would be experienced by the client as uncaring. The likelihood is that the client already understands that there are negative consequences to his or her behaviours and yet has still chosen the behaviours.

Rather than being rejected for those behaviours, he or she needs help in finding alternative behaviours that will have more positive consequences.

A second parameter is that anxiety often accompanies feelings of dislike for a client. The counsellor may feel threatened by client's behaviour that raises concern about his or her own unresolved issues or by the fear that the client's problems are beyond his or her ability to help. Excessive resistance by the client or power struggles in the counselling sessions can also trigger counsellor anxiety.

A third parameter is that some characteristics of the client may remind the counsellor of some other person for whom there are feelings of anger or resentment. In such circumstances the counsellor does not perceive the client with full accuracy but instead has some distortions in his or her image of the client.

Keeping these parameters in mind, working through dislike for a client requires that the counsellor gives honest answers to the following questions:

1. What characteristics of my client interfere with my ability to find him or her likable?
2. What do I think my client should be doing that he or she is not doing now?
3. How are my 'shoulds' affecting our relationship and my openness with the client?
4. If I am imposing 'shoulds', what am I missing about my client as a result?
5. Am I experiencing an anxious rather than a calm feeling with my client?
6. With whom in my life might I have important unfinished business?
7. Is my own unfinished business interfering with my ability to feel caring for this client?

These questions are very difficult for any counsellor to answer without the assistance of a professional colleague. For this reason it is strongly recommended that every counsellor have his or her own resource counsellor—usually either a colleague or a supervisor. Exploration of feelings of disregard for a client in conjunction with another counsellor will help the counsellor determine whether the disregard can be understood and replaced with a more helpful attitude or whether the client should be referred. The practising counsellor may also learn that his or her own unresolved issues are intrusive in enough counselling interactions that personal therapy may be needed.

Of course, an effective counsellor will experience positive regard for the vast majority of his or her clients. Although caring is usually not as directly expressed as empathy, it will become apparent to the client through the counsellor's spontaneous statements that acknowledge the validity of the client's struggle for a more satisfying life. As Ivey (1994) states, "the counsellor points out how, even in the most difficult situation, the client is doing something positive." Similarly, a client will usually detect the absence of caring fairly quickly, so the counsellor is well advised to deal promptly with such feelings.

6.8.3 Genuineness

Rogers (1942) originally defined genuineness as the characteristic of transparency, realness, honesty, or authenticity. He has also used the term congruence to suggest that a genuine counsellor behaves in ways that are congruent with his or her self-concept and thus consistent across time. The counsellor shares thoughts and feelings in ways that do not manipulate or control the client. Although genuineness does not give the counsellor license to ventilate his or her own emotions on the client, Rogers said that a counsellor who is having trouble liking a client would do well to share and try to resolve the feeling with the client rather than trying to hide it. It is cautioned that clients with deep wounds to their self-esteem may not be able to handle such honesty from the counsellor. Genuineness may have to be established through persistent congruence over a longer period of time.

Rogers believed that if the counsellor behaves consistently over time, he or she eventually will be perceived as real. Having this perception of the counsellor will help the client feel safer and develop a greater sense of trust and thus be more willing to engage in the intensive exploration work of counselling. Experiencing genuineness from the counsellor in a climate of safety enables the client to be more genuine and also encourages him or her to drop defenses, games, and manipulations. Transparency—that is, allowing the client to see into the counsellor's thoughts and feelings—reduces the client's concern that there are hidden agendas that the counsellor is going to try to manipulate the client into behaving in certain ways.

To be fully genuine in the sense described by Rogers, counsellors must know themselves very well. They must have a clear picture of their personalities and how the elements of personalities are expressed in significant events and relations with people.

The principle of genuineness dictates that the counsellor should never communicate dishonestly, never present information that misleads, and never knowingly present an image of himself or herself that deceives the client. However, the principle does not require that the counsellor impulsively disclose every thought, opinion, and feeling to the client. Sharing information about oneself is a decision, not an impulse, for both the counsellor and client. The counsellor decides what and when to disclose based on perceptions of the client's need for or ability to benefit from the information. For example, describing an emotion experienced in the client's presence or an observation about what is happening right now in the relationship (such as "I feel that you are unloading on me today") is immediacy communication that the client may have trouble working with during initial stage. In the next stage such responding may be appropriate because the client feels safer and is more ready to work with it. Disclosing a past experience that parallels the client's experience may help reduce distance and create a feeling of mutuality. However, going into a lot of detail about past personal experiences can quickly move into storytelling that can take the focus away from the client and block the exploration process. If the counsellor chooses to disclose personal experiences, he or she should disclose no more than is necessary to help the client see the parallels with his or her own experience.

Another type of disclosure that tends to diminish the client's perceptions of genuineness is opinions about other people's behaviour. Clients who experience interpersonal stresses sometimes want confirmation that they are right and others are wrong. They may try to draw the counsellor into taking a position. For example, with couples experiencing marital disagreement, each client may seek to gain the counsellor as an ally against the other. Because the counsellor cannot know all the circumstances or motives involved, and because talking about another person's behaviour is gossiping, it is wise for the counsellor not to express any judgment. A counsellor who makes the error of judging a third party's behaviour will be seen as a counsellor who will judge the client as well. It may help if the counsellor explains that he or she is not in a position to judge.

6.8.4 Concreteness

As Ivey (1994) states, "a concrete counsellor promptly seeks specifics rather than vague generalities. As interviewers, we are most often interested in specific feelings, specific thoughts, and specific examples of actions." Concreteness is not one of the Rogerian conditions of the helping relationship. In fact, the concept has emerged because it has been observed that counsellors who are empathic, caring, and genuine may still encourage a *portent* material. If the counsellor responds with equal interest to the statements "The weather has been very nice" and "The way my boss has been treating me and my other colleagues really hurts", the client is likely to be encouraged to elaborate on either statement as though they were of equal importance.

As stated earlier, it is the counsellor's responsibility to identify which of the client's statements are central to his or her reasons for being a client and to encourage talk about those issues. The client is still the person who determines what will be introduced as the content of the session, but the counsellor manages the process in such a way as to make it easier for the client to talk about what matters. What the counsellor responds to, the client will probably follow up on; what the counsellor ignores will likely be dropped. As diagnostic skills improve with experience, it becomes easier for the counsellor to identify important themes to be pursued, but even the beginning counsellor can easily distinguish between small talk and self-disclosure. Beyond initial social amenities that may contribute to client comfort, small talk wastes valuable counselling time.

Ivey (1994) suggests that concreteness can be increased by asking directly for specific examples of troublesome events. For example, the frequently heard phrase "She is always picking on me" tells little, but examples of specific interactions between the client and the other person will shed much light on the relationship dynamics. "Picking on me" may actually mean "Every time I don't have my work done, the boss calls attention to it in a public way and embarrasses me."

The language used by the client and by the counsellor can also contribute to unfocused discussion. Vagueness, abstractness, and obscurity are the opposites of concrete communication. Therefore, the counsellor should model direct communication as well as challenge the client to become more specific. The more fully and concretely the troublesome events in the client's life are re-created, complete with affective tone, within the counselling session, the more likely it is that new understandings and more positive feelings can be developed.

The following Example (6.7) includes three counsellor responses, each of which is at least minimally responsive to the client's statement. The responses increase in their level of concreteness and thereby increase in their potential to focus the client's self-exploration.

EXAMPLE 6.7

Client: "I feel so frustrated with my teenage daughter. She is completely out of control. No matter what I do she stays out till late hours and won't get up for school in the mornings. I've tried everything but it just seems hopeless."

Response with little concreteness:

• You seem very upset and worried.

Response with moderate concreteness:

• You seem pretty frustrated with your daughter's behaviour and are running out of ideas.

Response with a high degree of concreteness:

• You are frightened that your daughter is harming herself and feel powerless and hopeless. At the same time you haven't given up. You are here and ready to try to work out some other way to help.

Although the first response identifies something of the client's feelings, the second adds more of the client's meaning as well. The third response includes feeling and meaning in more detail, and it begins to structure toward hope that exploration might lead to new possibilities for helping. Any of the three responses would likely sustain the conversation, but the more concrete the response, the more likely the client will focus energy productively.

6.9 Summary

This chapter focused on specific counselling skills which are basic to the process of counselling and are used by most of the counsellors regardless of the setting.

The first thing is that the counsellor has to accept what the client brings to the counselling experience. Some may be willing to go through the process while some may be unwilling to do so. Both have to be dealt with appropriately in the counselling session. Different ways to invite communication and build the counselling relationship have been classified into non-verbal and verbal communication. Non-verbal communication is expressed by different modalities like using time, using body and using environment. The interpretation of non-verbal communication varies from person to person and also in the same person on two different occasions. The counsellor's non-verbal messages also have important role to play in determining the effectiveness of counselling process.

Verbal communication also makes important contribution to the process of counselling. To develop communication one should follow open-ended leads and be a good listener. The counsellor can use encouragers, echoing, repetition and reflection to indicate that he is listening. There are few listening barriers like fear of listening too well, listening for what one wants to hear, personal limitations, emotional reactions, lack of self-awareness, thinking ahead and self-consciousness, which need to be managed well. Certain qualities of the counsellor like tolerance and self-knowledge help the counsellor perform his job better. Core conditions of counselling include empathy, positive regard, genuineness and concreteness that have to be maintained for counselling to be effective.

The next chapter brings out the dilemmas that the managers have to encounter while they practice counselling in business organizations.

Review Questions

1. How does self-disclosure by the client during the initial phase enhance the effectiveness of counselling process? Discuss different kinds of apprehensions that clients have during the initial phase.

2. What are the different components of communication? How does non-verbal communication take place? How can a counsellor keep a control over his/her non-verbal messages?

3. How does verbal communication influence the counselling process? Discuss the issues that need to be kept in mind by the counsellor while communicating verbally with the client.

4. What is the difference between active and passive listening? What are some of the barriers to listening?

5. List and discuss the core conditions for counselling. Why are these important in the process of counselling?

Chapter 7

Role Conflicts in Counselling

In his novel *Nice Work,* David Lodge (1988) presents the two worlds of education (the University) and commerce (the factory) and uses the theme of 'shadowing' to show the differences between the two worlds. Throughout, the two main characters Robyn (a lecturer from the English department) and Vic (managing director of an engineering firm) struggle to understand and learn about each other's world. They start off with antipathy towards the world of the other and slowly begin to learn how one could influence the other and how values found in one could be of help of the other. Towards the end Robyn has a dream where both worlds meet:

> *"And the beautiful young people and their teachers stopped dallying and disputing and got to their feet and came forward to greet the people from the factory, shook their hands and made them welcome, and a hundred small seminar groups formed on the grass, composed half of students and lecturers and half of workers and managers, to exchange ideas on how the values of the university and the imperatives of commerce might be reconciled and more equitably managed to the benefit of the whole of society (Lodge, 1988)."*

If we changed the terms above to the two worlds of business and counselling, the underlying themes would be the same. Few texts struggle with the particular problems that arise among the underlying values, philosophies and policies of the world of business and the world of counselling. Some authors have reviewed the conflicting values between counselling and the contexts in which it is applied; for example, counselling in Nazi Germany (Cocks, 1985), and under the apartheid system in South Africa (Dryden, 1990). It is all too easily assumed by many counsellors that counselling will blend easily with whatever context and that the resulting marriage will be one of continual harmony. Warning voices have been raised (Bakalinsky, 1980; Lane, 1990) about introducing counselling into companies without consultation. Some organizations may not be ready for counselling provision.

Counselling can be integrated into industry for all sorts of wrong reasons resulting in unclear boundary issues and, in some instances, the 'hijacking' of counselling to cover managerial defects.

7.1 The Values of Counselling vs. Those of Business

Oberer and Lee (1986) articulate a major concern: "the most obvious [area of difficulty] involves the primary role of business vs. the counsellor's professional goals." Is there an inherent contradiction between the aims and purposes of industry and those of the counselling profession? Does working within industry compromise counsellors? There is no doubt that the aim of counselling is to promote growth and autonomy among the clients and to encourage clients to care for themselves, to be assertive and to develop their potential. But this is not always in accord with particular organizations that do not wish employees to be autonomous. Many organizations want teamwork rather than a concentration on the individual; many require 'passive employees' rather than 'active ones,' and many growth-orientated employees would clash with 'macho managers'. Orlans (1986) highlights possible conflicts:

"One difficulty with counselling within the organizational context is that the values and goals implicit in counselling (especially in non-directive approaches) are not easily reconciled with the economic, rationalistic models, which underlie organizational procedures and processes. Counselling is generally concerned with providing individuals with a greater sense of freedom, while an important organizational function is the control of its employees."

Nahrwold (1983) has traced the history of antagonism between counselling and business, showing scientists, especially in the mid-1960s "depicted businesses as amoral, greedy, polluting, exploitive (or even fascist) organizations that sacrifice human values and social responsibilities to increase profit." To counter criticisms portraying them as Dickensian villains, business people in turn have characterized social scientists as "naïve, bleeding head academics or crypto-Marxist social agitators seeking to overturn capitalism." While acknowledging the strong stereotypes put forward by both camps, Nahrwold upbraids counsellors for an anti-business attitude, which is sometimes expressed in the way they dress, and the way, they maintain hostile attitudes and professional arrogance. He suggests that the two worlds can exist and blend amicably if common sense, coupled with the desire to know one another and the roles involved, and an awareness of the politics of the organization, are used with good will.

Besides possible conflicts between counselling values and those of the organization, there may also be value conflicts within employees counsellors themselves where they struggle with their precise roles and responsibilities.

Which comes first: the individual client or the organization as a whole? Counsellors are trained primarily to deal with the individual and to put the welfare of the individual first. This may conflict with company norms and even policies. Moving from individual counselling, either privately or in other settings, to employee counselling in the work-place can be problematic for counsellors trained this way.

Counsellors and managers struggle to understand and be changed by the world of the other. Not only are some organizations reluctant to see a role for counselling within their ambit but also there are counsellors who view industry as simply against people and are concerned with making profit at the expense of individuals. Clashes in values among counsellors, clients, organizations and society have to be faced continually by work-place counsellors who are trying "to integrate outer-directed business values with the more inner-directed humanistic ones" (Puder, 1983). However, this is a generalization and not all work-places would agree that they were either profit-orientated to the detriment of their people, or that they are growing literature on the supportive and learning organization (Egan, 1994).

A key value question that runs through the literature on counselling within industry is, who is the client of the counsellors? Is it the individual client who makes his or her way to the counsellor's door, or is the organization the client? Clarifying roles with the individual client and within the organization becomes something of a difficulty, especially in the light of the expertise expected for the above. Work-place counsellors have to balance the fact that in many ways their clients are both individual employees and the organization from which they emerge. One of the earliest books on counselling at work in Britain (Watts, 1977) highlighted this area as needing special mention.

Where counselling takes place within an organization, however, the counsellor has to take into account its responsibility not only to the client but also to the institution, and to operate within boundaries set by the institution. This is especially problematic where the counsellor is employed by the organization. So long as he works only inside the one-to-one relationship he may be able to avoid being seen by the organization as threatening or subversive. Yet if he does this, he is inevitably defining problems as emanating from the individual rather than from the institution, where there is conflict between the interests of the two, all he can do is to accept the institution's needs and demands as given, and to help the individual to decide how to respond to them.

In brief, while theoretically there may well be value clashes between the world of work and that of counselling, in practice most counsellors are able to reconcile differences and work creatively within organizational settings. However, it seems that some caution is advised in taking for granted that the work-place readily adapts its values to complement those of counselling.

7.2 Counselling Service

The way the concept of counselling is used or understood within a particular company will determine what the goals of counselling should be, how counselling is practiced, and to what extent the model of counselling presented is really possible.

A survey of 20 companies in UK revealed that the majority use counselling in the context of performance review, both formal (appraisal) and informal inspired in one way or another by the idea that the employee may have something to contribute to the proper evaluation of his/her own work and may then be more open to corrective action.

Some use counselling as a part of their training methods, so that trainees may have the opportunity to assess their individual strengths and weaknesses.

The term is also commonly used in the context of career counselling and redundancy counselling; where the meaning most closely approaches the one that is adopted here, as does its use, for example, by a couple of UK airlines to describe the process of debriefing flight crews who have been under pressure. Other companies use counselling as part of their disciplinary procedures, sometimes mandatory, sometimes not.

7.2.1 Traditional Factors

Historically, the original pressures behind the establishment of employee counselling services in the United States were linked to the following three things:

1. The legislation held the employers responsible not only for their physical safety at work but also for what might be termed as *emotional damage*, especially where that was construed as leading to catastrophic effects in terms of illness or death.

2. The incidence of alcoholism and drug abuse, which were calculated by American industry amounting to quite astronomical sums.

3. The reaction of Health Insurance Company because it had to pay more in terms of health cost, it attempted to control the situation by correspondingly higher premiums and more stringent exclusion clauses. The agencies responsible for counselling services were also willing to modify this tougher approach for companies, and ran an employee-counselling programme.

7.2.2 New Factors

Now, according to the latest development, counselling services are linked to two things:

1. The economic recession in the world has put many companies under pressure to reduce and/or redeploys their workforce and at the same

time involve much more in people welfare. They have to take a long-sighted view of manpower requirement, to handle redundancies in a manager, to take steps to attract the key industrial employees they wish to retain.

2. To reduce the negative effects of stress on the grand scale arising from pressure, pace and fluctuations of modern life.

7.3 Dilemmas of a Manager Counsellor

When an independent counsellor is helping a client there is no conflict of interest, because once the contract between the two is agreed, the process is designed to satisfy only the interests of the client.

It is important for organization's counsellor, manager or anybody, to recognize that employers have a legitimate concern with performance. There will be an emphasis on action-positive change and measurable results.

The root of the difficulties, which managers and supervisors may experience, can be traced to certain ambiguities in the situation of the manager acting as counsellor. The same ambiguities are shared to a certain extent by those who have staff rather than line responsibilities. Most of the times, managers are not willing to take up the role of a counsellor for a number of reasons:

1. They fear that their assessing/controlling role will be undermined.
2. They believe that the subordinates will exploit a show of sympathy on their part.
3. They think that being sympathetic with a person means they cannot make any further demands on him or her.
4. According to some of them their job description doesn't include social work.
5. Some managers are reluctant to spend time as counsellors.

Leadership and management are both said to hinge on the desire and ability to make other people successful. The skills of counselling are subset of the skills of leadership. They may not be deployed everyday but one timely intervention by the respected boss or colleague can make a difference to the individual and he might learn a valuable lesson which will stay with him for the rest of his life and will also help him to make progress. Still there are certain role conflicts experienced by the managers when they are playing the role of a counsellor in an organization. Few of these are:

7.3.1 Different Priorities

First, managers and supervisors carry a natural responsibility to evaluate, control and improve performance. The company's objectives demand it; the way they carry it out is part of what they themselves are assessed on. Such pressures, from above and below, make middle management one of the most stressed groups in an organization. The calm listening, the reassurance and basic compassion of the counsellor are difficult to come by. The manager cannot refrain from making decisions, from passing judgment.

The manager and the counsellor may easily have different priorities. A manager may need to confront where the relative independent counsellor can afford to wait for the person to confront himself. The counsellor can perhaps afford to accept any one of the three solutions to a problem, but the manager may have to insist on only one. He or she may have to insist on one particular result, one outcome, however much freedom the individual is given to choose the means. The counsellor can usually be more relaxed about goals as well as means.

The gulf between the two perspectives may sometimes seem too wide to bridge. One might say that the counsellor works for the client, the employee works for the manager-counsellor. But this is to overdraw the difference in perspective. All sorts of people in authority have the same situation, the same dilemma. Teachers, nurses and, of course, parents play a significant management role with their charges. But they shift just as often into a helping, caring, counselling role too.

Likewise the manager may play now one and then the other role. What has often been missing from the manager's own education is training in counselling. Hence this book, which underlines at once both the techniques and the attitudes of good counselling. But the last thing it is intended to do is to shackle managers in their main duty, i.e., to manage. It is intended to show how they may do both at different times—and incidentally enhance their authority as managers.

7.3.2 Difference in Power

People often come to a manager because there is something or other he can do for them; there is something in his gift, so to speak. It is not necessary that they might always be seeking counselling. They might be interested in something as simple as—can they or can they not extend their sick leave, have a raise, go on flexitime, change their client-base, and postpone a deadline?

From the typical counsellor's point of view this may be an enviable position. The independent counsellor usually does not have the executive power to bring about a change in the situation, which will be beneficial to the client. Managers sometimes do. They can sometimes nip a problem in the bud simply by doing something. They may not need to counsel. If it makes sense the manager may simply say: Yes, you can (...go on flexitime, or whatever). They can arrange matters where the independent counsellor cannot.

Another major difference between the power of a manager and a counsellor is that the manager has the power to decide when to counsel and when not. For example, take the case of Bharat, the foreman, who wants to postpone a deadline. "There is no way we can get the stuff out on time", he says. Now, the manager has to decide what to do regarding Bharat's request.

There is one kind of Bharat who, when he says he can't get the stuff out on time, means he has run into unexpected problems which he will sort out with the minimum delay, but the manager is being given early warning that he will have to do some reshuffling on his own account.

There is another kind of Bharat who cannot meet a deadline because he cannot organize his workforce properly. Perhaps they fall behind because Bharat likes to handle all machine breakdowns himself. Perhaps that is what he likes to do best. Maybe he thinks the men respect him most for his technical skill, and is afraid he would lose their loyalty and respect if he did not continue to get his hands dirty.

In these situations, manager can take the decision regarding the problem but a counsellor can give only suggestions. In the former case deadline can be extended as the problem appears to be genuine, while in the latter Bharat needs counselling before he needs managing.

7.3.3 Owning the Problem

Another major problem is that the employee does not start by owning the problem. Bharat, the foreman in the previous example, does not actually think he has a problem. He believes there is a problem but he isn't part of it. Maybe he thinks it is the manager who is responsible for setting impossible targets. Perhaps it is the new generation of operatives who don't have (and never will have) the mechanical know-how to look after their own machines. He doesn't see that his own expertise came through experience, by being allowed to try things, by being shown, by experimenting, by learning.

He does not see there is anything he can do about the problem. That is why people say: if you are not part of the solution you are part of the problem. But Bharat does not see it that way. He does not own the problem.

The manager's first task would be to make him understand that it is his problem and not someone else's. Counselling is a delicate enough process. The need first to convince someone that they have a problem is even more so. This is typically the case with performance issues.

The redundancy counsellor too may face the same paradox. He or she is easily seen as the agent of the organization, which has given the person their problem, and can be the natural recipient of the welter of feelings which are involved such as, panic, resentment, bewilderment, and grief.

One may spare a thought in passing for the in-company redundancy counsellor. It can be an intensely demoralizing and conflict-provoking task, if it is not further complicated by the knowledge that theirs will be the next jobs to go. Professional counsellors are brought up to the recognition that they themselves need counselling from time to time. In-company counsellors often go without such support. Nor have they had experience and training to recognize and deal with the burden of other people's feelings in the office itself and, not to take them home with them, but rather to find ways of unloading them, as their professional colleagues usually can.

The manager, too, if he is to go behind surface problem will have to face the more emotional upheaval of dealing with the problem behind it. Bharat's real problem will not go away until his manager tackles it head-on. From a stress point of view that will be more demanding for the manager. He too may need some help. And maybe that is his real problem. He does not like asking for it.

7.3.4 Conflicting Views on Confidentiality

The reason most often given by employees why they are reluctant to accept counselling from anybody in the organization, even where there is no line relationship, is that they cannot be sure that what they reveal will not in some way prejudice their employment, either now or in the future.

Managers in their turn may want to refuse confidences because they are not sure they could maintain an unprejudiced personal attitude or an uncontaminated judgment of the individual from the company's point of view. Quite reasonably they may be afraid of having their hands tied, wittingly or unwittingly, by an employee's openness about a personal problem. For example:

EXAMPLE 7.1

> *One personnel manager I know is quite clear in her own mind which 'hat' she is wearing, and when talking with someone makes it quite clear which one it is. But most people are afraid that what they have under their hats leak unwanted into their heads.*

7.3.5 Ambiguity in the Situation

The individual manager might be a caring person, but company culture, policy or procedures are geared in such a way that he or she might be restricted from the outset in terms of the help they may offer. Such people may hesitate to get involved where the only response open to them is a kind of impotent sympathy which would leave them feeling all the more frustrated.

7.3.6 Ambivalence Towards Counselling

This is a more fundamental factor, which makes some people frankly unwilling to be involved in the counselling role. They may hide behind a protest about the kind of ambiguities just discussed but in fact it is more a question of personal ambivalence than role ambiguity. This may be for a variety of reasons:

1. Some people simply do not have a natural sympathy, warmth or caring for others.
2. Some would rather describe themselves as 'pragmatic', by which they mean they don't let their feelings affect their performances.

3. Some nourish the conviction that people (i.e. other people) are basically lazy or inept.
4. Some see counselling as encouraging malingerers rather than building trust and loyalty.

7.3.7 Ambivalence in Good Listening

There is another kind of ambivalence, which is rooted, in the genuine difficulty of good listening.

One aspect of it is the struggle anyone will experience when his or her own emotions or values are engaged by what someone is saying. Most of us can really only pay attention to one thing at a time. If our own vested interests are being challenged (however unknowingly) by the other person, we do not normally keep the focus of our attention on what they are actually saying. Good listening—for whatever purpose, be it counselling, negotiating or managing—needs to become second nature if we are not to become entangled in our own reactions.

A second and related aspect of this genuine difficulty in listening is that for many people there is something inherently competitive about talking. If someone tells me they nearly went under a bus, what is the most common reaction? I want to tell them the same thing happened to me. Most people don't listen for long before they start to itch to get in their own similar experiences.

There may be something here, something even more basic in many people, which is a reluctance to listen, from the belief that if they listen they may be forced to agree, that if they see the other's point of view they may have to give up their own.

In fact it is not true, but many people believe it. Not just with managers, but with negotiators. It is not only present in the boardroom, but also present in the bedroom. Listening is felt to be the same as giving in. If there is anything competitive in a relationship between two people, there will be a conflict or a struggle about listening. The struggle is about making sure the other listens first. "I'll go in and tell him when he's ready to listen", says the employee. And the boss? "I'll listen to him when he changes his tune".

7.4 Summary

The values of counselling differ a great deal from the values of a business. The businesses are for profit whereas counselling focuses more on the welfare of the employees. The use of counselling services in industry has existed for a long time and has served well. A manager playing the role of a counsellor in a business enterprise has to confront a number of dilemmas as the priorities of a manager are different from the priorities of a counsellor.

Some of the dilemmas that the manager has to confront are that the manager has to carry a natural responsibility to evaluate the subordinates while a counsellor does not have to do it. Employees expect a lot from the managers in the form of both tangibles and intangibles. The third dilemma is that the employee does not start by owning the problems. Fourth is the issue of confidentiality and then there is always an ambiguity in the situation. Some managers are unwilling to be involved in the counselling role and there may be ambivalence towards good listening. These dilemmas make the role of manager very difficult in the organizations.

Chapter 8 identifies and discusses the general principles followed in administering counselling, and the specific techniques used by the counsellors to counsel different types of employees.

Review Questions

1. How do the values of counselling differ from the values of business? Can these differences be reconciled? How?

2. List and discuss the traditional and modern development of counselling in the world of work.

3. Why are managers not willing to take up the role of counsellor in the work organizations?

4. What are the possible reasons for the conflicts between the role of a manager and a counsellor?

Chapter 8

Changing Behaviours Through Counselling

After going through the previous chapters it has been established that the counsellor has helped the client considerably. Many problems have been clarified, emotional reactions have been explored, and various alternatives and their consequences have been considered. For some clients this help is enough; they may be ready to move forward without any help. Clients often need more direct assistance if they are to follow through from gaining greater insights and self-understanding to reaching practicable solutions. Counselling should help clients to think differently, behave differently, to talk in a new way and to feel differently. There are a set of general principles that need to be accorded to if the counselling process has to succeed effectively.

8.1 General Principles of Counselling

Sometimes clients need to be supplemented by the specific techniques to help them. Certain general principles are useful in helping clients to change. Some of these are:

Setting Goals: When the counsellor aims to bring about changes in the behaviour of the client, the first job of the counsellor is to get his client to be clear and specific about his or her goals. Breaking a general goal into smaller more manageable ones and to plan practical steps towards a goal may help to achieve it.

Gaining Commitment: It is best if the client chooses and specifies his or her own goal, for he or she is then more likely to work hard to achieve it. But if counsellor has a good working relationship, he can propose a number of goals but ensure that the client commits himself or herself fully for achieving the goal and accepts responsibility for it. If the counsellor neglects to do this, the client will blame him for the failure. Most of the skills of the responding and leading stage might be helpful of get a commitment. The skill of influencing and confronting can be used. Sometimes the counsellor might find it helpful to formalize an agreement beyond the client's oral statement. It may be possible to ask the client to write down the goals and actions to implement on it in the form of a written statement or contract. The counsellor and clients plan such contracts jointly.

Anticipating Situations: Having generated the client's commit-ment to a precise goal, the counsellor's next job is to help him or her to plan exactly how, when and where the change process will start in earnest. Everything should be planned carefully. One should be helped to choose the best time and place to start, to decide exactly what to say or do, to imagine how one wants to look and feel, to consider likely reactions of others, and of himself or herself and to anticipate ones response to these different reactions. Such matters should be fully discussed so that the client feels very secure in what one is planning to do. The counsellor should encourage client to anticipate success, even if it might be unpleasant for him/her to think about the situation beforehand.

The prospects of failure should also be discussed because it would be foolish for counsellor to guarantee success. The client should be encouraged to think of failure as *nothing lost* and as an opportu-nity to make better plans for the next occasion.

Assessing Results: As soon as possible after the client has worked according to behaviour change plans, the counsellor should discuss the experience with him or her. The factors that led to success should be identified so that he or she is encouraged to try it again. The counsellor should also discuss, how the client felt, and remind him or her of the satisfaction one had when the goal was achieved. The client should be encouraged to re-experience these pleasant feelings as vividly as possible, as these will act as inducement for him or her to repeat his or her first success.

Making Records: Recording is a simple but very important skill because it provides one of the most powerful means of prompting behaviour change. Recording should be focused on one or two observable behaviours that are at the centre of the issues and that can be counted. It is hardly a counselling skill, but it is such a valuable aid to making good decision about change that its importance must be stressed.

8.2 Specific Techniques

It is often necessary for the counsellor to help a client to try out different ways of behaving. There are few specific techniques available, which the counsellor may use depending on the requirements and demands of the specific clients. Some of these techniques are:

8.2.1 Using Rewards

There is much current interest in finding out how to change individual's behaviour in various settlings (families, work places, institutions) by systematically altering the associations between events or bits of behaviour. The name of this method of changing behaviour is **reinforcement**, which refers to the way in which one can increase or decrease the likelihood that certain events will occur. As a general rule, the behaviour, which is regularly and immediately followed by pleasant experience, tends to be repeated. Such behaviour is said to be positively reinforced. On the other hand, behaviour, which is ignored or has unpleasant consequences, becomes less likely to appear.

One of the problems with the ways one reinforces is that generally one observes the inappropriate behaviour more readily than the desirable ones. Frequently in such situations all desirable behaviour passes unnoticed and without commendation of any kind, and the only adult reaction is to misbehaviour. The more effective way of dealing could be to ignore the misbehaviour and instead make pleasing comments about appropriate behaviour.

A counsellor should help clients to plan changes based on careful observation of exactly "What is reinforcing what." The combination of rewarding desirable behaviour and ignoring inappropriate behaviour is especially powerful, although it may be sufficient or appropriate in all cases. Most of the counselling skills used in the beginning and the middle stages include rewarding effects. Good eye contact and minimal encouragers are rewarding in the way that they help a client feel accepted and induce her to keep talking. Understanding and reflections of feelings have similar effects. Almost all techniques in the initial stage like rewarding, intimacy, sharing, problem-exploration, and a search for solution help the client to feel better.

A counsellor should use the technique to help a client similar to those of a successful teacher or parent uses the technique to help a child, i.e., by reinforcing certain remarks and rewarding others. By talking about or showing interest in client's remarks, which refer to insights and plans, for instance, the counsellor is rewarding problem solving and positive attitudes. If at the same times the counsellor ignores or cuts off long complaints and harrowing tales (i.e., does not reward them) he is discouraging irresponsibility.

The counsellor should remember that reward techniques can operate in either direction, and that a client may use them on the counsellor, as well as vice versa.

8.2.2 Providing Model

Modelling means providing a good example or pattern of behaviour for the client who does not know how to act appropriately in some situations. At one level, of course, modelling could means simply showing a physical example. Usually, modelling refers to actions, which seem very complicated. For this reason modelling is usually demonstrated in two ways, i.e., completely, without a break, to show the total effect, and also in segments to show that the separate skills can be isolated for observation and practice. The counsellor can act as a model; even a colleague or a peer can act as a model in client's ordinary social setting. After the model has been presented the client should be asked to attempt to imitate the model. He or she should be encouraged to rehearse the behaviour, with counsellor giving immediate feedback in the form of positive comments and suggestion about needed improvements. He or she should be reminded of the importance of such behavioural rehearsals in his or her own time.

8.2.3 Role Playing

Role-playing means acting out how a person with a particular title or function usually behaves. It is obviously akin to modelling and behaviour rehearsal, and all these are often used in conjunction with one another. But role playing usually implies a less prescribed way of behaving. The emphasis is more upon feeling what it is like to act in a certain manner, sometimes with the further implications that the role, being different is unfamiliar. It is not necessary for the roles to be played for long, three or four minutes is all that is desirable.

When people play somebody else's role, they might begin to experience what another person feels or thinks. In both role playing and role reversal the client should be encouraged or even coached, to throw himself or herself into the parts he or she plays, with all the feelings, gestures, words, tones, and volume that typically are used, or that he or she wants to experiment with. The more convincingly the roles are enacted, the greater the number of learning opportunities and change possibilities that are offered to the client.

8.2.4 Bodily Awareness and Relaxation Activities

As part of the processes by which behaviour is changed, it can be very helpful for people to become aware of and in control of their bodily sensations. Heightened awareness can help clients to identify their feelings more precisely. It can also help clients to gain more control of themselves. Relaxation is an especially useful skill for this. Transcendental meditation, yoga, biofeedback, and hypnosis are few examples of techniques with similar purposes.

Relaxation is achieved by gradually loosening muscles in all parts of the body so the there is no tightness or tension anywhere. Full attention is required, so that different parts of body are relaxed in sequence. It is possible to obtain total relaxation or partial relaxation. Relaxation can be used in preparing for some especially tense situations, such as, an interview, examination or important meeting. Counsellor should encourage clients to use partial relaxation skills while actually in tense situation. The following set of directions is typical of those used to attain a deep state of relaxation. Counsellor who often use relaxation methods usually have such directions readily available for clients in pamphlets form and recorded on cassette tapes:

1. Lie flat on the back, placing the feet about 18 inches apart. The hands should rest slightly away from the trunk, with the palms up.

2. Close your eyes and gently move all the different parts of the body to create a general feeling of relaxation.

3. Then start relaxing the body part by part. First think of the right leg. Inhale and slowly raise the leg about one foot off the floor. Hold it fully tensed. After 5 seconds, exhale abruptly and relax the muscles of the right leg, allowing it to fall on the floor on its own. Shake the leg gently from the right to left, relax it fully, and let it rest and concentrate on the other leg.

4. Repeat this same process with the left leg, and then with both hands, one at a time.

5. Abdomen, chest, shoulders and all other parts of the body are then followed for relaxation.

6. Slowly, gently, turn the neck right and left, right and left, and then back to centre, mentally relaxing the neck muscle. Follow it up with facial muscles, lips, cheek muscle, and nose and forehead muscles.

7. Now, you have relaxed all the muscles of the body. To make sure of this, allow your mind to wander over your entire body, reach for any point of tension. If you come across any spot of tension, concentrate upon and it will relax. If you do this mentally, without moving any muscle, you will notice that the part concerned obeys your command.

This is complete relaxation. Even your mind is at rest now. Observe your thoughts without trying to take your mind anywhere. You are a witness not a body or a mind but an ocean of peace and tranquillity. Remain in this condition for 5 minutes. Do not become anxious about anything. When you decide to wake from this conscious sleep, do so quite slowly. Imagine that a fresh energy is entering each part of your body then slowly get up. This exercise helps create refreshed and peaceful feelings for the body and mind. Try to do this one to three times a day, especially upon arising and retiring.

Physical activities can reduce the many stresses that come from modern living—mentally and emotionally demanding experiences and boring, solitary, and sedentary occupations. Similar functions can be served by many other pursuits such as, dancing, hobbies, games, arts and crafts, and playing and listening to music.

8.2.5 Thoughts and Imagery

The client's thoughts, ideas and perceptions are obviously important throughout counselling, so much so that their uses in changing behaviour are often overlooked. The counsellor can tell the client to recall or imagine events and situation when indulged in relaxation technique. This imagery encourages the loosening of muscle tension. Physical tightness in body may be reduced if client can call up images associated with calm, comfort and rest.

Some clients seem to have too active an imagination and most of their difficulties seem to arise from the way they concentrate on relative aspects of their thoughts. These people become more and more anxious and resistant to change because they constantly anticipate failures, and as a result they avoid facing up to things. In whatever way he can, the counsellor should stop these clients from dwelling on these aspects. He can reinforce talk about alternatives, he can ignore references to negative aspects, and he can point out in rational manner the self-defeating nature of such thoughts.

Some counsellors, in trying to change the client's behaviour, also use a rather dramatic technique called **thought–stopping**. It is sometimes used with clients who indulge in unproductive talks. Suppose if a client expresses his doubts or fears for the tenth time, the counsellor may interrupt him and say firmly 'stop that, right now' and emphasize his point with a gross movement, such as thumping his chair, standing up or turning away. He might succeed in directing his talk in some constructive direction. Obviously the success of this depends upon sound counsellor and client relationship and upon the judgment by the counsellor. It may be used in more subtle ways. He can encourage the client to devise a thought-stopping signal for himself.

8.2.6 Desensitisation

This approach to changing behaviour uses several techniques together, including, thinking, relaxing and imagining. In effect the counsellor tries to inoculate the client against fears and anxieties that have become very intense in a particular situation. There are several considerations and distinct stages in this process.

1. This is used with clients who are anxious about only one specific matter, e.g. exam fears, a dread about travelling in aircraft, fears of height etc.
2. All the client's feelings should be explored in advance. Until the client accepts that change is possible and most fears can be learnt and can be unlearnt, the process will not work.
3. Then the counsellor should make the client believe that the change for the better is possible, and they should together work out a list of events that are associated with fear. These are arranged in a hierarchy from least feared to most feared. It is useful to sort them on a scale, assigning a value of 0 to the least and 100 to the very worst.
4. Counsellor describes the lowest item in the fear hierarchy. If the client signals that it is distressing to imagine that event (i.e., by raising a finger) he helps him to relax and concentrate on other pleasant images until he feels that the client is able to cope with the things he fears. Not giving a distress signal means that he can tolerate that event. The counsellor then introduces the next item. And soon the client achieves a state of deep physical relaxation. In this way the two of them gradually work up the hierarchy.

8.2.7 Rational Emotive Behaviour Therapy (REBT)

Work stress can have disastrous effects on the quality of life and the quality of work life. Being boundary less, it can affect men and women, executives and presidents, Indians and Americans with equal intensity. Majority of the employees concede that stress is one of the most serious problems in the workplace today. Moreover, most people are on the job that they don't love. The benefits provided by the organization act as a bondage for a person to continuously being tied up with the irrespective of his or her liking to it. No predictions can be made in advance with respect to the kind of job and the organization which would be more suitable and of liking to the person. We get to know the positive and the negatives of the job and the organization only when we start working there. Some of the factors that have a bearing on the level of stress in an organization are:

Factors specific to the job: Nature of workload, variety and meaningfulness of the work, autonomy, working hours, general environment and the kind of team and people you are working with

Role in the workplace: Role conflict and role ambiguity

Career growth: Promotion, job security, lack of career planning, job uncertainty

Relationships at work: Relationship with superiors, colleagues, subordinates, stakeholders, clients and others

Organizational culture: Office politics, gossips, lack of proper direction, leadership

Unrealistic expectations: Excessive workload, learning new methodologies and technologies, excessive travel

Every individual in an organization has varying levels of resilience. Some of us perform reasonably well-under pressure, while others tend to give up. Further, it is not always possible to avoid stressful situations. Some of the common and general symptoms of stress are anxiety, nervousness, frustration, anger, insomnia, anorexia, decreased motivation and failure to concentrate. However, if the intensity and the length of stress exceeds the threshold levels of individuals, it may result in severe disorders in the form of depression, tremors, substance abuse, problems in the family life, harming others and suicidal tendencies. At the organizational level, these further result in low employee morale, low productivity, high absenteeism and high employee turnover.

Management of stress is one of the most important responsibilities of the managers today in work organizations, especially if he or she also adorns the role of being counsellor. Besides other techniques, one of the best ways to cope up with the work stress is to use the Rational Emotive Behaviour Therapy (Ellis, 1962).

Rational Emotive Behaviour Therapy (REBT) is based on the premise that the source of stress and anxiety in any context is not because of that particular event, but is because of the belief that we hold towards that event. Our emotional disturbances are the result of our perception and evaluation of a particular event and not the event in itself. The theory assumes that people have tendencies to think both rationally and irrationally depending on their experiences and learning in life. When someone thinks rationally, he or she makes a logical and objective assessment of the situation, self and others. Rationality and objectivity result in achievement, conflict resolution and a state of happiness. On the other hand, irrational thinking results in distortions and misinterpretation of reality, resulting in high state of anxiety and emotional suffering.

The origin of both rational and irrational thinking can be traced back to process of bringing-up and socialization. Humans make conscious decision to think rationally or irrationally. According to REBT, it is the propensity of an individual to think, behave and feel irrationally which is the source of anxiety and stress in humans. As a result of irrational thinking, humans suffer from inner conflicts, interpersonal conflict, reduced tolerance for frustration and low self-esteem, resulting in further discomfort. It has been found that humans have strong innate biological energy to think irrationally, and these beliefs keep on growing exponentially as a result of exposure to the environment which keeps on reinforcing it. But there is positive side of human nature as well. Humans also have the ability to change these dysfunctional beliefs into more positive and functional beliefs.

REBT is one such process in which the counsellor facilitates the client to focus on these irrational and self-defeating beliefs, and change them into more rational and self-promoting thoughts. The client with the help of the counsellor develops a more positive perception of situations, objects and people and moves out of unrealistic and illogical thinking. It proposes that whenever client is faced with an adverse situation, he or she has a choice of either feeling healthy, positive, motivated and encouraged or unhealthy, disappointed, frustrated and annoyed.

The sources of irrational beliefs in our life are the self-angering philosophies and ideas that we develop in ourselves with the passage of time. These self-angering philosophies and ideas get manifested through certain *shouldings* and *musting* in life. These irrational ideas can be classified into three categories:

IRRATIONAL IDEAS 1

The first type of irrational ideas comes from the focus on self, i.e., the beliefs that one must always do well in life to be identified as a successful person. The person with these beliefs think that he or she must always have the love and approval of others all the time from all the people. Further, he believes that he should be an achiever in life and the universe around him should be in perfect order, certainty and predictability. This environment will give him/her an edge over others to be able to perform adequately.

IRRATIONAL IDEAS 2

The second type of irrational ideas focuses on 'others' in life which include, family, friends, colleagues, boss, subordinates and many others. These ideas exemplify certain expectations from other people towards self. Individuals with these ideas believe that others should treat them kindly in a manner that they expect them to. If they don't do it, the society or the system should blame them and punish them. They also expect that others should not be critical of them, and if they criticize they should not get anything from the life. These people should be treated as rotten people and life should not be fair to them.

IRRATIONAL IDEAS 3

The third set of irrational ideas is about the world in which we live. The person in this category wants everything in this world to be in order as per his or her expectations. Some of the irrational ideas the individuals have at this level are the expectations that everything in the world must be arranged in a way that he or she wants. Further they expect that everything should fall in line as per their expectations and availability. There should be correct and perfect solutions to their problems and of the people they care for. If it does not happen, there would be catastrophe and horror.

FRAMEWORK FOR REBT

REBT basically relies on ABC format which gives an insight of an individual's three important components of behavioural patterns. The 'A' in this is for activating events, which could be in the form of difficult and challenging situations that the person is going through. These include dissatisfying work, misunderstanding with a friend, stressful situation, misconduct of an office colleague, boss or subordinate which are the cause of dissonance in our personality. 'B' in this stands for irrational beliefs, which evolve from the event being experienced by the person, and are the real cause of discomfort. 'C' is the consequence, which is the behavioural response that arise as a result of irrational beliefs.

Generally, it is not the activating event which is the cause of pain for us, but it is the belief associated with the event which becomes the major cause of disturbance. The role of the counsellor is to help the client challenge and dispute the irrational belief, and try to convert them into rational beliefs. With the rational beliefs about the event, there is a possibility that the client may start experiencing positive emotional reactions and reduce his or her dissonance.

ABC Framework

Unpleasant Event (A) → Irrational Belief (B) → Unhealthy Negative Consequences (C)

Unpleasant Event (A) → Rational Belief (B) → Healthy Negative Consequences (C)

EXAMPLE:

Situation: I find it very difficult to see my drunken fellow students/ colleagues in the college/office functions, singing loudly, and raucously and using lots of foul language on the party night.

This being put in the ABC Format.

Reaction 1

A—Drunken fellow students/colleagues in the college/office functions, singing loudly and raucously, and using lots of foul language on the party night.

B—Drinking and then misbehaving does not match up to our value system. When will the youth of this country realize that it is not going to help them at all?

C—Feeling miserable at the state of affairs

Reaction 2

A—Drunken fellow students/colleagues in the college/office functions, singing loudly and raucously, and using lots of foul language on the party night.

B—I hate people who drink. These people should be punished by the authorities in due measures.

C—Extreme anger and discontentment

Reaction 3

A—Drunken fellow students/colleagues in the college/office functions, singing loudly and raucously, and using lots of foul language on the party night.

B—This is a personal choice of an individual. I have no right to infringe on their personal choices.

C—Neutral

It can be inferred from the above analysis that 'A' does not cause 'C'. It is 'B' that causes 'C'. In the first case, it is not the behaviours of people, but your own value system, which in this context seems irrational, the cause of misery. In the second case, it is the hatred towards people who think is the reason for anger and discontent. In the third case, the event is not disturbing you, and therefore, you remain calm and neutral.

COGNITIVE ERRORS

Disturbed evaluations of situations often occur through cognitive errors. Cognitive errors often arise from faulty assumptions or misconceptions. Some cognitive errors that cause unhappiness (Burns, 1999) are as follows:

- *Overgeneralization:* When individuals over generalize, they have a tendency to believe that anything wrong that is happening to them once, is going to be repeated over and over again all throughout their life. If they fail once, they start believing that they can never be successful in life ever. A single unpleasant event may be perceived as the complete recurring reality of life.

- *Polarized thinking:* In this, the individuals have a tendency to think in terms of all-or-nothing thinking, or dichotomous thinking. Events, objects and people are viewed in extremes. The situation can either be good or bad, right or wrong, ethical or unethical, success or failure, and there is no other way. An employee feels that if he has not got an excellent rating he is the most useless person in the organization. This thinking assumes that everything in this world is absolute which actually is an unrealistic perception.

- *Catastrophizing:* It is a process in which the individual has a tendency to either blow things out of proportion (magnification) or undermine it totally (minimization). Catastrophization turns ordinary negative events into nightmares, and leads to frustration intolerance. In case of magnification, a very small problem or issue is exaggerated and assumed to be unmanageable (for example, minor achievements of self or someone else's small mistakes), while in minimization, the tendency is to convert a big achievement into nothing (such as their own mistake, or someone else's achievement).

- *Mental filter:* This includes magnifying the negative elements in a situation and dwelling on it exclusively, at the cost of positivity associated with it. For example, if you got a 'C' grade in Finance, you start thinking it to be terrible even though you have 'A' grade in all other subjects.

- *Generalizations:* This involves creating a completely negative self-image based on your or other's errors. The individual has a tendency to look at one or two negative qualities and give it a global judgment. It is also referred to as 'labelling'. The individual has a tendency to attach a unhealthy label to self or to other people instead of trying to look at the situation from some other perspective.

- *Mind reading:* This involves making guesses about another's behaviour and being convinced about it without really checking the reasons for the behaviours. If another person does not reciprocate out greetings we may like to conclude it by saying that the person does not have the basic etiquettes. We try to read is as being done deliberately rather than any other factor by claiming that we can predict the behaviours of others.

- *Fortune-telling:* Individuals with this cognitive error start believing that they can make accurate predictions of the future based on their perceptions. They also believe that these predictions are the realities. For example, believing that one is not going to get anything in life because he or she can see the future.

- *Personalizing:* Personalization is a distortion where a person starts believing that whatever others say or do is somehow as a result of the person himself or herself. They have a tendency to assume responsibility for a negative event, even though they have no role to play in that. For example, if a large number large of student fail in the paper taught by the person, the person will start believing that they failed, because he or she is a poor teacher. Though students might not have done well because they did not work hard.

- *Blaming:* Under this error, we have a tendency to blame other persons for our failures in life or start blaming ourselves for anything wrong that happens. For example, "My child did not do well in the exams, because I could not devote much time on his studies." In reality no one can make us feel that way as we are the only ones who have control over our emotional reactions.

These inflexible philosophies of 'shoulds', 'musts', 'ought to', and 'needs to' have to be replaced with more flexible and self-helping attitudes by challenging the basic ideology. The healthy alternative to being demanding is unconditional acceptance of humans.

ACCEPTANCE

To be emotionally healthy, we must accept reality, even when the reality is highly unfortunate and unpleasant. Three types of acceptance which may help to accept the reality are:

- **Unconditional self-acceptances:** We have to accept that we are not perfect human beings with our strengths and follies. Everyone has flaws and weaknesses and one is no more or no less worthy than any other person.

- **Unconditional other-acceptance:** We have to accept other people as they are and understand that they will treat us unfairly at times. There is no reason why one should always be treated fairly. Everyone is as worthy as any other human being.

- **Unconditional life acceptance:** We have to accept life as it is. It does not work out as per our convenience. It will not always be pleasant but will not be totally miserable too. At times it has to be just lived as it is.

Therefore it can be summarized that REBT helps us to believe that:

- To be able to achieve mental and psychological well-being, it is important to unconditionally accept self, others and life.
- The world and the people living in the world are fallible, and therefore, it is suggested that we should be accepting of the hassles and unfairness of others "as they happen to be".
- Humans are too complex to be judged as they are a blend of both positivity and negativity with their good and bad attributes.

● Whatever feeling of self-worth that an individual has are only meant for himself and have no substantial empirical evidence.

DISPUTING OUR IRRATIONAL BELIEFS

The outcome of REBT is based on the counsellor trying to convince the client to change his or her irrational belief system into something more rational. This can be done by focusing on certain 'musts, shoulds and have to' in client's life. For example, the counsellor can challenge the client by asking 'Why must or should' he have approval of others always?" "Why should she be treated fairly by others always?" These questions will help the client to challenge his or her assumptions of self and allow them to dispute their own beliefs. An extension of ABC model is by adding 'D' and 'E'. 'D' is the Disputing of ABC model. When the client disputes these irrational beliefs, he may begin to see situation in a newer light by accepting that it is not important for others to always treat him or her fairly and approve of their behaviours. This will result in effective new thinking, adding 'E' to the existing model.

It may not always be possible to eliminate all irrational beliefs form our thinking, but we can attempt to reduce the frequency and the intensity of these beliefs. It can be done by not getting upset by holding inflexible beliefs as we continue to feel upset because we cling on to the old irrational beliefs. The only way to get better is to work hard at changing our beliefs and it requires only practice.

A-B-C-D-E MODEL

Situation 1

Activating Experience (A):   I have been treated unfairly by Dr. Goel

Irrational Belief (iB):   "How awful! He should not, must not treat me in that manner"

Inappropriate Consequence (iC):   Anger and Rage

Rational Belief (rB):   "I find Dr. Goel's behaviour deplorable and unfortunate".

Appropriate Consequence (aC):   Frustration and Displeasure

Disputing and Debating (D):   You detect your iBs and begin disputing and debating them by asking yourself questions that challenge your interpretations or beliefs regarding people's treatment of you.

Cognitive Effect of New Philosophy (cE):   I can see no reason why he MUST treat me fairly even though I would definitely prefer it.

Behavioural Effect (bE):   Loss of anger, relief, and return to appropriate Consequence (aC): feeling of sorrow and disappointment

Irrational Anger: If Dr. Goel's unfairness is viewed as awful or totally bad and you view him as a 'bad person' you exaggerate reality (unrealistic thinking); experience anger, fury and wrath about Dr. Goel and his behaviour.

Rational Anger: Extreme annoyance, irritation, frustration of displeasure in response to unfairness

Situation 2

Activating Event (A): The boss shouted at me in front of my colleagues. He was screaming and was really abusive and rude.

Irrational Belief (iB)

- Whenever I commit a mistake, he overreacts and humiliates me in front of my colleagues.
- Someone in the office must have poisoned his mind against me and that is the reason he is always on a fault-finding process.
- He does not have basic decency and respect for his fellow employees.
- My reputation is ruined in this company.
- This will certainly impact my promotion this year.

Consequences (C)

- Feeling downright miserable
- Feeling impatient and stressful
- Feeling insecure of losing the promotion or the job
- Feeling disturbed because of humiliation

Dispute the Irrational Beliefs (D)

- Why do I think he only shouts at me? He is generally aggressive with most of the people in the company.
- Why do I think my reputation is ruined? He alone cannot bring down my reputation.
- Why I do not remember the occasion when he has been appreciative about me? He has acknowledged my contribution to the company on number of occasions.
- My promotion is not based on one single event like this.
- May be it was one of my bad days today!

Effective New Thinking (E)

- No one can be a perfect employee. All of us make mistakes sometimes.
- I should look at this situation as a way to improve my aptitudes and skills at my work.
- In future I should try to avoid making mistakes of these types as they become a source of stress. This stress can be damaging for me as well my family.

- Nowhere is it mentioned that I should make a good impression. It is not possible to everyone to like me and my work all the time. If they do so, it's great, if they don't it's not the end of the world.
- Just because my performance was not up to the mark it doesn't make me a worthless person.
- I am too hard on myself. If I try to be perfect, I feel stressed, and disappointed with myself.

Result: Feeling less miserable

ADVANTAGES OF REBT AT WORKPLACE

It is aptly clear through the discussion that people in organizations do not respond to the event, but to the beliefs associated with the event. REBT can be effectively used in work organizations to help employees change their self-defeating behaviours which generally interfere with personal and organizational goals. It can help us develop a workforce which does not get deterred by minor crisis situation, and learns to take stressful situations and events in stride and dispute the irrational beliefs associated with them. It helps people solve their personal and professional problems, improve their relationships with others in the organization, enhance the performance and productivity of employees, and help them become motivated and effective managers and leaders.

8.3 Summary

The objectives of counselling is to help clients think differently, behave differently and to talk in a new way. A set of general principles like setting goals, gaining commitment, anticipating situations, assessing results and making records are essential for effective counselling. Some specific techniques that are used by the counsellor to bring about changes in the client include using rewards, providing models, role playing, bodily awareness and relaxation activities, thoughts and imagery and desensitisation. These techniques can be used in isolation or they can be combined with each other depending on the requirements of the clients.

Chapter 9 focuses on the application of counselling skills in business organizations in some specific areas.

Review Questions

1. Before the onset of counselling for the client, the counsellor is required to set up a few general principles to help the client to change. List these principles and discuss with examples.

2. Discuss some of the specific techniques which could be used by the counsellor to help alleviate the stress and anxiety of the client.

3. What is Rational Emotive Behaviour Therapy (REBT)? What are the principles governing REBT? How does it help the client manage his/her anxiety?

4. What are cognitive errors? How do they impact the evaluation of a situations leading to higher state of anxiety?

5. It may not always be possible to eliminate all irrational beliefs form our thinking but we can attempt to reduce the frequency and the intensity of these beliefs. Discuss how A-B-C-D-E Model helps us to reduce the intensity of irrational beliefs?

Chapter 9

Organizational Application of Counselling Skills

A manager who uses counselling skills effectively will address problems when early warning signs become apparent, and will encourage people to come to him or her with problems before they become major issues, thus making the department run more smoothly in the long term. Managers will also benefit from approaching problems, which appear to be completely personal, and not work related. It is not possible for employees to totally separate their work lives from their outside lives and outside problems do eventually have an effect on work performance. There are some specific areas in the organization where counselling skills can be applied.

9.1 Change Management

In order to create and maintain competitive advantage, companies have to be flexible about changing, and yet continuously uphold the highest level of performance and productivity from employees. Implementing positive strategies to ease the pressures of upheaval and uncertainty is absolutely necessary. Given people's resistance to and natural fear of change, managing it is not an easy task. Employees require counselling to cope with and adjust to changes.

Managers should use counselling skills not only to support and motivate subordinates during periods of change, but also to create the environment towards which organizations are attempting to change. Many companies have benefitted from changing from being downwardly operating, hierarchical, directive and slow to change to being upwardly operating, flatter, facilitative and more flexible. Using counselling skills is essential in order to implement this cultural change effectively (rather than just giving it lip service), so an ideal time to institute the top-down training of managers in counselling skills has to be a part of change management programme.

9.2 Downsizing

Just as organizations change their products, services, or administrative systems to stay competitive, so too do they alter the size and basic configurations of their organizational chart, i.e., they restructure. In many cases, this has meant reducing the number of employees needed to operate effectively, a process known as **downsizing**.

Typically, this involves more than just laying off people in a move to save money. It is directed at adjusting the number of employees needed to work in a newly designed organization, and is therefore also known as **rightsizing** (Hendricks, 1992). Whatever you call it, the bottom line is painfully clear. Many organizations need fewer people to operate today than in the past—sometimes far fewer.

Another way organizations are restructuring is by completely eliminating parts of themselves that focus on the non-core sectors of the business, and hiring outside firms to perform these functions instead—a practice known as **outsourcing** (Tomasko, 1993).

Handling the process of downsizing in the most humane manner possible is worthwhile both for the sake of the organization and for those made redundant. When a large number of people are made redundant, employees will require counselling at many levels. Besides the redundant employees, others who will need help include the remaining employees and the managers who must communicate the changes and then adjust to running a new organizational structure.

Taking steps to make sure that the remaining staff stays motivated and committed will improve their morale and reassure them that the company cares about them. It preserves the internal company image. Immediately following a large-scale redundancy is an opportune time to institute top-down training of managers in counselling skills. Feelings, which are likely to need to be dealt with by using counselling skills, include resistance, lack of trust, anger, fear, demotivation, hostility and a disinterest in the future.

9.3 Managing Diversity

Diversity can be defined as a mixture of people who vary by age, gender, race, religion and/or life style (Thomas, 1992). One management challenge is to help people understand diversity so that they can establish productive relationship with people at work. Effectively managing a diverse work force means adopting practices that recognize all aspects of diversity. Perhaps nothing has greater implications for managing diversity than the changing characteristic of the work-force. The make of the work-force is changing at a very high pace. Most of the multinational organizations have diverse work force comprising men and women of different races, national origins and ethnic backgrounds. Organization like Hewlett-Packard conduct workshops for all employees in which the emphasis is on educating and encouraging managers to understand culturally different employees and to create an environment that fosters productivity.

Work-forces in Asia, Western Europe, Latin America and North America are growing more complex and diverse. Thus, managers need to recognize differences resulting from this diversity, particularly in terms of what employees want from the job. According to De Luca and McDowell (1992), some of the challenges that an organization faces with a diverse work-force are as follows:

Language Differences: Unless employees can understand each other, communication is difficult or even impossible. Employees cannot train each other or work together if they can't communicate. Language barrier, therefore, poses real and often serious problems, which could lead to misunderstanding regarding performance standards, work methods, safety measures, and other essential working conditions.

National Ethnics Groupings: Sometimes employees tend to form strong ethnic groups on the basis of similarities. Although such grouping develops a strong sense of teamwork within the group, it doesn't promote working with others who don't share the same language and cultural heritage.

Attitude and Cultural Differences: Most people have developed attitudes and beliefs about others by the time they seek a job. However, some attitudes and beliefs create frustration, anger and bitterness in those at whom they are aimed. Managers who want to foster employee tolerance are opting for major change. In many organizations, women and minorities are bypassed when important, formal decisions are made. Informally, these people often are left out when others go to lunch or a sporting event. These informal get-togethers give older employees a chance to counsel junior employees about coping with problems. For managers to effectively create an environment where everyone can contribute to the organization's goals, attitudes must change.

Employees are adapting too much more heterogeneous work environments (race, class, sex, religion and culture). Using counselling skills is a way to manage diversity. Adopting a counselling style of management will set an example of how to communicate, learn from one another, and get the most from everyone.

9.4 Equal Opportunities

The use of counselling skills can be invaluable in organizations, which are implementing equal opportunity policies. It can assist in tapping and developing the resources of female employees, and also in helping men and women to adjust to one another and work together most productively.

Women may require counselling as they move up the ladders, often alone, into uncharted territory with few role models. Women have not been conditioned for the traditional work environment in the same way that men have been. Counselling can help to provide them with much needed support and confidence.

However, women's conditioning can help them to excel as managers using counselling skills in a modern, co-operative work environment. Men may require counselling in order to adapt to organizational cultures, which are becoming less patriarchal and masculine. In the past to get to the top an employee had to repress feelings, adapt to hierarchy, even deny reality. Emotions were not shown at work, and certainly not discussed. Counselling can help men to break out of old habits and thinking which could hold them back in modern environment.

9.5 Entrepreneurism/Intrapreneurism

Venture capitalists, bankers, small business and business start-up consultants and managers whose subordinates are entrepreneurs (managing start-up ventures within the organization) can all benefit from applying counselling skills to help the intra-or entrepreneur. Developing and guiding entrepreneurs require a balance of high support levels along with a high level of challenge. Using counselling skills make this balance achievable.

The concept of the person's ownership of the business idea, plan or problem resolution is especially applicable to entrepreneurs who tend to see their business as their baby and have difficulty accepting outside advice. These entrepreneurs should do the following:

1. Use listening skills to build trust and get employees to open up, and to detect problem areas, which they may be initially reluctant to reveal.
2. Challenge the employees in a pulling fashion in order to get them to consider the problem rather than defend. They should use counselling skills to help them to take action when they are blocked.
3. Work through decision-making and problem-solving processes with entrepreneurs, so that they can then continue to use these themselves and with their own subordinates.

9.6 Mentoring

Mentoring programmes pair more senior people in the organization with people who are junior, in order to help them to learn the ropes, advance, and grow and achieve in their career. Mentors help mentees with personal objectives and effectiveness, self-confidence and self-awareness as they apply to organizational objectives, directly or indirectly. The role involves a mixture of counselling, coaching and advising.

The mentor-mentee relationship is less directive than the manager-subordinate relationship. Within the mentoring relationship, mentors are less concerned with their own and departmental objectives and less worried about loss of professionalism. Subordinates may want to paint the best possible picture for their manager, who is their immediate boss and can affect their pay cheque. They are more likely to open up to a mentor. Successes and failures, personal strengths and weaknesses, and problem areas and difficulties can be discussed and analyzed in a relationship, which feels safe. Therefore, effective counselling skills are especially vital for a mentor. Services that mentors provide include:

1. Helping the mentee to understand how the organization works.
2. Helping the mentee to understand organizational politics.
3. Providing specific knowledge about the broader aspects of the business and the industry.
4. Helping the mentee to set development goals.
5. Helping the mentee to achieve full potential within the organization.
6. Helping the mentee to explore and identify learning needs.
7. Determining with the mentee ways of meeting those needs.
8. Acting as a neutral and non-judgmental sounding board for new ideas.
9. Providing coaching in particular skills.

9.7 Team Management/Conflict Resolution

Counselling skills can be used very effectively to facilitate groups in problem solving, decision-making and conflict resolution. Group counselling is similar to facilitation, but there is more focus on feelings and emotions. It can greatly improve the way teams work together.

When individual project team members suffer from personal problems, which affect their ability to work, other team members' ability to work is often affected as well. Sometimes a team will have difficulty working together, even if there are only one or two problem-causers.

A manager or a consultant trained in counselling skills can use a counselling process to address these situations. Someone outside the team has no investment in the work or the outcome, and will be freer to offer interpretations about the group process (the way the team interacts) and to help the team clearly define and communicate expectations. Following are some of the aspects of group process, which can be addressed (Kolbe, Rubin and McIntyre, 1984):

Goals or Mission:

(a) How clearly defined are the goals?
(b) Who sets the goals?
(c) How much agreement is there among members concerning the goals? How much commitment?
(d) How clearly measurable is goal achievement?
(e) How do group goals relate to broader organizational goals? To personal goals?

Group Norms:

    (a) What are the group norms?

    (b) Are they implicit or explicit?

    (c) Who sets the norms?

    (d) Are they being followed by the individual members?

Leadership:

    (a) Who is the formal leader of the group?

    (b) Who is the informal leader?

    (c) What style does he use?

    (d) What power base does he use?

    (e) Is he effective?

Decision-making:

    (a) How does it happen?

    (b) Is everyone satisfied with how it happens?

    (c) Is there a better way?

Role Expectations:

    (a) Role ambiguity—Are people clear about their own and others' roles within the team?

    (b) Role conflict—Do any team members feel pulled in different directions due to dual or multiple roles?

    (c) Role overload—Are the responsibilities of the roles manageable?

When using counselling skills with teams it is necessary to encourage group members to speak up about their feelings, even when those feelings are vague and unfocused and people feel unsure about them. Insist that the participants listen to one another and try to get them to use 'I' statements to express their own feelings rather than make accusations.

9.8　Counselling for Older Adults

Across the period of thirty years or so (age sixty to ninety and above) that we refer to as older adulthood or the third age, there is a fairly predictable set of experiences that all of us encounter. These experiences come as the inevitable and irreversible consequence of biological, sociological, and psychological aging. Some of the developmental tasks of later life are:

Adjusting to Decreasing Physical Strength and Health:　By middle age most adults begin to notice that certain activities, such as moving and that recovery after strenuous activity takes longer. In older adulthood, declines in physical agility and sensory acuity accumulate so that simple tasks, such as climbing stairs become a challenge for some. Sexual capacities decline, even though sexual functioning remains important to most. As systems of the body decline, we become more subject to acute (sudden-onset and usually temporary) illnesses such as colds and the flu, and we also acquire chronic afflictions, such as cardiovascular disease, diabetes and osteoporosis. As physical strength declines and illnesses accumulate, the older person's attention is inevitably drawn to contemplation of his or her own death.

Adjusting to Retirement and Reduced Income: Employment provides for a sense of accomplishment, and identity in the world of commerce, an arena for social discourse, a basis for structuring time into a daily routine and money. It may also be physically and emotionally stressful and limit one's time and energy for other pursuits. In an idealized view, retirement may be seen as having completed life's work, freedom from required toil, opportunity to be free of a major responsibility and to pursue other interests, a time to reap the benefits of a life of working and saving. For some, many of these benefits, along with improved health and an opportunity to invest anew in relationships with spouse, children, and grandchildren, do in fact materialize, and the period of adjustment is satisfying and growth producing. For others, the end of employment signals a sense of uselessness, a loss of personal identity that was intertwined with occupation, a feeling of having nothing of consequence to do and time languishing, and a sense of loss of valued human contact. Needless to say, retirement is a life transition of major importance because of apparent loss of finances, status and power.

Adjusting to the Death of a Spouse: For most older adults, the loss of a spouse means the loss of a longtime companion who had chosen to share all the sorrows, joys and burdens of life. A household that was organized around the needs and interests of two individuals must now be reorganized with new daily routines and the absence of an in-house partner for social and sexual intercourse. Patterns of friendship that were previously shared by the couple do not work when one becomes single, and isolation from friends and silence that follows after the funeral is over adds to a profound sense of loneliness. All these changes in life routines are superimposed on and exacerbate the experience of grief that comes from the loss of the one person who has usually been the most important person in one's life. Needless to say, in cases of second marriages, the duration of relationship is often shorter and there is not as much shared history. Still, many of the same adjustments are required though perhaps to a lesser extent.

Establishing an Explicit Association with One's Age Group: Throughout our life, it is probably so that most of our friends are near about our own age group—at least roughly in the same cohort. However, with the withdrawal from work and perhaps community involvements of one kind or another, opportunities to interact with younger people outside the family decrease. It is often helpful for older persons to seek new opportunities for social interaction with other seniors, sharing a common hobby, working on political issues of value to older citizens, or simply sharing recreational time together. Even so, it is a typical experience of the oldest of the old that in their social circle of persons their age diminishes, especially if they are still living in the community.

Adopting and Adapting Societal Roles in a Flexible Way: As older adults give up the roles of the generative period of midlife and younger old age, each person must decide what new roles are rewarding and what changes may be made in roles that will continue. One person may take on new responsibilities in a church, assume a role as an officer in his or her condominium association, or join a book club to expand reading horizons while gaining social interaction. Another may assume a very active role in bringing up and taking care of the grandchildren. Still others seem satisfied to devote their time and their energies (often depleted) to the simple tasks of maintaining the comfort and quality of home life.

Establishing Satisfactory Practical Living Arrangements: A major goal of most senior adults is to maintain the maximum independence possible in their living arrangements. For some, this means hanging on to the home in which they have spent the majority of their adult lives. Others are ready to shed the responsibilities of maintaining a home that was suitable for rearing a family but now has unused and unwanted space. Still others recognize the need for assistance with living that can be acquired only by moving in with a family or going to an assisted living facility.

Opting for Pre-retirement Counselling: Retirement is a major life transition. Because retirement will be such a significant change in lifestyle, it is worthwhile for employees to prepare for it in advance. Individual counselling (or counselling for couples) can be offered as a complement to a group educational programme. There are likely to be issues that people will prefer to discuss privately.

Specially trained professionals best offer retirement counselling. However, some employees will want to talk to their managers about the approaching retirement, so having an understanding of what happens during retirement counselling is useful.

Retirement counselling should relieve employees' negative thoughts, build their confidence and be informative. The employee's feelings should be discussed in order to help them to accept the change and its losses, and to anticipate the future in the most positive light. Not enough people realize what an opportunity retirement can be. Some people look forward to reaching retirement age. Positive feelings about retirement include:

1. Freedom from demands of work and parenting
2. Opportunity to expand on favourite hobby
3. Opportunity to try something new
4. More time to spend with family

Some people dread retirement. Signs of apprehension about retirement are depression or tiredness. Negative feelings about retirement include:

1. Loss of identity and status
2. Lack of purpose/usefulness in life
3. Awareness of negative attitudes towards older people
4. Loss of income

5. Lack of friends outside present work
6. Boredom
7. Concern about future health

Providing the employees with information on what to expect (normal reactions to the transition) is helpful. Retired people will often go through three stages as they adjust to their new lifestyle, i.e., initially a honeymoon phase, and then approximately 6 to 12 months later a period of disenchantment, followed by reorientation and stability.

9.9 Crisis/Trauma

A crisis is defined as a situation of excessive stress. The frequency of violent and traumatic crises in the workplace is unfortunately increasing. Examples of traumas include accidents leading to serious injury or death, bomb blasts, theft/hold-ups, fire, raids, kidnappings, extortion and other natural disasters such as floods and earthquakes.

People who have been involved in or exposed to a traumatic event experience a range of symptoms:

1. Shock
2. Unexpected frightening thoughts or visions
3. Nightmares
4. Loss of interest in everyday life
5. Inability to concentrate
6. Insomnia
7. General depression
8. General anxiety
9. Disorientation
10. Fears of insanity or nervous breakdown

The effects from trauma last much longer than is realized. Often people will attempt to conceal their symptoms. For example, thinking about what could have happened is often very disturbing, but people are likely to be reluctant to share this with others at work.

Managers will want to get back to business as usual and as quickly as possible. However, if the managers are unaware of post-traumatic stress syndrome then the employees who underwent traumatic experience will not be treated in a considerate manner and resulting treatment will further add to their trauma. On manager's part taking time off from their busy work schedule to support the traumatized employees will make the employees return to normalcy much sooner than expected.

Experienced trauma counsellors should be summoned when a severe crisis occurs. Their specialized knowledge of fighting trauma and its effects will allow them to recognize employee's state and identify those who are severely traumatized. However, whether or not professionals are called in, it will be useful for managers to have some knowledge regarding post-traumatic stress syndrome, which they can utilize in case of crisis.

9.9.1 Working With Clients in Crisis/Trauma

Generally thought, as James and Gilliland (2001) emphasize, the term crisis refers primarily to "a person's feelings of fear, shock and distress about the disruption, not to the disruption itself." When the clients realize that they do not have the resources in the form of coping skills or support system they enter into a state of crisis (James and Gilliland 2001). The techniques that worked well in the past do not work anymore. Since the person is not able to resolve the dilemma, the extent of tension and anxiety is on the increase. As a result of this, there is a feeling of helplessness, disturbance, shame and guilt, and inability to reach a decision for self as well for others. Crisis interventions have been defined in terms of availability of resources that can aid the client in restoration of his or her levels of equilibrium (Aguilera, 1998).

Aguilera (1998) has developed a paradigm (Figure 9.1) that shows what happens when a person in a state of equilibrium is confronted by a stressful event. As a result of this stress, there is disequilibrium which needs to be restored. If the person perceives the event accurately, and has adequate support and coping skills, the problem is resolved and crisis is avoided. In the absence of accurate perception, situational support and coping skills, the problem remains unresolved gives rise to crisis.

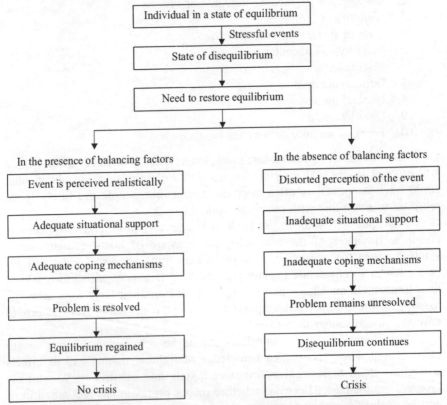

Figure 9.1 The effect of balancing factors in a stressful event.
Adapted from D.C. Aguilera, *Crisis Intervention: Theory and Methodology*, 8th ed., p. 34.

It is difficult for the counsellors to preempt as to which situations can give rise to crisis in the client's life. People even with best of the coping skills and support system tend to experience crisis in certain situations like loss of a person' entire family in a fire or a major accident causing the death of many family members which cannot be easily managed as they are extremely traumatic. The attacks on the Taj Hotel and other places in Mumbai on 26th November were traumatic for many people, especially the ones who lost their near and dear ones and also for those with prior history of trauma and the time spent watching the reenactment of those events in the media.

9.9.2 Purpose of Crisis Intervention

The purpose of interventions of crisis is to facilitate the client to move out of the traumatic zone and learn to live a comfortable life (Aguilera, 1998). The client has either got to solve the problem or learn to live in a situation that he is currently in. If the job is gone, one must try to search for another job to overcome the crisis. In case of loss of loved one, one has to learn to live without the physical presence of the person. One of the most important thing to remember is that crisis intervention is oriented in today's context and the history of the client's past experience can only help us to understand his or her behavioural patterns, and also his coping abilities as he has dealt with the problems in the past.

9.9.3 Stressful Events Leading to Crises

There are many events that may be responsible for precipitation of stress or crisis among people. It is important to realize that crisis is sometimes caused by an event that affects an important person in the client's environment. Some of these events which could lead to stress are:

- Losing a loved one in life
- Health and well-being
- Disruptions of intimate relationships
- Violence
- Disruptions of work or school
- Natural and environmental disasters
- Financial emergencies and homelessness and many more

Besides situational crises, crises may be precipitated by a range of developmental transitions, and these developmental crises are managed the same way. The major changes in the normal life pattern of an individual can be source of crisis. The examples would include starting school, or college, entering the world of work, marriage, having children, retiring, and many more. These events should ideally be source of joy and happiness for the person, but if he or she does not have the coping skills to manage with these major transitions, he or she may experience major crisis.

Steps in Crisis Intervention

While offering counselling services during crisis situations, the counsellor needs to operate in certain definite manner so that they do not disturb the stress level and anxiety of the client. For this they will have to follow some specific steps. These are:

1. *Develop a relationship of help:* During this step of crisis intervention it is important for the counsellor to basically rely on the core counselling skills like listening and responding (as discussed in Chapter 6) so as to create a comfort zone for the client where he or she is able to freely express the fears and anxieties present. This would help the counsellor develop an enhanced understanding of the triggers that could be leading to crisis and stress in the client (James and Gilliland, 2001). This may provide the client with a reassurance that he or she is being attended to and also being understood by someone who could be a strong support base too. This may help alleviate the discomfort in the person. In addition to this, the counsellor can use the other aptitudes of empathy, positive regard, genuineness, and concreteness to enhance the effectiveness of the process.

   The counsellor's posture in maintaining the calmness is an indicator to the client about the maturity of the counsellor. In situation of crisis, the counsellor is expected to maintain his or her poise and encourage the client to regain the emotional strength and reassure him or her of the protection. In this way, they both can collectively figure out the next step that is to be followed to take the client out of crisis. A direct statement such as, "We will work something out that will help you face this situation better," bolsters hope. Hersh (1985) also recommends special attention to a comfortable environment, privacy, and the absence of time pressures.

2. *Creating safe and secure environment:* One of the important requirements of the crisis intervention is to assure safety to the client. Since the client is in a very vulnerable state, the threat of danger from anywhere can be quite overwhelming for him or her (James and Gilliland, 2001). The client may also be in danger from someone else. Also there could be a fear of some loved one being in danger from a third party. In such situations it becomes important for the counsellors to ask direct questions to the client about the fear being experienced and the reactions emanating from it. There is a possibility of reducing the tension of the threat by just talking about it. In case the client is perceived to be damaging self as a result of the crisis, it may be important to appraise the family or friends about it. It is believed that sharing of the concerns may sometimes act as alternatives to actually carrying out the act (Patterson and Welfel, 2000).

In case of severe disruption, the counsellor is required to seek help from other reliable sources. Trying to deal with an extremely adverse situation by oneself increases the risk of burnout for the counsellor (Figley, 1995). It could become a very difficult situation for the counsellor to deal with severely impacted clients, and may result in intellectual and emotional dissonance for the counsellors. The counsellor would be in a situation to assure safety to the client when he himself feels safe and secure in the situation.

3. ***Conduct an assessment:*** To carry out the process of assessment the counsellor needs to obtain information about the events that led to crisis, and how has it impacted the client (Aguilera, 1998; Hersh, 1985; Roberts, 2000). Further an assessment of support system available to the client can aid in the process. This information will help the counsellor to identify the triggers of the crisis and the capability of the client to cope up with it. Aguilera has developed a paradigm, which has been discussed earlier showing how people react to stressful events that introduce disequilibrium.

   The behaviour of the client including the mood, speech patterns, appearance and the attention span are the indicators of the degree of stress that he may be going through. Counsellor can also make some prediction about how the client is able to take the extreme pressure resulting from stress by making an assessment of the general ability of the client to be able to handle normal levels of stress. This will help the counsellor to design effective strategy to deal with crisis with the mutual consent of the client.

4. ***Providing support:*** It is also important to find out people who are the part of the client's support system. These are the people who care for him and have a favourable opinion about him. In the situations of lowering self-esteem and confidence, these sets of people can be a substantive support for the client and help him manage the crisis more successfully. For example, providing financial support for needed medical attention. In all situations counsellor should be able to give the reassurance to the client that there is someone who really cares for him or her.

5. ***Implementing action plans:*** In crisis interventions, it is assumed that client is not in a mental state to be able to manage his concerns, so the counsellor is expected to play a more active role and be directive in his approach to deal with the client (Aguilera, 1998). The counsellor here is expected to identify and develop a strategy which will help the client to return to his or her exact level of equilibrium. He should be able to list a number of alternatives and then encourage the client to make a choice of one or more actions within his or her range of accomplishments.

   The attempt of the counsellor should be to help the client resolve the problem now and be equipped to face other problems of life in future (James and Gilliland, 2001). It is expected from the client to own up a plan of action so that he or she can regain control over his or her life. The help and support from another person provides hope to the client and encourage him or her to take the actions that have been planned and reduce the tension. Sometimes, it is quite useful to invite a friend or loved one to be a part of the termination meeting so that client is reassured that there will be people in life to support him even in the absence of the counsellor whom he had begun to rely on so much. But this should be done in agreement with the client.

6. *Arrange for follow-up:* Roberts (2000) also proposes to conduct a follow up meeting or a telephonic call to check on the client's progress towards resolving the crisis. It is also suggested to have this meeting within one month of the last session so as to be able to evaluate the proposed changes and take any other corrective action, if it is not providing any positive results.

9.10 Consulting

In many industries, counselling skills are extremely useful for working with clients as well as with subordinates. Of course, as a consultant a manager can't use a counselling style completely as usually a consultant is hired to give answers but he can use counselling techniques like listening and questioning while interviewing a client or a subordinate to collect as much 'real' information as possible, and then later on based on this he can offer his expert advice and findings to help the client to find ways to tide over the crisis.

9.11 Upward Feedback

Upward feedback is feedback from subordinates regarding their managers' performance. It involves establishing two-way communication, and respecting subordinates by listening, valuing and considering their input. However, upward feedback is difficult for managers and supervisors to receive. The best way to manage this sensitive situation is for the manager or supervisor's own manager to talk about the issues, which arise from upward feedback in a counselling style.

It is useful to use an upward feedback software system, where subordinate's appraisal, the manager's own self-appraisal, and the counsellor's appraisal can all be viewed along each dimension on a chart or graph. Later concerned manager being assessed can be asked to comment on the data.

9.12 The Learning Organization

A new paradigm is sweeping the business environment across the world. In this emerging paradigm, terms like information, communication, knowledge and learning have acquired a critical relevance to an understanding of the nature of contemporary business. In other words, the business world is moving from its tangible based assets on intangible ones (Sonnerberg, 1994). The libelous, the abstract, the impalpable appear to have begun to increasingly matter more than do the things one can touch, feel and hold in hand.

Since mid 1980's there has been a sudden avalanche of a new kind of vocabulary. Corporations, which so far had been economic entities, are being described as information-based organizations (Drucker, 1988), educated organizations (Handy, 1990), knowledge creating company Nonaka, (1988) and learning organization (Senge, 1990). Instead of product market strategies, one has started talking about core competencies, intangible assets, knowledge-based capabilities, etc. Processes are replacing tasks; (re-) engineering has now less to do with tinkering with machines and more with reconceptualizing the very nature of business. Even the practical, down-to-earth business world has suddenly become obsessed with terms like Brain-Power, Intellectual Property Rights (IPRS), and Intellectual Capital and their corollaries in patents, brands, trademarks, etc.

Since knowledge is the end product of all learning, any organization aiming to compete through knowledge must, by necessity, develop learning capabilities, namely, becoming a learning organization. The concept of knowledge-based learning organization has captured the attention of executives and academicians alike. There is an increasing emphasis on the need to build a learning organization which facilitates the learning of all its members and continually transforms itself (Pedler, Boydell, and Buryogne 1989). An extensive survey (Dodgson, 1991) has concluded that corporate learning is necessary to retain and improve competitiveness, productivity and innovativeness in uncertain technological and market circumstances. Senge (1990) has described a learning organization *as a place where people continually expand their capacity to create the results they truly desire, where new patterns of thinking are nurtured, where collective aspirations are set free and where people are continually learning how to learn together*. The practices and processes in a learning organization do not conform to conventional managerial wisdom. Together they define an entirely new view of an emerging form of organization. The biggest challenge in building a learning organization lies in replacing the traditional mental model with a new one. Thus, the greatest challenge in the future will not be quick adaptation or creation of new practices and technology; the greatest challenge for organization will be to develop the capabilities to learn new ways of operating and re-creating themselves. Those that will be able to do so will emerge as learning organizations.

According to *The Learning Organization Journal*, a learning organization is an organization which facilitates the learning of all its members and thus continually transforms itself. A learning organization, therefore, aims for continuous business improvement. Learning organizations adopt a very dynamic management style, building a culture, which encourages all employees to develop and learn.

It has been discussed as to how a manager can use counselling skills to develop individuals. The same concepts and skills can be used at team, department and organizational (senior management) levels to encourage self-responsibility for growth, learning, problem solving, etc., in order to continually develop the company continuously.

9.13 Organizational Development

In order for an organization to develop, effective training in counselling skills is required to be introduced as a normal part of its mainstream management development programme. In order for the subsequent use of counselling skills to be effective, however, the company culture must really support the use of these skills, i.e., really value its people. Otherwise the skills will be used manipulatively, which will cause even more underlying problems.

Every organization has an unstated culture consisting of unwritten rules and norms, which guide how people are expected to behave. It is essential that the organization's unspoken messages to employees match up with and back up its spoken messages. Unwritten beliefs and rules (even though often only based on tradition) are very difficult to change, but they have at least as much if not more effect on employee behaviour than do spoken and written rules.

Two aspects of culture to monitor for health include:

People's Receptiveness to Problems:

(a) Is bad news shared or is there a tendency to shoot the messenger?
(b) Is admitting to feeling stressed tantamount to admitting weakness, failure, or lack of capability?
(c) Are staff and managers openly rewarded for bringing up problems and difficulties rather than for burying their heads?

The Way that Conflict is Handled within the Organization:

(a) Is conflict viewed as negative?
(b) Is the environment over competitive? Is conflict seen as a situation in which one must win, or beat the other, rather than an opportunity for learning and growth? In such a climate, everyone is out for themselves, feeling a bit paranoid, always protecting themselves, being defensive and passing the buck.
(c) Is conflict repressed, or smoothened over and avoided? Problems may be avoided temporarily, but under the surface are anger, discomfort and frustration.
(d) Or are people always questioning in a non-blaming manner, looking for ways to improve? If managed properly, conflict can be a resource for better ideas and approaches.

Unsteady messages about leadership are communicated through the ways in which managers are appraised and remunerated like who is actually promoted, and who is spoken well of. It is important to consider how managers will be rewarded for making changes. Will managers really be rewarded or will they be subtly penalized for using counselling skills and for helping the employees and in the process helping the organization to progress? For example, is there a payoff for managers who empower and develop their subordinates to the point where they leave the department and move on to something else? Is the achievement acknowledged from above? Or does the manager's own department simply suffer from the loss? People are very much in tune with what they will be rewarded for in reality.

9.14 Counselling Women

Women are the primary consumers of counselling services. The concerns and issues that may require counselling for women are different from the ones related to men because of their different biological patterns and socialization process (Cook, 1993; Hoffman, 2006; Huffman and Myers, 1999). The issues related to counselling women are many, ranging from sex discrimination and sex role stereotyping to career choice and support services for women combining a profession and a family and for those reentering the work force. The focus on counselling of women in increasing to enable counsellors to assist women with the new personal and professional choices which are making.

During the last few years, our society has become increasingly aware of the extent to which women have been victims of discrimination. Sexist attitudes have permeated our social, religious, business and educational institutions. The workplace is structured in such a way that sometimes it is highly discriminatory, and, in fact, has negatively impacted most women entering the work force. In this fight against sex discrimination, there is an increasing awareness about the negative impact of sex role stereotypes. Women throughout the historical development, have been expected to play traditional feminine roles. As a result, the business organizations which have a relatively different perspective have difficulty in adjusting with the new empowered women. Women also find it difficult to shed their feminine roles and adapt to new environment. This socialization has presented difficulties for women as they enter the workforce and has seriously limited the opportunities available to them.

Expanding career options for women into non-traditional, male dominated occupation have important implications for counsellors. Women choosing non-traditional careers have been significantly influenced by their home environment, and they appear to possess androgynous personality characteristics. Since career decisions are made by many women at the level of schools, intervention must begin in the early years (Chusmir, 1983). Counsellors must design interventions that help young girls develop positive self-concepts. A preventive approach combined with a continuous focus on expanding the definition of sex role has to be designed to make women feel more powerful and capable of handling the demands of multiple roles they face.

Another concern is regarding the sex discrimination practices. Counsellors too have been brought up in the similar kinds of institutions which have promoted sex bias and sex role stereotyping; hence many of these attitudes have become part of their value structure and surface in helping relationships. In one of the classical studies by Broverman, et al. (1970), trying to find out if the counsellor would judge a client's mental health on the basis of the sex of the client, it was concluded that the standards applied by the counsellors to judge the mental health of men and women were different basically leading to the interpretation that counsellors at times also operate through their own stereotypes and biases. Characteristics ascribed to mentally healthy males included achievement, aggression, dominance, and counter-reaction; those attributed to mentally healthy females included nurturance, patience, play, submission, and abasement (Neulinger, et al., 1970). In a study by Scholossberg and Pietrofesa (1973) it was found that while trying to make a choice between a traditionally masculine occupations like engineering, and traditionally feminine occupation, like teaching, women subjects were discouraged by the counsellors in order to take up engineering as their career choices.

These studies basically support the belief that many counsellors are sex-biased in their counselling practices. It is important for the counsellors to eliminate these biases and help women develop a positive self-concept and make choices that are a reflection of the wide range of skills and abilities that women bring to the professional environment. Counsellors must be trained to help women to cope up with the issues of accomplishing their personal and professional choices. A woman is generally expected to make a softer choice of her career keeping in mind the factors such as limited time, importance of husband's career, limitation of geographical movements and responsibility of child rearing. Women who combine a career with the family have to deal with the conflicting societal demands, and resolve the conflict between roles and other psychological problems experienced by her. For this, they require emotional support from others. Counsellors dealing with women clients have to be knowledgeable about the kinds of problems experienced by women and be able to assist in the development of coping strategies. Some of the important skills with which the counsellor should be trained are time management, realistic goal setting, and assertiveness. While counselling women, counsellor should guide them in creating effective support systems and maintain intimate friendships. Women need support for meeting their own needs and encouragement for choosing satisfying relationships in which they can get the emotional and psychological support they need to survive daily stressors. They have to be informed to choose their friends carefully so that the time spent with them is rejuvenating.

9.15 Summary

There are certain specific areas in organization, which may require the use of counselling skills. Some of these specific areas where counselling skills may be used effectively are change management, downsizing, managing diversity, equal opportunities, entrepreneurialism, mentoring, team management, conflict resolution, counselling for older adults, crisis/trauma, consulting and upward feedback, learning organization and organization development.

Chapter 10 will focus the attention on issues of dealing with Problem subordinates in the work organizations.

Review Questions

1. How can counselling skills be used to help manage changes and the issue of downsizing in organizations? Discuss with examples.

2. The issue of managing diversity is relatively a new development in the work organizations. What are the major concerns of diversity management and how does the use of counselling skills address these concerns?

3. Identify and discuss the developmental tasks associated with old age. How can counselling procedures and skills help the people in this category to handle these tasks more effectively?

4. Crisis and trauma have become a part of living for everyone. List and discuss some of these crisis situations and explain how counselling skills can help in managing the anxiety associated with crisis?

5. Discuss the process to explain the state of disequilibrium for a person leading to crisis.

6. The women in work organizations are exposed to lots of dilemmas which affect both their personal and professional lives. Discuss how a counsellor can help women employee in the corporate overcome their dilemmas and be more effective in their performance.

Chapter 10

Dealing with Problem Subordinates

Most of the managers today in business organizations tend to acknowledge the presence of problem subordinates. If asked whether they have them or not, the response is generally in the form of cynical 'yes'. So if there is one universal truth about managers, it is that all of them have problem subordinates. If there is a second truth, it is that the stories they have to tell about these subordinates often reflect a good deal of disparagement and despair.

Here are a few examples of typical tales of woes of managers describing their problem subordinates:

EXAMPLE 10.1

Manager: ...*Talking to that man is like talking to a rock! I know he is very bright, some say an electronic genius, (but) and it's impossible to carry on a normal conversation with him. He intimidates the hell out of most people by just staring at them.*

EXAMPLE 10.2

Manager: *This woman is very charming and personable. She seems to have talent and yet more often than not, she disappoints me. I give her a major assignment and she comes up short. Quite often, I end up picking up the pieces. Surprisingly, she always seems to land on her feet...she generally has a plausible excuse for what she's done, or not done...I'm never sure how much I can count on her.*

EXAMPLE 10.3

Manager: *He seems to be unplugged from the socket. I mean, really, he seems to be disconnected from the realities of his job. He tells me things that make no sense whatsoever and I really can't rely on him to complete a job of any importance. If he weren't so close to retirement age I might do something—maybe put a bomb under his chair? (Laughs)*

On first reading, one feels that these subordinates have chronic defects and that their bosses would be much better off just getting rid of them than dealing with them. After all, who would want to put up with any one of them? But are they really as unsalvageable as they are portrayed? Certainly, in the opinions of their exasperated bosses, they are. One thing is clear, however. Unless and until some corrective action is taken, the prognosis is not encouraging.

How can such individuals thrive in today's corporate world? How can they be tolerated, or even ignored, in light of the potential they have that can and do wreak on the organization? Perhaps the answer is that they have become so pervasive that they are an accepted fact of life. It has been lamented by few bosses that there are a certain percentage of subordinates who, regardless of the amount of human relations training forced on them, are difficult to get along with by nature. Or, maybe it is because all of us have been problematic from time to time; therefore, we make allowances. After all, nobody is perfect. Although such arguments have a ring of truth, they tend to mask the real problem: we are actually unwilling to confront problem subordinates.

Who is the real victim here? Is it the boss for having to live with such a difficult subordinate? Or is it the subordinate, who no doubt is doing something that causes problems but who may also be suffering from his or her boss's reluctance to confront and try to correct such behaviour?

In many cases, problem subordinates are as much a result of mismanagement (or failure to manage) as they are of personal shortcomings. Hence, both parties are victims and both are to blame. Clearly, managers at all levels need to examine their role in creating problem subordinates and determine preventive measures to be taken. Senior managers who are derelict must take the lead and discipline themselves and then offer advice to the problem subordinates.

10.1 Identifying Problem Subordinates

When managers are asked to describe in details the case histories of their problem subordinates, their response consists of only in putting the blame on them. Blaming others is the easy part: "He's a liability to the company" or "She's a game player." Going beyond the superficial and describing how these people actually behave proves difficult but enlightening. In some cases, the managers are amazed at how little evidence they are able to collect. In others, the evidence often involves very subtle behaviour which is sometimes easy to describe and sometimes difficult to describe. The initial descriptions are usually based on how the problem subordinates make their bosses feel—"she drives me nuts!"—and not in terms of behaviours that causes the feelings. This exercise illustrates that while problem subordinates are discussed and thought about frequently, such musings rarely produce useful information for providing effective feedback. And operating on pejoratives and half-truths only make matters worse. Using limited and selectively perceived information they focus on a single trait, to the exclusion of many positive attributes the problem subordinates might have had on being questioned.

Not too surprisingly, when the managers attempt to reconcile their stories with what they report at performance appraisal time, the gap is significant. The managers usually respond by saying that they keep two sets of books. One is the public record, which is generally circumspect and vague, and the other is the private record, which contains how they really feel. And it is the latter one, which they rarely share, except with confidantes, but which influences their thinking when they make decisions that affect the individual's career.

10.2   Why are Problem Subordinates Avoided?

More often than not, problem subordinates described are not as problematic or ineffective as their portraits are made. Managers have a tendency to overreact whenever emotions are generated because of these problem subordinates. They tend to produce an autistic hostility, an emotion not entirely grounded in reality but still painfully real. As described by one of such manager (refer Example 10.4).

EXAMPLE 10.4

Manager: *On the drive home, he would be on my mind ... I would get so damned mad at him and myself for not saying anything that I would work myself into a rage. Sometimes it would take me over an hour to calm down. And then I'd come back to the all-too-familiar dilemma: Do I take some action or do I try to put it out of my mind for now?*

For these distraught bosses, their anger was, in effect, feeding upon itself—the subordinates need not have done anything at all. The angrier these bosses became about their own inability to confront the problem the more they blamed their subordinates for making them feel that way.

Although such emotions are common, they are often exaggerated by the intense anxiety a manager experiences when thinking about confronting a problem subordinate. Ideally, such feelings need to be transformed into constructive action. Unfortunately, however, these feelings are often rationalized away, further exacerbating already difficult situation. Thus, while anger often plays an integral role, such self-inflicted misery begs the question. Why do managers from the executive ranks down to first-line supervisors avoid confronting the source of their pain? Could it be that managers, especially top executives, just do not have the guts to talk to their people face to face? The basic reasons for avoiding the problem subordinates could be outlined as:

1. *Some managers avoid confrontation because they are afraid that they will jeopardize a long-term friendship.*   First of all, it is too simplistic to attribute being chicken as the primary reason for such

avoidance behaviour. Certainly, some managers avoid confrontation because they are afraid that they will jeopardize a long-term friendship—the most common reason given—or they are afraid they might create an even worse relationship, for example, "She's so defensive that if I confront her, she could just get worse or even turn on me." Others experience guilt (refer to Example 10.5).

EXAMPLE 10.5

Manager: *Just after Satish's wife died we decided not to promote him as planned. I felt he needed some space to get his life in order. As I look back on it now, it was shortly after these events that Satish's attitude turned sour and I never—well knew how to approach him after he blamed me ....I know I should have, but I hoped that time would straighten him out.*

2. *Some managers feel frustrated.* In some cases, the managers feel frustrated or hopeless. When things don't work out properly the frustration is likely to creep in. As a result they give up and don't try counselling their subordinates at all (refer to Example 10.6).

EXAMPLE 10.6

Manager: *I have tried repeatedly to point out to her that she has to be more sensitive to other managers' feelings, but after a few weeks, she's right back into bulldozing everyone ... I don't see how I can change her personality.*

Manager: *If you want legal backing, the person has to be more than a pain-in-the-neck to get fired in my shop. So what's the point of trying?*

3. *Sometimes managers are insecure.* Some managers feel that the other person with whom they are dealing is much superior to them and, therefore, feel insecure in his or her presence (refer to Example 10.7).

EXAMPLE 10.7

Manager: *She knows more about running this place than I do!*

4. *Some managers are reluctant to play God.* Some managers want to keep away from any emotional or personal problems of their subordinates as they feel that it is not appropriate for them to be God to them and, therefore, avoid counselling them (refer to Example 10.8).

EXAMPLE 10.8

Manager: *I don't want to be the one to push him over the edge. This wouldn't be the first time someone has considered suicide or gone on a rampage after a poor performance review.*

5. *Some managers want overwhelming proof before taking action against a problem employee.* This is a tendency often reinforced by personnel policies designed to avoid litigation and thus severely restrict managerial response. One manager from a major corporation confided that the major reason he had not confronted a problem subordinate was because there was no documentary proof to support his concerns (refer to Example 10.9).

Example 10.9

Manager: *If I screw up in following to the letter corporate procedure, it's going to be a problem for me. Personnel expects me to maintain detailed contemporaneous notes on all discussions I have with the employee and a carefully documented history of any infractions....What I want to know is how the hell are you supposed to do that with a subordinate whose primary fault is being arrogant and insensitive?*

Thus, gathering detailed evidence is often perceived as so onerous that it is rarely done. In the absence of convincing evidence, and the desire to avoid a libellous confrontation, managers feel their hands are tied up and, therefore, continue to give conflicting signals to problem subordinates. Quite often the feedback is inconsistent with how the managers feel—sometimes it is a complete fabrication—but it is justified as reasonable given the lack of hard evidence. Having thus committed to a course of faulty and erroneous feedback, managers often believe there is no turning back and, in an effort to reduce their feelings of dissonance, they begin to justify a continued strategy of avoidance, thereby becoming trapped in a self-reinforcing pattern of behaviour.

10.3 Types of Problem Subordinates

The classification of the problem subordinates can be done based on the two criteria:

1. Job performance, i.e., whether or not the individual performed above or below the boss's expectation.
2. Interpersonal skills, i.e., whether or not the individual worked effectively with others.

Combining these two themes results in the grid shown in Figure 10.1.

In one of the studies (Veiga, 1988) the most pervasive problem subordinates were classified into three types: the talented but abrasive (cited by 40 percent of the executives) the charming but unreliable (cited by 33 percent), and the plateaued but indifferent (cited by 20 percent). The fourth type on the grid, the ideal subordinate, represents the talent mix that manager's desire—one that performs up to expectation and works effectively with others. A discussion on each of the types of the subordinate as presented on the grid follows:

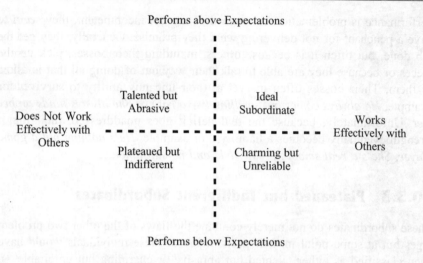

Figure 10.1 Types of Problem Subordinates.

10.3.1 Talented but Abrasive Subordinates

These subordinates are generally described as very bright and gifted performers who are insensitive to others and lack interpersonal skills. Most are perceived as superstars of comers and yet because they play solely to their strengths and are either unaware of or ignore their weaknesses, they are eventually labelled everything from arrogant know-it-alls and pushy, unreasonable and demanding. In some instances their behaviour is excused because of the responsibility they are willing to shoulder and also because they are talented: *She is always willing to take more responsibility* or justified: We needed someone to take the responsibility and he is the man for the job. Some of them are similar to the label of abrasive personality, although the term *personality* often connotes to the layperson a permanent and, therefore, unalterable condition, which in these cases is not so. Because abrasives subordinates are usually quite good at their jobs, they tend to become impatient with anyone who can't keep up with them. In some cases, this impatience shows itself in both verbal and non-verbal behaviours such as the caustic remark or the silent stare. These individuals are also perceived as having a talent for making politically insensitive remarks, which is often further exacerbated by their general unwillingness to concern themselves with issues of political sensitivity. Paradoxically, by trying to avoid encounters or tune out abrasive individuals, bosses and co-workers often unwillingly reinforce such unwanted behaviour.

10.3.2 Charming but Unreliable Subordinates

These subordinates are in many ways the exact opposite of the abrasive individuals. The charming subordinates are perceived as interpersonally skilful—what one manager called **personality plus**—but their job performance is problematic. Although they are not incompetent, they seem to have a penchant for not delivering what they promise. Generally, they get the job done, but often it is because others, including their bosses, pick up the pieces or because they are able to talk their way out of doing all that is asked of them. Their bosses often marvel at their uncanny ability to survive, for example, *He always comes out smelling like a rose* or *She always lands on her feet*. Unfortunately, because the real deficit goes unaddressed, their major strength eventually becomes a liability. For example, *He's nothing but a game player, She's a real smoothie—all style and no substance*.

10.3.3 Plateaued but Indifferent Subordinates

These subordinates do not merely combine the flaws of the other two problem types but at some point in their pasts, many of these individuals would have been classified as either talented but abrasive or charming but unreliable—a time when they should have been dealt with. They are typically viewed as interpersonally ineffective because others refuse to take them seriously. Traits that at one time would have produced pejoratives are now seen as harmless; e.g., *Her bark is worse than her bite*. And while their performance is below expectations, it isn't perceived as pre-retirement aged plodders who either has not kept up or can't be counted on because they are generally given unimportant, make work assignments or expected to do the bare minimum. Their indifference is as much the result of how they are treated as if it is a chosen state of mind. Although their co-workers accept that these individuals are just biding their time until retirement, they are far less forgiving when asked to carry part of what should have been the indifferent subordinate's workload—much to the boss's chagrin.

10.4 Dealing with Problem Subordinates

Regarding dealing with problem subordinates, there are no easy answers that one can give with complete confidence. But one thing is clear; however there are many alternatives a manager can exercise besides getting rid of a problem subordinate or just doing nothing. Just because certain individuals are talented does not mean that a manager must tolerate abrasiveness or treat such individuals as special. Neither is there any reason to avoid straight talk with the unreliable performer or listen to plausible excuses offered by him. The ultimate responsibility for initiating action lies squarely on the boss's shoulders. Following are some maxims for dealing with problem subordinates, offered by the experienced managers, which all managers must heed.

10.4.1 Confront Directly

Contrary to the usual prescriptions offered for helping a person with a problem, most of the managers believe that candour promotes credibility and that problematic individuals cannot be handled with kid gloves or in a detached, counselling-like way. This is no time to offer a positive sandwich, i.e., praise followed by criticism, followed by praise again—because most subordinates are smart enough to perceive its contents as baloney. The goal is to clarify the unwanted behaviours and the consequences. From the start, be prepared to take a tough stand; take the risk of owning up to your position first, then be prepared to be receptive. Blaming and fault-finding will not work. Both parties must accept the fact that each is responsible at some level for allowing the situation to continue. The manager should remember that he is dealing with individuals who probably know they disappoint him. Thus, the manager's attempt to unravel this illusion about the subordinate's performance calls for straight talk. Clear-cut expectations must be established such as, make clear what is wrong and what you expect to see changed. Offering psychological safety to the subordinates and support to encourage even a small but new step is very essential. Help these individuals face the central question: why do they behave as they do? Are they unsure of themselves? Are they having trouble managing their time or establishing priorities? Are there legitimate, personal reasons or priorities that have caused them to behave as they do? Or are they having trouble admitting that they are not well suited to their jobs? As the following two cases illustrate, a big first step taken in that direction is starting with honest dialogue.

CASE STUDY 1

The Talented but Abrasive Engineer

Hitesh was a very bright industrial engineer; he had a master's degree in engineering and had been promoted to senior engineer at the age of 25. The problem was that every time he worked on a project with manufacturing personnel, he caused trouble. He knew more than the foremen he worked with and let them know it in many ways. Since his ideas were too good to waste, his boss Rajan had to intervene on his behalf. Rajan would present Hitesh's ideas to the foremen; drop a lot of his statistical analysis, and generally win their acceptance. Even though Rajan valued Hitesh's contributions, yet it seemed to Rajan that Hitesh was meddling with the work often. When Rajan called Hitesh in for his annual performance review, he decided it was time to confront him. At first Hitesh told him it wasn't his fault that there were so many stupid people in manufacturing. Rajan told him that's why they hire "smart engineers", to help those less fortunate. He also told him that his ideas were no better than his ability to implement them; that was what he was paid for, and he would no longer smooth the way. Hitesh wanted to focus on what was wrong with the manufacturing personnel, but Rajan reminded him that if he could get his ideas accepted, it must have something to do with how he presented his ideas. He reluctantly agreed to meet the next day with Rajan and one of the foremen he had trouble with to explore his problem. In that meeting, he found out that his attempts to impress the foremen with his statistical prowess were seen as an attempt to put the foreman down. The foremen told Hitesh, "I don't need to take crap from a smart-mouthed college graduate. I know my job and I do it well. When you accept that fact, you might be able to see that I have just as much to contribute as you do. Sure, I don't understand the numbers, but I do know my people and how things work, and you don't."

When the meeting was over, Hitesh was angry. He didn't say anything but it was clear that he felt ganged up on. Rajan thought he might lose him until about two weeks after the meeting when he asked to see him. When they met, he asked his advice on how he could present a new cost-cutting idea to the plant manager. While he never talked about the earlier meeting, it was clear that he had heard the message. As it turned out, this was one of several meetings he and Rajan would have.

CASE STUDY 2

The Charming but Unreliable Plant Manager

Raman is the manager of one of the five assembly plants and reports to Shekhar. He's been in the job for five years. Shekhar had managed the plant before him and supported his promotion. Raman had always struck Shekhar as a pleasing and hardworking guy and he liked him ...he was honest and loyal. After one year, Raman's plant became the poorest performer in their division. When Shekhar ran this plant it had regularly been number one or two out of the five.

When Shekhar noticed this slippage in productivity, he began to question Raman. In the beginning he made promises to turn things around. He told him how some things he was working on showed real promise. He sold Shekhar and Shekhar believed it. During the same time, he had also made a lot of friends in the company than Shekhar did. But his promises never materialized. He was getting on Shekhar's nerves. But invariably he did nothing. Because they were good friends, some of the other plant managers believed Shekhar was protecting an old buddy.

Initially, when their boss would question Raman's performance Shekhar would make excuses for him. Soon it became clear to him that his ability to manage Raman was being called into question. He began to cut his annual salary increments. Raman said he understood but still did nothing. Finally about a year ago Shekhar decided he had to take some action. He knew that if he got angry with him that would do no good. But he felt the need to lay all my cards on the table. He carried out many dress rehearsals through his mind. But when the time came he was surprisingly calm. He talked and Raman listened. He told him how he had grappled with the problem and had tried to avoid it and how he felt? Raman and Shekhar had to begin addressing what was happening. You know what? He agreed. He told him how lousy he felt that he was unable to get his plant moving. How he hated to come to plant manager meetings, especially when performance issues were talked about. How he had begun to seriously doubt his career choice. They met again and talked some more. At that time Shekhar asked him to develop a plan that would improve his performance over the next two years. They agreed that this would be a good way to rest his potential as a plant manager and a way to provide the evidence as to whether he should continue on his present career track or look for a reassignment more suited to his ability. One year has gone by since the plan was developed. So far the results are not too encouraging. Shekhar has serious doubts that he will improve. But two things are different now. First, they are talking openly about what's happening and secondly, Shekhar is convinced that he will be much more receptive to a job change. In the meantime, their boss is very pleased with Shekhar's approach to manage Raman.

Unfortunately, attempts such as these are rare. Instead, managers often bungle the job by exerting subtle pressures on the subordinate rather than directly confronting him or her. In many cases, the subtle pressures, such as, irrelevant or undesirable assignments or excluding the subordinate from management seminars and retreats—eventually are escalated to the not so subtle pressures, such as, holding back on salary increases or other tangible perks. Unfortunately, these kinds of pressures drive a wedge between the boss and subordinates. On the surface relation between the two appears to be cordial, polite, and even friendly, but beneath the surface, both are getting further mired in the deception. Clearly, action must be taken to break this self-reinforcing pattern of behaviour. As we saw in the case studies, both parties benefitted from confronting the situation, even if the final resolution was uncertain.

10.4.2 Avoid Frozen Evaluations

All too often, ability and potential become inextricably tied to past performance. This is especially true when subordinates do not live up to the expectations of their bosses. As one manager observed: "In organizations we label people…it's a gradual, insidious kind of process…but, over time, labels stick and become well-known, unspoken fact." Such labelling gradually reduces the confidence a boss will show in a subordinate and eventually may threaten the subordinate's self-worth. Once this happens, both the charming but unreliable performers and the talented but abrasive individuals are likely to start making extra efforts to prove their value by engaging in activities that place greater emphasis on their strengths—in most cases, whatever they do well they will try to do more often. In turn, the boss will assign them less important projects or compensate by monitoring their work more frequently. As one engineering manager narrates:

> *When he took over the engineering department, there was one engineer who spent several hours a week running a sports pool all over the plant. Everyone liked this guy. He had helped the department*

many times by greasing the skids with other units. Anytime a sell job
was needed, they used him. Unfortunately, he had to check his work all
the time. Eventually, he had to put him on unimportant projects to
avoid serious mistakes and save my time.

Labelling subordinates based solely on past performance rests on the
faulty assumption that people are unable to change over time. Who would say
that the engineer described above would not make an excellent customer
service representative or liaison with purchasing? Moreover, such unchanged
or frozen evaluations are unfair and in many cases are merely excuses for the
boss to do nothing. Once previously held views are put aside, the potential for
new insights can be enormous. As one boss explained:

He used to tune this woman out because she grated on him. The more
he tuned out, the more she would push her point. Finally, one day he
started to listen. As painful as it was, he kept telling himself, this
woman is bright; just try to see her point of view. Eventually, he got
past his negative reaction and she started to behave less abrasively.
What he needed to do now was to help her to see how her desire to be
heard and have her ideas appreciated was causing her to be too pushy
and triggering many of the problems she had with others.

10.4.3   Attend to Early Warning Signals

Many problem subordinates start out with great promise due to their charm.
Some are so pleasant that initially at the start of their career their shortcomings
are easily overlooked: *She's so pleasant to work with I'm sure it's only a*
matter of time before she comes up to speed. Others are so talented that their
few eccentricities are hardly noticed: *He is just a little strong willed.*
Overlooking these warning signals can prove insidious for the organization.
All too often, bright and/or charming young subordinates seem to be given a
special dispensation by their seniors. Many problem subordinates will continue
working the same way till they take on a major management responsibility.
The prognosis is likely to be more promising in early career when the
individuals are the most malleable and the damage minimal. This is the time
when they are most easily turned around or redirected.

It is a proven fact that it is going to be difficult for the managers to
challenge youthful brashness because such attempts can backfire. If the
manager's efforts become too threatening, he could be faced with a hostile and
uncooperative subordinate. He might also find himself trying to convince the
client to stay or worse, he could stand accused of causing the problem. The
manager should not wait for all the evidence to accumulate before he starts a
dialogue. When in doubt, he should trust his instincts. Most managers have
good instincts but often fail to follow them. Early coaching can make a
difference, like, waiting until the warning signs can no longer be ignored
because it is a mistake. In fact immediate attention to the warning signals is
required.

10.4.4 Don't Neglect the Problem Subordinates

Shelving an individual in mid-career because of shortcomings that should have been dealt with years before is inexcusable and continuing to write him or her off as deadwood is also wrong in many of the cases, but, undoubtedly an attitude of why bother prevails, leaving both the boss and the subordinate feeling helpless, believing the situation is outside their control and there is little hope of escape. Judging by the long history of neglect from which such cases have evolved, both parties are right and little can be done to change what has already happened and little can be done at this stage in the problem subordinate's career to offer major redirection. But does that mean that these individuals deserve continued neglect?

Often the plateaued but indifferent subordinate has potential and talent. The counsellor's job is to identify it and to fully exploit it. Just as anyone would be unwilling to drive an automobile running on fewer than all its cylinders, the manager should also be unwilling to allow any human resource to be under utilized. In the beginning, these indifferent subordinates must be involved in mainstream activity, no matter how trivial their part is. At a minimum, they should be asked to carry their fair share of the workload. Find out what interests them and encourage them to follow through. Not all the staff has to do the same thing. Try to juggle the workload to match individual interests and talents. These subordinates may be ideal candidates for retraining or job rotation. As the following case illustrates, sometimes a small effort, even in late career, can make a difference.

Case Study 3

The Plateauted but Indifferent Subordinates

Kanika manages a group of designers. Many of them love creating new ideas but lack the patience for the detail work after the initial design is accepted. One of her designers, an older woman named Mary, hadn't been assigned any major projects for several years. Mary was considered good designer in her days but she had not kept pace with the times. Other designers refused to work with her because she was considered a 'nit-picker' and that disturbed their creative flow. As a consequence, Kanika had to assign her to minor projects.

One day a couple of her best designers approached her with a complaint....They felt it was unfair that they had to do projects that Mary should be doing. They were especially unhappy about doing the additional burdensome detail work...That meeting gave her an idea. She decided to experiment by assigning Mary to do the follow-up detail work on accepted designs. This would free up the other designers to do what they loved to do best. It turned out to be a perfect marriage after some encouraging and nudging on Kanika's part. Mary's attention to detail resulted in her finding minor flaws in the accepted designs and saved them production glitches. The other designers began to respect her 'eye for detail' and seek her advice during the preliminary stages of design. This gave Mary a greater sense of ownership in the project.

To be sure, there are also a number of plateaued but indifferent workers who, for whatever reasons—cynicism, despair or apathy—are less willing to respond to such change attempts. The counsellor manager, however, has to learn to recognize that helplessness conditioned by years of neglect requires a patient response from his side; don't give up too easily. As one executive summed up, *There are no easy answers when you deal with human beings... If there were, we wouldn't need managers.*

10.4.5 Accept the Mistakes

The manager regardless of the type of problem subordinate he comes across should first of all start examining his own involvement in the process. How big a part has he played in creating the problem or allowing it to continue? When is the last time he paid attention to a problem subordinate or took the time to find out how he or she feels about the job? Sadly, such attempts are frequently affected by a simplistic cost/benefit decision.

Another mistake on the part of the managers is that they will invest energy in a subordinate when the payoff is substantial but are unwilling to do so when it is not. However, writing off another human being as a bad investment is not only a dereliction of a manager's responsibility to develop human resources—it is dehumanising as well. Although the manager cannot undo past practices or necessarily fix what is broken, there are many instances where effective interventions have made a difference.

The manager can also begin to accept this mistake by recognizing that the metaphors they sometimes use to describe problem subordinates often create more hostility in them and frustration in you that is uncalled for, and that such metaphors, whether derogatory or despairing tend to guide and colour the views when providing counselling. They should also try to recognize that such actions detract from their primary mission of developing productive human beings.

When Don Quixote thrust his lance at monsters created out of windmills, it was funny. Similarly, when managers allow themselves to be hassled by monstrous kinds of behaviour, some real and some imagined it is not acceptable. Perhaps it is time to recast these metaphors to produce more positive images such as a subordinate with a problem, rather than a problem subordinate, could become a potential challenge and not a threat, a mismatch and not a misfit. And perhaps it is time to stop passing the buck, arguing that "It's not my fault, I inherited him (or her)." Managers don't inherit people, but they do inherit responsibility for their performance and development, a rule to which most managers subscribe but for which few are willing to foot the bill.

But, there are no quick fixes or guarantees. It is sheer hardwork and depends on the skills of the manager. One week of training is not the answer, nor is a simple heart-to-hear talk. The manager must accept the fact that the problem solving process will be a long haul. Establishing a pattern of coaching, counselling and feedback, perhaps supplemented with training takes time. In some situations the behaviour patterns are well entrenched if not permanent. In these cases, it may be nearly impossible to promote change or it may take some major crisis to break the pattern. As one CEO explained, "The threat of a takeover made us all pull together...survival was at stake. Each of us learned a valuable lesson in humility and teamwork." Some changes take time to be implemented: others will never occur. Sometimes you may be too big a part of the problem and might have to change as well; other times, the only answer is reassignment or termination.

In the final analysis, managerial vitality depends on the ability to see something new in the old and the familiar. Therefore, all managers must be willing to take another hard look at problem subordinates and themselves, and be prepared to face both. Unless and until all the managers accept this charge, they will continue to be victimized and continue to be blameworthy.

The counselling managers should bear in mind that they are not expected to be a miracle worker but are expected to shoulder the responsibility of improving the work performance as well as dealing with the problem subordinates or a subordinate facing a problem.

10.5 Summary

Problem subordinates are part and parcel of any organization. Every manager has to deal with them. They are generally avoided because managers want to abstain from direct confrontation or are reluctant to play God. Some of them may feel insecure or frustrated. In organizations, different types of problem subordinates include talented but abrasive, charming but unreliable and plateaued but indifferent. While dealing with problem subordinates, the manager will have to confront them directly, avoid frozen evaluations and learn to attend to various signals. They also have to understand not to neglect the problem subordinates and also to accept their own mistakes. This will help the manager to enhance their personal relationship with subordinates and convert them into ideal subordinates.

Chapter 11 discusses the concept of performance management and the use of counselling skills in performance appraisal.

Review Questions

1. Define problem subordinates. How can they be identified at the workplace? Are they the result of mismanagement or personal shortcomings? Discuss.

2. Why do managers in organizations have a tendency to avoid problem subordinates?

3. Identify and discuss the types of problem subordinates and describe the ways to deal with them?

Chapter 11

Performance Management

The term performance management is often used to describe a revamped appraisal system or a performance-related bonus scheme. Performance management, however, needs to be looked at in a much larger and more comprehensive context of continuous improvement in business performance. The holistic performance management system takes into account several ongoing and integrated processes within the framework of achieving overall business strategy. Most of these processes involve the use of counselling skills.

Figure 11.1 shows the interrelated nature of the aspects of performance management. Setting objectives lead to determining what human resources are

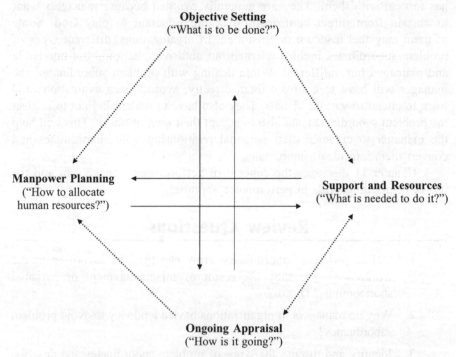

Objective Setting
("What is to be done?")

Manpower Planning
("How to allocate
human resources?")

Support and Resources
("What is needed to do it?")

Ongoing Appraisal
("How is it going?")

Figure 11.1 Components of Performance Management System.

needed to meet the objectives, and what supports and resources the staff of a business organization will need to meet their individual objectives. Then achievement and progress need to be assessed, both formally and decisions are to be made regarding how to allocate human resources in the future.

Once the system is going, the aspects become interrelated, feeding back and forth to one another. For example, appraisal gives rise to new training and support requirements as well as vice versa, and appraisals give rise to new objectives as well as assessing how well old ones were met. Manpower planning decisions, such as recruitment and redundancy give rise to new training or counselling needs, and the growth that arises from supporting and developing people engenders the need for succession planning and monetary rewards. All the aspects must work together, with continuous feedback to one another, in order for the system to work.

The performance management system promotes self-improvement at both the level of the employee and of the organization. Thus, each aspect of the performance management system must be considered at both these levels. Objectives are set at the level of the organization (strategies) as well as at the level of the individual (how the individual will contribute to the strategies). Human resource requirements are considered relative to the company's needs to promote, downsize, transfer or recruit, and on the individual level, where career aspirations are taken into account. Resources and support for achieving objectives must be procured for the company like information and communication technology, building space usage, large-scale training programmes, etc., as well as for individual's own specific training, resources, coaching and counselling requirements. Appraisal must also take place at both levels, monitoring both organizational and individual capability.

The following sections discuss how counselling skills are used at the individual level within the different processes of the performance management system.

11.1   Setting Objectives

There are two main areas of opportunity for using counselling skills when setting objectives. First, while corporate and departmental objectives will usually be determined by management (with or without employee input), the manager's counselling skills can be used to encourage the subordinates to think about how they are going to contribute to meeting the objectives. In case they do not agree with the corporate objectives, counselling services can help them to take a second look at these and find out how they can be aligned with their personal objectives. Secondly, the manager or the counsellor can use counselling skills to help his subordinates come up with additional objectives of their own, as well as plans for meeting them. Counselling skills may also be helpful in getting subordinates to suggest ways of measuring their progress and performance.

11.2 Support and Resources

In this aspect of performance management, there are the obvious applications of counselling skills to training, coaching, mentoring and counselling subordinates. There is another area worth mentioning in more detail—training needs analysis.

Training Needs Analysis: Counselling skills can be used to pinpoint the exact areas where improvement is necessary, as well as for determining which modes of support will be most useful. For example, if the subordinate needs to improve their supervisory skills then the manager or the counsellor can use counselling skills to determine more precisely what exactly his difficulties are, and which particular supervisory skills are weak. Then the manager or the counsellor can use counselling skills to determine whether a training course, coaching or counselling will be most helpful, or some combination of these. Too often the response to a developmental need is to send the subordinate on a course that sounds as if it will help cover the area for which help is needed. Using his expert counselling skills, the manager or the counsellor will be able to ascertain the exact nature and depth of the need, and to determine together a method of learning which will be most suited to that need.

11.3 Human Resource Planning

An organization's human resource planning should be performed alongside career planning for individuals. The supply and demand of human resources are matched so that skills are utilized to the best possible advantage, and the aspirations of the individual are taken into account. This co-ordination of organizational and individual needs is becoming more common as companies recognize that they have to make the best use of human resources and that staff turnover is expensive. This component of human resource planning is referred to as succession planning.

A manager or a counsellor should keep in mind that this expert counselling skills will be useful during the part of the succession planning process which involves talking to your subordinates; in other words, during career counselling.

11.3.1 Career Counselling

Career counselling is a specialized forms of counselling, and indeed a career in itself. The manager as a counsellor should always remember that he can only be involved in career counselling peripherally and that he is likely to have difficulty remaining neutral regarding the subordinates' decision-making. However, if he can work with subordinates to help them achieve their own goals as well as company objectives, they will be much more happy and productive.

Career counselling involves looking at alternatives and making choices in order to get people from where they are at present to where they want to be. Although he may not be able to assist them regarding career opportunities outside the firm, he can provide information about opportunities and options which exist within the firm, and help them with self-assessment, generating realistic alternatives, and decision making like

1. He can provide information regarding:
   - (a) job description
   - (b) personal qualities and educational levels necessary for jobs
   - (c) realistic estimates of future organizational requirements
   - (d) resources for further information
2. He can assist in self-assessment regarding their:
   - (a) general abilities
   - (b) special aptitudes
   - (c) strengths and weaknesses
   - (d) interests and job needs
3. The manager or the counsellor can also assist in generating options.
4. He can assist in the decision-making processes both for long-term and short-term decisions.

Career counselling will take different slants depending on the stage the subordinates are at in their careers. Early career issues involve finding one's area of contribution, learning how to fit into the organization, becoming productive, and seeing a viable future for oneself in the career. Mid-career issues involve choosing an aspect and building one's career around it (specializing vs. generalizing). Late career issues involve becoming a mentor, using one's experience and wisdom, letting go and retiring.

11.4 Appraisal

The most effective appraisals meet subordinates' needs as well as those of the manager and the organization. In addition to being opportunities to assess, develop and motivate, appraisals are an opportunity for subordinates to pursue their own issues and concerns.

Appraisals will have one or more of the following objectives:

1. to provide feedback on performance by giving subordinates information and assessment on achievements and results such as praise and formal assessment of unsatisfactory performance
2. to ask subordinates how they view their performance
3. to review the job to see if there is a better way of carrying it out
4. to set new objectives and targets
5. to improve performance
6. to determine future potential and discuss career development opportunities and plans

7. to assess training and development needs such as identifying strengths and weaknesses, and identifying how to improve skills
8. to plan future promotions, pay and successions
9. to motivate staff by providing positive feedback on objectives achieved and personal strengths gained, for suggesting plans for improvement and by setting personal targets such as giving people direction and something to aim for
10. to provide a fair standard for comparison
11. to provide an opportunity for constructive conversation between manager and subordinates

The skills required for conducting an appraisal include obtaining information, providing feedback, problem solving, motivating and counselling. Depending on the nature of the appraisal, these skills will be used in varying degrees, but all of the objectives above can best be achieved by using counselling skills to some degree.

There is a current trend towards emphasizing the future in appraisals. The process is less likely to be a manager's assessment than of a subordinate's past performance, as was common in the past. Instead, appraisals are now more likely to be mutually participative, which leads to a greater ownership of the outcome on the part of subordinates, and therefore makes them more likely to improve. The most effective way to do an appraisal is to focus it mainly on the subordinate, i.e., to get the subordinates to do as much of it as possible themselves, which is synonymous with the counselling style. This is idealistic in some cases, however. Although the manager and the counsellor want the appraisal to be as objective a process as possible, it is impossible to have no judgments or opinions involved. Nevertheless, since the success of the appraisal is very dependent on the subordinate's perception of its fairness, it is important to elicit and consider his or her thoughts. If appraisal schemes are not handled well, they can be worse than useless in that they can actually worsen both performance and working relationships.

One way to increase perceptions of the fairness of appraisals is to rate everyone in similar positions along the same criteria. Another way for the manager or the counsellor is to use their counselling skills is to persuade subordinates to air their views and concerns.

11.5 Performance Counselling

Performance counselling is an integral part of performance appraisal. Any organization interested in administering a good performance-appraisal system that aims at developing employees must practice effective performance counselling. Although performance counselling can be provided by anyone who is senior to the employee being counselled in competence, knowledge, experience or hierarchical position but it is generally the manager who counsels his subordinates more often. In this context, performance counselling can be defined as the help that a manager provides to subordinates in analyzing their performance and other job behaviours for the purpose of increasing their job effectiveness. A manager can provide counselling at any of various stages in a subordinate's development (for example, soon after a subordinate has been hired or when the subordinate faces difficulties or problems).

The objectives of performance counselling are as follows:

1. to provide a non-threatening atmosphere in which the subordinate can freely express tensions, conflicts, concerns and problems
2. to develop the subordinate's knowledge of his or her strengths and weaknesses
3. to enhance the subordinate's understanding of the work environment
4. to increase the subordinate's personal and interpersonal effectiveness by giving him feedback about his behaviour and assistance in analyzing interpersonal competence
5. to review the subordinate's progress in achieving objectives
6. to identify any problems that are hindering progress
7. to assist in generating alternatives and a final action plan for dealing with identified problems
8. to encourage the subordinate to set goals for further improvement
9. to try to provide whatever support the subordinate needs while implementing the action plan
10. to help the subordinate realize his or her potential

11.5.1 Conditions Required for Effective Counselling

Counselling is a means rather than an end in itself. A subordinate's performance does not automatically develop in positive ways because counselling takes place. But when done effectively, counselling can be quite useful in helping a subordinate to integrate with the organization and to develop a sense of involvement and satisfaction. The following conditions are necessary if counselling is to be effective:

1. *A general climate of openness and mutuality.* At least a minimum degree of trust and openness is essential. If the organization or the unit in which the subordinate works is full of tension and mistrust, counselling will not be effective.

2. *A helpful and empathic attitude on the part of the manager.* The manager as counsellor must approach the task as an opportunity to help, must feel empathy for the subordinate being counselled, and must be able to convey both helpfulness and empathy to the subordinate.

3. *The establishment of an effective dialogue.* Counselling is collaborative rather than prescriptive. It is based on the subordinate's achievement of performance goals set in concert with his or her manager. Consequently, the counselling process should be one in which both the manager and the subordinate participate without inhibition and engage in a discussion that eventually results in a better understanding of the performance issue involved.

4. *A focus on work-related goals.* Work-related goals should be the exclusive concern of a counselling effort; attention should be given only to behaviours and problems that directly relate to the subordinate's achievement of those goals. During the course of the discussion, issues that are not work related may arise; but when this happens the manager should refocus the dialogue on improvement in the organizational setting.

5. *Avoidance of discussion about salary, raises, and other rewards.* The purpose of counselling is to help subordinate plan improvements in performance, but discussing the linkage between performance and rewards may interfere with this purpose.

11.5.2 Tips for Effective Counselling

The following are useful tips for performance counselling that managers should follow:

1. *Make sure that the subordinate is willing to learn from counselling.* On some occasions a subordinate does not ask for performance counselling, but is, in effect, forced into it. When counselling is provided without having been sought, it may be of limited value and frustrating to the manager as well as the subordinate. In such a situation the manager would do well to forget about performance counselling and instead talk to the subordinate about his or her interest or lack of interest in growth. If the manager establishes the proper climate, such a discussion can lead to openness on the part of the subordinate. However, if the subordinate has serious difficulty in dealing with the manager, a problem-solving session should be the first step.

2. *Encourage the subordinate to function independently.* Sometimes subordinates are so loyal and their manager so protective that they become totally dependent on the manager. From time to time every manager should reflect on whether he or she is unintentionally fostering this kind of relationship. It is important to allow subordinates to make their own decisions and thereby increase their autonomy. The same principle holds true in a counselling situation, such as the subordinate should bear the main responsibility for determining what action to take.

3. *Make sure that the subordinate understands the purpose of the counselling.* If the subordinate does not understand the purpose or has unrealistic expectations, he or she may not receive the manager's message in the proper perspective. If it is obvious that the subordinate has some misunderstandings, it is a good idea to spend the first session addressing them; then another session can be scheduled for the actual counselling effort.

4. *Minimize arguments.* One argument is sufficient to make both the

manager and the subordinate defensive. The manager should try to accept everything the subordinate says and build on it. Acceptance is the best way of helping the subordinate to achieve self-realization.

5. *Ensure adequate follow-up.* Good counselling sessions will ultimately fail to produce effective results if follow-up is inadequate. When the manager follows up through informal exchanges, this approach goes a long way toward communicating interest in the subordinate. But when the manager fails to follow up, the subordinate may feel that the counselling was artificial and, consequently, may lose interest in improving the performance at issue.

Specific areas in which counselling skills will help the manager to do an appraisal include:

1. Putting the subordinate at ease if their body language indicates tension.

2. Being aware of both your own and the subordinate's likely feelings, which will help the manager to establish rapport at the beginning. Some of these feelings which may be generated during counselling include:

   (a) For the manager,

      • Positive feelings such as to be helpful and understanding and to be kind and tolerant.
      • Negative feelings such as fear of carrying out the interview ineffectively or fear of unleashing powerful emotions.

   (b) For the subordinate,

      • Positive feelings such as to be liked and accepted and to get help with problems.
      • Negative feelings such as fear of criticism and punishment.

3. Giving subordinates advance warning of appraisals, requesting them to think ahead about certain topics which will help them to feel more prepared and confident and more aware of what to expect.

4. Getting the subordinate to volunteer as much information as possible and then probing areas that they don't cover. Some subordinates may want the manager's point of view instead (the 'that is what managers are paid for' attitude) but they are in the minority compared to people who would prefer to assess and criticize themselves constructively. People are sensitive to criticism from others and tend to reject it, even when it is justified and there is valid proof or evidence. Operating in a counselling style (trying to get the other person to bring up and discuss their weaknesses) is often much more effective in getting them to consider seriously and accept areas which need improvement.

If the main objectives of the appraisal are to enhance the subordinate's motivation and development then counselling skills must be used as much as possible. If the objective is to pass on information about poor performance or to explain why a promotion is not to be given then counselling skills are necessary to help the subordinate determine how to improve or to move forward once the feedback has been given.

The following are some suggested open questions to commence a counselling style conversation:

1. How might you perform more effectively?
2. What are the ways of going about this improvement?
3. What are your development needs?
4. What solutions do you recommend?
5. How can we work together more effectively to improve your performance?
6. Describe the situations where your job goes well.
7. Describe the situations where your job does not go well.
8. What aspects of the job are difficult?
9. What objectives have not been met?
10. What changes or challenges are likely to occur in the near future?
11. Where do you feel satisfied with your efforts? (Ask for examples.)
12. Where do you not feel satisfied with your efforts? (Ask for examples.)
13. What are your career aspirations?—Aims, interests, changes since our last discussion/new aspects.
14. What are your feelings about the position and your future potential?

As with any counselling situation, follow-up is a very important aspect of appraisals. The meeting must produce a basis for future action. Following it up with subordinates shows that their conversation has been taken seriously and that an appraisal is meaningful, not just a formality.

Another important trend is operating in ongoing appraisal process which consists of three components such as regular feedback regarding day-to-day operations, periodic meetings in order to keep up-to-date, proactive communication regarding the broader and longer-term context; and formal annual appraisals for record keeping and managerial decision-making. Rather than waiting until the formal appraisal time rolls around, counselling skills can be used in continuing assessment, communication and trouble-shooting processes.

As organizations become more and more interested in avoiding costly turnover and initial job training, a greater emphasis will be placed on performance counselling as a means of retaining employees. Performance counselling is a difficult, intense task for a manager; it requires patience and the use of several particular skills. But it is well worth the effort. Over time it can enhance an employee's strengths, minimize weaknesses, and help the employee to realize his or her full potential, thereby benefiting the employee, the manager and the organization as a whole.

Human resource development professionals can help managers to become acquainted with and acquire the skills that are essential to effective counselling; and in the future they will be asked to provide this help more and more often. As they do so, they will not only provide a valuable service to organizations but will also promote their own credibility.

Other areas in which counselling skills are involved in managing performance are during pre-disciplinary meetings and grievance interviews.

11.6 Pre-disciplinary Action

The term pre-disciplinary is used because the use of counselling skills is not a substitute for disciplinary action. Instead, the use of counselling skills precedes, and is complementary to disciplinary action. Using counselling techniques at an earlier stage before initiating disciplinary action can often prevent the need for that action; using counselling skills along with the formal disciplinary procedure can help subordinates to take ownership of and responsibility for resolving the problem.

Personal problems, of course, should be allowed to remain private unless the person is willing to talk or the problem is adversely affecting their work. In fact, managers may feel uncomfortable about initiating a conversation with a subordinate whose work has not yet been very adversely affected by their problem. However, if attempting to tackle the problem early might avoid it's getting much worse, then giving it a try is worthwhile. Refer to Example 11.1.

EXAMPLE 11.1

A normally polite and pleasant customer service representative was known to have a personal problem, which was making him edgy and sharper than usual when dealing with people. This developed to the stage where his approach to the customer became unacceptable and the first step of discipline had to be taken. A counselling session set up by the individual's manager or supervisor when an enduring problem first became apparent would perhaps have prevented more drastic steps.

If the offer is rejected, do not push the subordinate. Simply point out that the situation cannot be allowed to continue indefinitely if it is having a negative effect on the company, and then continue to monitor performance. The manager can offer help again later on.

Pre-disciplinary counselling sessions fall into different categories— sometimes the manager has the facts, and at other times he has to do investigatory work. If he has the facts then he needs first to communicate the problem clearly and concisely. Then use the counselling skills to try to establish agreement on the existence of the problem, and to help the person to decide on courses of action. If the manager asks too many questions before sharing the reasons for the meeting, he will appear furtive.

Pre-disciplinary counselling sessions are difficult because of the emotional content. In response to the statement of the problem(s), the manager is likely to face an emotional outburst, denial of a problem or deflections away from his point.

The manager should use his counselling skills to listen to the person's emotional outburst and let them take their time. He should acknowledge their feelings and reflect back the emotional content. He should not make any judgments about their feelings, such as "you are right or wrong for feeling upset/angry", he should rather just say "you are upset/angry about that." In order to avoid getting caught up in deflections, the need to have a very clear idea of what the issue is and be sure to keep coming back to it.

Reflection can also be used in a pre-disciplinary situation to play back any ridiculous statements that subordinates make in defense of themselves. Often they will then admit they are not being straightforward. For example, if a subordinate with an absenteeism problem brings up her new puppy when the manager refers to her attendance record he could say, "Your puppy has stopped you from coming to work regularly over the past few months?" Then she is likely to realize what a weak excuse it sounded.

11.7 Grievance Interview

When a subordinate comes to the manager with a grievance, he can use a mixture of investigatory and counselling skills to get to the heart of the matter. If he treats the situation completely logically without using counselling skills (for example, 'just give me the facts') then he might miss important information, and also an opportunity to help the subordinate possibly to resolve the situation by a method other than following a formal grievance procedure. Sometimes after talking through a situation with a sympathetic listener, a subordinate will want to go away and think again about how to handle the situation.

11.8 Summary

Performance Management is a process of continuous improvement in business performance. The component of performance management system include objective setting, human resource planning, utilization of support and resources and ongoing appraisal system. While setting objectives both corporate and individual objectives should be kept in mind. Counselling skills are also needed in training, coaching and mentoring. They are also useful in human resource planning which also includes succession planning. During the appraisal process counselling would be required to provide feedback, solve the problem and motivate.

Performance counselling is an integral part of performance appraisal. To conduct the performance counselling certain conditions required are a general climate of openness and mutuality, a helpful and empathic attitude on the part of the managers, establishing an effective dialogue, a focus on work related goals, and avoidance of discussion about salary raises and other rewards. Some tips for effective counselling are given to enhance the process. Counselling can also be used as a part of pre-disciplinary action and grievance interview.

Chapter 12 identifies and discusses one of the major problems confronting the society in general and business organization in particular—Alcoholism and other Substance Abuse.

Review Questions

1. How does performance management system integrate into the framework of achieving overall business strategy? What are the components of Performance Management System?

2. What is the role of appraisal in performance management? What are its objectives? How can it be made more effective?

3. What is performance counselling? What are the conditions required for effective performance counselling? Give a few techniques to make this process more conducive for the subordinates in organizations.

4. How can counselling skills be used for a per-disciplinary action and a grievance redressal procedure?

Chapter 12

Alcoholism and Other Substance Abuse

The relationship of human beings to drugs is a long one, antedating recorded history. Drugs have been used for religious, medicinal, hedonistic and social purposes. Cultural and legal attitudes towards drugs vary. For example, a drug, such as alcohol may be highly exalted by one society (e.g., France) and at the same time prohibited by another (e.g., Libya); or another drug, such as cannabis may be widely used by one segment of a community and severely frowned upon by another part of it. Furthermore, over time a community's attitude toward a drug may reverse itself; for example, opiates were legally accepted in the United States prior to World War I and legally prohibited, except under strict regulation, after that time. The current drug problem all over the world is not a new phenomenon, although now it is more complex than it was previously.

The increased complexity of the drug problem is related to scientific advances in the field of pharmacology over the last thirty years. Society today has at its disposal drugs that cover the whole spectrum of human behaviour. Besides the contraceptive pill, we have others to sedate us when we are nervous, to excite us when we are sick, and to make us sick when we are well. Thus, on one hand, drugs can enhance our ability to function more effectively, but on the other side, they can carry our minds out of the realm of reality into loneliness, despair and hopelessness.

In discussing such an emotionally charged area as drugs, it is imperative to maintain a rational perspective. Miracle drugs of the antibiotic family (such as penicillin), steroids, insulin and other such sort of drugs have brought a revolution to the treatment of many of diseases affecting humans. Thus, drugs in a generic sense have achieved widespread acceptance in all countries, whether obtained by prescription or over the counter. The mass media in western society is filled with advertisements of chemical agents that will remedy many of our problems, whether they are body odour, headache, bad breath or digestive upset. Yet any drug or chemical agent can be misused with negative consequences to the individual and society. Fortunately, there are few drugs out of the thousands available that are consistently misused by any significant portion of the population (Pittman, 1974).

12.1   Drug Terminology

Much confusion surrounds the scientific and the social terminology used in reference to drugs. The first problem centres on the question, "What is addiction?" Authorities disagree as to what actually constitutes addiction, and as a result, which drugs are addictive.

One reason addiction continues to puzzle scientists is the multifaceted character of the phenomenon. Addiction to drugs (of which alcohol is one) is typically the result of many interacting factors. It is not just the effect of the drug on the person, but the social-psychological state of the individual that is crucial, i.e., how he or she reacts to the drug in his or her particular environment.

Since there are many different addictive drugs, and many factors influence a person's becoming addicted, it is difficult to discover any direct cause-effect relationship for addiction. Thus, it is not a sufficient reason to state that a person has become addicted to drugs because he or she took excessive amounts of a certain drug. One must also consider the drug in question, the laws regarding it, the society's attitude toward the chemical agent (which is not always reflected in the laws), the individual's attitude toward it, and the physical and psychological makeup of the individual. Stated differently, knowledge of the drug per se is necessary for understanding addiction, but it is not sufficient for a full comprehension of the pathology (Glatt, et al. 1967).

In drug research field four terms frequently appear: *addiction*, *habituation*, *dependence*, and *abuse or misuse*. These terms are not mutually exclusive, and there are frequent disagreements about their precise meaning as will be observed from the following discussion.

12.1.1   Addiction

There are three properties that a drug must have before it is considered addictive, i.e., it must produce tolerance, abstinence (withdrawal) syndrome, and craving. **Tolerance** means that the drug must be taken in progressively larger doses in order to achieve the desired result. Simplified, tolerance develops when a person taking one grain of drug A daily, finds that at the end of several weeks the drug no longer affects him or her in the same manner. He or she then increases the dosage to two grains daily. After a month or so, the person again realizes that drug A no longer produces the desired effect. He or she, therefore, increases the daily dosage to three grains, and so on.

If this person is suddenly prevented from taking any more of drug A, he or she experiences an **abstinence** syndrome. These symptoms vary from one drug to another and depend on the amount of drugs being taken. The abstinence syndrome is characterized by physical symptoms, such as stomach cramps, diarrhoea and irritability.

The person taking drug A starts developing a ***craving*** for the drug that is not only due to the physical effects that the drug has on his or her body but also due to fear of the abstinence syndrome. Two, he or she may develop a psychological craving that is not fully understood. Typically, many addicts who have been successfully withdrawn from a drug develop a strong desire to begin taking the drug again. This is one of several reasons why the relapse rate after treatment for addicts is extremely high.

12.1.2 Habituation

There are many habit-forming agents that some people use, such as coffee, tea and tobacco. Also some drugs are habit-forming. Simply stated, all addictive drugs are habit-forming, but not all habit-forming drugs are addictive in the pharmacological sense. Habituation is primarily psychological, as a physical abstinence syndrome does not develop when the agent is suddenly withdrawn from the individual. There are, however, habit-forming drugs, such as certain amphetamines, where tolerance does develop, but there is no abstinence syndrome. In short, habituation may consist of tolerance and craving (primarily psychological), but it is never followed by an abstinence syndrome.

12.1.3 Dependence

In 1964, the World Health Organization released a report published by its expert committee on drugs which combined the terms *addition* and *habituation* under one term, *dependence*. This committee felt that the scientific literature reflected much confusion between addiction and habituation, and as a result, the classification of a drug as addictive or habit-forming was difficult. The WHO Committee suggested that each drug should be described by its particular type of dependence, for example, "drug dependence of the alcohol type". Thus, the substitution of the word *dependence* for both addiction and habituation is an attempt to clarify drug terminology.

12.1.4 Abuse or Misuse

Almost all drugs that have been produced for medical or scientific use as well as beverage like alcohol have their consumption controlled by legal statutes. People, who use drugs illegally or for some purpose other than that for which the drug was commonly designed or in a manner other than prescribed by the physician, are said to be abusing the drug. Generally speaking, people who are dependent on drugs are also abusing them. However, there are some people who take drugs but never become dependent upon them. In a nutshell, persons who use drugs for other than the generally accepted reasons or who take them illegally but are not dependent on them are classified as **drug abusers** or **misusers**.

12.2 Concepts of Alcoholism

Fundamental to any discussion of alcoholism are the orientations held by various researchers and clinicians to this condition. The World Health Organization defines alcoholism as, Alcoholics are those excessive drinkers whose dependence upon alcohol has reached such a degree that it results in noticeable mental disturbance or in an interference with their bodily and mental health, their interpersonal relations, their smooth social and economic functioning, or those who show the signs of such developments.

The American Medical Association defines alcoholism as an illness characterized by significant impairment of physiological, psychological or social functioning that is directly associated with persistent and excessive alcohol use.

The late Professor Jellinek differentiated the species of alcoholism into five major types; namely, alpha, beta, gamma, delta and epsilon, indicating that the types of alcoholism vary in frequency in reference to the cultural context. However, a major schism in reference to the concept of alcoholism exists in North America.

There are two concepts regarding alcoholism. First that alcoholism is a symptom of an underlying mental condition, defect, or pathology (this position is sometimes reflected in the statement that alcoholism is a mental disease); or second that alcoholism is a chronic illness. The symptom orientation develops from psychoanalytic theory and has permeated the psychiatric and social work professions in particular. A telling critique of this position is found in the article on social workers' attitudes toward alcoholics by Bailey and Fuchs (1960), who state:

> *It seems possible that there is a relationship between the pessimism and frustration of these social workers and their tendency to regard alcoholism as a symptom rather than a disease. The helping person's concept of the nature of alcoholism will determine the orientation of his therapeutic efforts. If he regards alcoholism as a symptom then the treatment program will be designed to resolve the underlying emotional problem. This position is entirely logical, but in practice it resembles searching for the causes of a fire while the blaze itself goes unchecked.*

There is a further logical extension of the alcoholism as a symptom orientation that is rarely verified clinically. If alcoholism is caused by underlying psychopathology, a resolution of this conflict by the patient in a therapeutic context should allow the individual with his or her revised personality to return to normal or social drinking. This phenomenon, as we know, rarely occurs; therefore, we should critically evaluate the merit of this unadulterated psychoanalytic position in reference to our concept of alcoholism.

The competing view is that alcoholism is a chronic disease, the etiology of which is not yet established. Alcoholism is caused due to prolonged intake of alcohol in toxic quantities and due to this certain biochemical, physiologic, metabolic or genetic defects in the organism result, which are hypothesised as possible etiologic factors.

The disease concept of alcoholism, however, has implications for treatment process. When the alcoholic is viewed as suffering from a chronic illness, general practitioners and internists begin to assume more responsibility for the patient's case instead of providing blanket psychiatric referral. Hospital staffs, because they are prepared for the chronic nature of such illnesses as heart disease, ulcerative colitis and gastric ulcers, can better accept the relapses of alcoholics. Just as crucial is the fact that the sick role can be a signed to the alcoholic instead of a role that has overtones of moral responsibility.

Despite the pervasiveness of the disease and symptom viewpoints toward alcoholism, the counsellors should not overlook the possibility of other orientations toward this condition. For example, alcoholism may be a secondary disorder that results from the convergence of an array of intrapsychic tensions, normative orientations toward drinking, and alternative mechanisms of tension reduction.

Unfortunately, the line between alcohol abuse and alcoholism in individuals is sometimes difficult for the clinicians to discern. Almost all diagnosed alcoholics invariably have specific medical, social, and psychological problems. On the other hand, not all individuals who have specific problems show the consequence of drinking beverage alcohol are alcoholic. Perhaps this is most apparent in some individuals who are arrested for driving while intoxicated. Some of these persons are only social drinkers who become intoxicated and are imprudent enough to operate a motor vehicle. Thus, all individuals who have problems vis-à-vis the use of alcohol should not be diagnosed as alcoholics.

12.2.1 How is Alcoholism Diagnosed?

Doctors may overlook the possibility of alcoholism in a patient. Symptoms such as memory loss might be the result of ageing rather than a symptom of alcoholism. Because alcoholism usually involves denial, alcoholics may tell their doctors about related medical complaints, but hide their alcohol abuse.

If alcoholism is suspected, the doctor will take a medical history and ask questions about the patient's use of alcohol and its effects on his life and people close to him. If answers to those questions suggest alcoholism, the doctor may perform a short screening test using a standardized questionnaire. A history may be obtained from his family or friends if he is reluctant or unable to answer questions.

The consulting doctor will also perform a physical examination to look for medical problems associated with alcohol abuse. Laboratory tests may be performed, including various tests of blood and urine. A toxicology screen or measurement of blood alcohol level will confirm recent alcohol ingestion. This doesn't confirm alcoholism, however, because these tests show recent alcohol consumption, not long-term usage. Other blood tests measure the size of red blood cells, which increase with long-term alcohol use, and a factor called carbohydrate-deficient transferrin, which may indicate heavy alcohol consumption. Liver enzyme changes, such as a high level of gammaGT, are an indication of chronic alcohol intake.

12.2.2 How is Alcoholism Treated?

Only 15 percent of alcoholics seek treatment. Most alcoholics undergo screening or start treatment reluctantly because they are in denial about their disease. Often alcoholics agree for treatment only after their family, friends or doctor persuades them to do so. Intervention is a process whereby concerned people close to the alcoholic step in and make a concerted effort to help the person accept the need for treatment. If a person is considering intervention for a friend or family member, he should first discuss how best to go about it with a professional experienced in this area. An alcoholic cannot be forced to get help except under certain circumstances, such as when his behaviour results in crime or following a medical emergency.

The first step in treatment is to determine whether the person seeking treatment is alcohol-dependent. If he is an alcoholic then complete abstinence (cutting out alcohol altogether) is always necessary for successful recovery.

Alcoholism usually requires treatment programmes that include medical supervision and counselling. Treatment may involve an outpatient programme or a residential inpatient stay.

A typical treatment programme includes:

Detoxification and Withdrawal: Detoxification, which takes about four to seven days, involves the withdrawal of alcohol in a supervised setting. Tranquilizers called benzodiazepines (e.g., Valium or Librium) are often prescribed to control withdrawal symptoms. These are most common in the first five days after stopping alcohol.

Recovery Programmes: Recovery or rehabilitation programmes provide support after detoxification to maintain abstinence from alcohol. Counselling, psychological support and medical care are usually available within these programmes. Education about the disease and its effects is part of the therapy. Many of the professional staff involved in rehabilitation centres are recovered alcoholics who serve as role models.

Medical Assessment and Treatment: Medical assessment and treatment of common medical problems associated with alcoholism also needs to be carried under the care of an expert physician. Some of the alcohol related medical disorders include obesity, blood pressure, diabetes and heart related disorders.

Psychological Support and Psychiatric Treatment: Group and individual counselling and therapy encourage recovery from the psychological aspects of alcoholism. An important aspect of counselling and treatment is to recognize and modify behaviour patterns that cause a person to drink. Depression or other underlying mood disorders should be treated concurrently. Because alcoholism also creates adverse impact on people close to the alcoholic, involvement of the family is essential for effective recovery.

Emphasis on Acceptance and Abstinence: Effective treatment is impossible unless a patient accepts that he is addicted and cannot afford to risk drinking.

Drug Treatments: In addition to tranquilizers given to help the patient move through safely through the withdrawal stage, a second type of medication is used to help him remain sober. An alcohol-sensitizing drug, disulfiram (Antabuse), produces a physical reaction that includes flushing, nausea and headaches in case one drinks. Naltrexone (ReVia or Depade) is a new drug that blocks the alcohol 'high', and reduces the urge to drink. This medication lessens the craving for alcohol and helps prevent relapses.

Additional Ongoing Support: Even if alcoholics have been sober for a long time, they may relapse and must continue to avoid alcohol. Many recovering alcoholics and their families find that joining support groups, most notably Alcoholics Anonymous (AA), is an essential part of coping with the disease. AA is a self-help group of recovering alcoholics that offers emotional support and an effective model of abstinence. A doctor or counsellor can refer the patient to an AA group, which is also listed in the phone book and local newspapers and on the Internet.

General Health Improvement: And last but not the least eating a balanced diet with vitamin supplements and doing regular exercise are important as far as improving health is concerned.

12.2.3 What is the Outcome of Alcoholism?

Treatment programmes have varying success rates. Studies show that only a few alcoholics remain sober one year after treatment, while others have periods of sobriety alternating with relapses. Many alcoholics relapse several times, but this does not mean that a patient cannot eventually achieve long-term sobriety. The longer one abstains from alcohol, the more likely he is to remain sober. He may feel a desire for alcohol throughout his life, however. Some alcoholics are unable to stop drinking for any length of time.

Alcoholism is a major social, economic and public health problem and reason for over half of all unnatural deaths and almost half of all traffic fatalities. A high percentage of suicides involve the use of alcohol in combination with other substances. Additional deaths are related to long-term medical complications associated with the disease. The life-span of an alcoholic is shortened by an average of 15 years, as a result of the various complications of the disease.

If a person stops drinking, alcohol-associated health problems can often be controlled or prevented. However, some kinds of damage, such as to the liver or pancreas, may be permanent and even fatal.

12.3   Alcohol Abuse and Industry

The relationship between alcohol abuse and alcoholism and decreased industrial productivity is an intimate one. Although statistics are not precise, between 4 and 8 percent of the work force are alcoholics; they cost business around billions of rupees yearly in poor job performance, accidents, absenteeism, inaccurate decisions at all levels of the business command, and related costs.

Alcohol abusers are found at all levels of management and in all positions in the general work force of a company. No industry can make the statement, as some still do, that they have no alcoholic employees or executives. The same fact is true of labour unions, whether it be their hierarchy or mass membership.

Business has a unique ability to increase alcoholism rehabilitation activities, generally under the terms of the 'employee assistance programmes' or the 'troubled employee programmes'. These endeavours, which carry the implicit fear of the loss of job unless the worker or executive does something about his or her alcohol problem, have had recovery rates for the participants of 60 to 80 percent.

The first industrial programme to deal with alcoholic workers within the rehabilitation framework was instituted by the Du Pont Corporation as part of company policy, followed later by Eastman Kodak Corporation. But the old company policies of firing alcoholics or denying that they existed, the trade union's position of covering up the indiscretions of the alcoholic, and the military's reluctance to state that alcoholics were in the Armed Forces were slow to wither away. Now these traditions of denial of alcoholism in the work force have begun to collapse at an accelerating rate. In the past few years major 'troubled employee programmes', serving mainly alcoholics, have commenced with such activities as the jointly sponsored General Motors-United Automobile Workers programme covering 400,000 workers, the Department of Defence's announcement in 1972 of a rehabilitation program for all military personnel, and the United States Congressional mandate in 1970 that the Civil Service Commission would establish alcoholism treatment programs for all federal civilian employees.

The impact of these 'employee assistance programmes' will mean that more individuals will obtain help for their alcoholism probably long before they reach the terminal phase of their illness. However, the doctors and the counsellors should not assume that such programmes solve the primary problems of the prevention of alcoholism, which are anchored in general cultural and social attitudes toward alcohol use in the society, possible genetic predisposition and psychological variables.

12.3.1   Symptoms of Alcohol Users

Some of the symptoms of alcohol users at workplace are:

1. The alcoholics are frequently absent from the job, especially on

Friday and Monday mornings because of late partying and suffering from hangover in the mornings.

2. They generally come to work with alcohol on their breath.
3. While in the office, they have a tendency to sit behind the closed doors, as they want to avoid their colleagues or superiors who may be trying to help them out.
4. They would go a great length to hide their problems from other people.
5. Their moods are generally unpredictable and they get irritated at the slightest of provocation.
6. When someone at the workplace tries to point out their errors to them, they generally turn hostile or defensive and try to cover up for their problems.

As a result of all these behaviours the quality and quantity of their work starts suffering.

12.3.2 Recommendation for Alcohol Users

Few recommendations for the alcohol users are:

1. Don't play good guy or good friend with the alcohol users, as then they would try to hide their habit all the more and avoid discussing it.
2. Whenever a doctor or a counsellor should decide to try to discuss the issue with the problem employee, they should try to have facts in their hands. They should try to have specific evidence in the form of right information otherwise the patient or the client will try to defend it.
3. The doctor or the counsellor should be firm in their approach, but positive. Organization wants the competent employees to stay and employees need the job. When dealing with the alcoholics, the doctors and the counsellors should state firmly the following:

   • there is a problem
   • the problem has been recognized
   • it is affecting the job performance
   • the employee will no longer be allowed to continue to work under present circumstances
   • the treatment for the problem is present

   Don't lecture, moralize or argue. Let the facts speak for themselves. Send one message clearly to the person that if he or she continues with the same sort of behaviour, he or she may lose his or her job eventually.
4. The doctor or the counsellor should give him or her reasonable time to recover, as the path to correction is not an overnight trip. But a definite time period has to be decided in which either the employee has to accept the help or has to resign from the job. Maintain

understanding with firmness. There may be relapses in some cases. But if the boss has given the errant employee a warning of terminating his or her job, in case if he or she continues to misbehave, he should take the warning seriously.

12.3.3   Symptoms of Drug Users

Some of the symptoms of drug users at workplace are:

1. The performance of the drug user continues to go down consistently. His or her performance becomes less and less effective as the duration of addiction increases.
2. He or she is frequently found be absent from the job or is generally late with a good excuse.
3. The drug user may make or receive innumerable phone calls to try to contact the supplier or other users for his regular supply of the drugs.
4. He or she makes countless visit to the washrooms.
5. The mood of the drug user is generally very erratic and unpredictable.

12.3.4   Recommendation for Drug Users

Few recommendations for the drug users are:

1. Insist that the drug user should get the help as the situation worsens if timely action is not taken.
2. A manager should ask the addict to seek professional help. He should not try to counsel him or her as he is not qualified to render the special services which the addict requires.
3. A manager should advice a change in the job assignment of the addict. Drug addiction is sometimes found to be an escapist behaviour. Individual may get addicted to it to avoid heavy job demands or to escape the competition he or she faces or the inability to meet the taxing deadlines. The counsellor should suggest redesigning the job.

12.4   The Counsellor's Role

Counsellors work with alcohol and drug-related problems in both educational, industrial and community settings. Depending on the particular setting and role and responsibilities, counsellors should be prepared to offer services with three primary thrusts. The first thrust of the counsellor's service should be on *prevention* of drug abuse and for this he should organize a drug education programme. The counsellor must be informed regarding all aspects of drug use and abuse and should be prepared to present accurate information about drug usage. Many new drug-related curricula and instructional media are available. As part of a 'drug education programme' counsellors may choose to organize peer group activities in which experts speak about drug related problems with the employees in the organization. Drop-in, 'rap', or informational centres are also possibilities. These centres can be staffed by the counsellor or by trained employees.

The second major thrust of the counsellor's service should be *therapeutic*. It is essential that the counsellor who is providing counselling for individuals with drug-related problems have a grasp on the pharmacology involved. Drug abuse is often accompanied by other personal, psychological and emotional problems, however, and the counsellor's therapeutic skills are essential in establishing a climate that allows all aspects of the client's functioning to be discussed. Frykman (1971) has emphasized the importance of confidentiality, patience, acceptance, support and trust in counselling youth about drugs.

A third major thrust is for the counsellor to become *sensitive* to the impact of alcohol and drug abuse on the day-to-day functioning of individuals. School counsellors, career counsellors, marriage and family counsellors, and counsellors in various other roles need to become aware of the characteristics of the drug abuser so that they can more readily identify those who are in need of specialized treatment. Related to this is the need for counsellors to be aware of the treatment programmes available in their communities, so that appropriate referrals can be made.

In conclusion, the rapidly increasing use of drugs and alcohol in this country is a national concern that requires innovative programmes, both preventive and therapeutic. Counsellors working in both educational, organizational and community settings should be prepared to respond to drug-related problems with sensitivity, understanding, and valid information if they are to play a primary role in fighting the drug problem in our society.

12.5 Summary

Alcoholism and drug abuse are major problems confronting the business organizations today. The different drug terminologies, which are used to define this problem, include addiction, habituation, dependence and abuse or misuse. Alcoholism needs to be diagnosed and treated immediately in organizations. A typical treatment programme includes detoxification and withdrawal, recovery programme, medical assessment and treatment, psychological support, emphasis on abstinence, drug treatment, ongoing support and general health improvement.

The outcome of alcoholism has major social, economic and public health impact and billion of rupees are lost due to this problem. Organizations have to resort to alcoholism rehabilitation activities with the help of employee assistance programme. Different symptoms of alcohol users and drug user and recommendation to deal with these are discussed. The counsellor's role in such instances can be preventive, therapeutic and being sensitive to the needs of the patient.

Chapter 13 highlights the ethical issues related to counselling services.

Review Questions

1. The usage of drugs for prevention and cure of illnesses has been existing for a long time. How does this usage become an abuse? Discuss the terms associated with misuse of drugs.

2. What is alcoholism? Discuss the ways by which alcoholism can be diagnosed. What are its symptom and what recommendations can be given by a counsellor to an alcoholic?

3. What are the symptoms of a drug user? What recommendations can be given by a counsellor to a drug addict?

4. Discuss the counsellor's role in prevention and cure of alcoholism and drug abuse.

Chapter 13

Ethics in Counselling

Effective counselling requires that a client be capable of self-disclosure and self-exploration and motivated to change attitudes and behaviours. Successful counselling also demands skilled, empathic and trustworthy counsellors to guide and support the client through the change process. Counsellors, who violate their clients' trust, are insensitive to clients' needs and values, use their power exploitatively or experiment with counselling interventions for which they have no training or experience are acting unethically. In each of these situations, the counsellor is not working according to the best interests of the client, the highest priority, and is instead serving some other purpose—usually self-interest. Whenever this happens, the counsellor's behaviour is defined as unethical. For example, suppose a counsellor named Sonia shares confidential information from Mukesh's counselling session with friends at a party because it makes such a funny story, Sonia is putting her own needs to impress her friends ahead of Mukesh's welfare and she is also humiliating her client publicly, though in his absence. One partygoer may recognize the client's name and decide not to offer the client a job, or another may repeat the story so that eventually Mukesh hears it from some stranger and feels betrayed by the counsellor he trusted. Mukesh may even resolve never to visit another helping professional again, regardless of his distress. In several ways, then, negative effects may come to a client when the counsellor's self-interest is placed above the client's welfare.

Counsellors have two other broad ethical obligations, i.e., to be loyal to the institution that employs them and to promote the good reputation of the counselling profession. Sonia, the talkative counsellor, not only violated the interests of her client but also tarnished the reputation of the counselling profession and undoubtedly violated the rules of the counselling service for which she works. Others who heard her story at the party may conclude that this is typical behaviour for professional counsellors in general or for those who work at that agency. As a result, they, too, may be reluctant to seek counselling for themselves or recommend it to others. This example represents a rather obvious breach of ethics that all responsible helping professionals would condemn, but other counsellor behaviours are not so easily identified as ethical or unethical.

The following cases illustrate more complicated dilemmas that require more than good intentions and good sense to resolve ethically:

1. A counsellor's spouse's boss asks the counsellor to see her disturbed college going son in counselling because he is confused and lonely. The spouse is being considered for a promotion. The counsellor works at the college the son attends.

2. The parents of a tenth grader see a school counsellor because they want her to counsel their son, who is dating a girl of another caste. They say they're old-fashioned and believe that people should stay with their own kind.

3. A seventy-nine-year-old man sees a counsellor because he wants to maintain his own home, but his children and neighbours insist that he can no longer take care of the property. He threatens suicide if he loses his home but admits to having some problems with independent living.

4. A colleague at a counselling agency routinely uses diagnostic categories more severe than the client's actual difficulties to get the most insurance reimbursement possible and give clients the full benefit of counselling.

5. A counselling session with an adult client ends at dinnertime. This client came to the counsellor because of difficulties in social assertiveness. He asks the counsellor to join him for dinner at his parents' restaurant.

In each of these dilemmas, it is not easy to discern what really promotes the welfare of the client, the employer or the profession. The counsellor who 'fudges' diagnoses for insurance purposes appears to be attempting to promote the welfare of her clients. But is she really? The person who counsels the boss's son may truly help him in his life choices. Should the personal connection with this young man stop the counselling from taking place? After all, the connection to this young man comes only through the counsellor's spouse. Would accepting the client's dinner invitation facilitate trust in counselling and reward the client's social assertiveness, thereby helping the client, or would it jeopardize the counsellor's objectivity and therefore risk harm to the client? This chapter sorts out these and other ethical dilemmas by discussing the ethical standards and principles that underlie the counselling profession and make counsellors better equipped to act responsibly in such situations.

13.1 Making Ethical Decisions

Ethical decision-making is a process which requires integral trait, like moral courage, integrity and a sound character in addition to the knowledge and skills required to carry out the task effectively (Welfel, 2006). Generally, counsellors operate with their personal ethical standards and guidelines rather than following any established set of rules. Sometimes in a given situation there are no 'best' solutions which create a dilemma for the counsellor in terms of being ethical or moral (Swanson, 1983). In such situations a lot of ethical concerns arise that lead to heightened anxiety, doubt, hesitation and confusion in determining their conduct. Unfortunately, when they act, their behaviour may turn out to be unethical, because it is not grounded on ethical code or it is grounded in only part of a code that they have extracted to justify their behaviour.

Hayman and Covert (1986) in their research identified five major dilemmas that counsellors have to encounter while being in the process of counselling. These are:

(a) Confidentiality
(b) Role conflict
(c) Credentials and competence of counsellor
(d) Conflicting relationship with employer or institution
(e) Danger in a situation

The conclusions drawn from the research proved that the element of danger in the situation were the easiest to resolve but the one's dealing with the counsellor's level of confidentiality and conflicting roles were the most difficult to resolve. The astonishing finding was that less than one third of the counsellor respondents conceded to rely on published professional codes of ethics while trying to overcome the dilemmas. Most of the counsellors had a tendency to rely on 'common sense', which can prove to be unethical and at best unwise.

Therefore, it is suggested that counsellors should be aware of the codes and principles of ethics by referring to books, write ups on ethics and experience of senior professionals from the same area to be able to handle any form of confusion, dilemma and ambiguity (Welfel, 2006). These resources come to the rescue of counsellors in situations of controversies, like taking extra money, indulging in multiple relationships, and working with clients whose value systems do not match with the value system of the counsellor.

While making ethical decisions, keeping the context in mind, counsellors should take decisions which seem to be professionally appropriate (Tennyson and Strom, 1986). Certain ethical principles which could guide the decisions of counsellor are:

13.1.1 Beneficence (doing good for others)

This ethical principle, beneficence, is at the core of the profession. As members of a profession whose justification for existence is to do good for others, counsellors have deeper ethical responsibilities than ordinary friends or confidants who receive no payment for their trust and do not purport to have any special training in counselling. Counsellors publicize themselves as expert helpers, and people therefore, come to seek their help precisely at those moments when they think the support of loved ones won't be sufficient to help or when they are desperate to get out of a situation they can't cope with. Counsellors must do all they can to help. Moreover, counsellors' status as paid professional helpers means that leaving clients at the end of counselling in the same place where they began is also inconsistent with counsellors' role. Sometimes counsellors try to project their skills and competence to a degree that does not match with reality. They exaggerate their abilities to handle clients with all kinds of emotional disturbances. In a way, they falsely advertise their expertise. Of course, there are times when counselling has negative outcomes. What is important in these cases is to ensure whether the counsellor did all within his or her control to assist the client. Counsellors need to ask a question, "Is this course of action likely to benefit the client?" to ensure that the particular course of action is ethical or not?

13.1.2 Non-maleficence (not harming others)

The ethical principle in the form of taking the responsibility to not to worsen the state of the client by reckless action or incompetence of the counsellor is 'non-maleficence'. This principle is also at the foundation of biomedical ethics (Beauchamp and Childress, 1994). Some have argued that it is the most fundamental ethical principle guiding all human service professions. Precisely because counsellors profess to be helping professional, they have a duty not to make a client worse if this outcome is avoidable. In the past, scholars thought that counselling was not a risky activity; they admitted that it did not always help but suggested that it could not really hurt a client either (Eysenck, 1952). More recent evidence has overwhelmingly contradicted that perception (Hubble, Duncan, and Miller, 1999; Lambert and Barley, 2002; Seligman, 1995). Counselling and therapy can are very powerful tools which could be either used to benefit the client or even to harm him or her substantially. It is one of the major responsibilities of the counsellor to assess the problems of the clients accurately, to choose their strategies properly and also evaluate the outcome of these processes on the client effectively. It is this ethical principle that underlies the statements in the ethics codes about practising within the 'limits of one's competence', that is, dealing with client problems with which one has been trained and using counselling strategies with which one is skilled unless under supervision. This ethical principle is also at the core of the requirement that clients not be exposed to research or experimental treatments with high risk and little hope of real benefit. Thus, in addition to evaluating the ethicalness of an action, it is also important to identify that no harm is done to the client in the process.

13.1.3 Autonomy (respecting freedom of choice of others)

Respect for autonomy is an individual's right to self-determination. Individuals have a right to think as they wish, even if others don't like their choices. Autonomy must be respected, with two restrictions. First, the right of an individual ends where others' rights begin. In other words, a person's freedom is only to the extent of his or her jurisdiction, and should not invade into other person's territory. Second, respect for autonomy assumes that individuals are capable of understanding the implication and consequences of the choices they make. This ability to comprehend the meaning of choices is called competence. Society gives a little autonomy to children because, at their developmental level, they are unlikely to understand the implications of their choices. Similarly, the autonomy of people with severe organic brain damage or psychotic episodes and not oriented to reality can also be restricted because these individuals are at least temporarily unaware of the meaning and consequences of their choices.

Let us again return to the example of the aging man (as discussed at the beginning of the chapter) to illustrate the role of respect for autonomy in resolving ethical dilemmas. The principle of 'Autonomy' suggests that the person has a right to live wherever he wants to live, if he understands the meaning of the choice. His choice need not be logical or even in his ultimate best interest as long as he understands its meaning. In this case then, the principle of autonomy obligates the counsellor to first evaluate the man's competence to make autonomous choices. If the man is competent, then the counsellor must respect his choice as a priority, even if the counsellor doesn't approve of it. The issue is not whether the counsellor should decide for him what is best, but rather how the counsellor can help him to live the way he wishes with the least possible risk to him and help him resolve the conflicts with those worried about him. Counsellors need to avoid acting paternalistically, that is, in the role of a parent who knows better than the adult client. Potential conflicts are in the areas of women's rights, abortion rights and social justice. A client may believe that wives should be submissive to their husbands in all things, and the counsellor may believe in equality between marital partners. The principle of autonomy suggests that it would be inappropriate for the counsellor to impose his or her ideologies or philosophies on the client or force the clients to get to see the 'hings in their way, which is the right way'. Client's beliefs and values can and do change during counselling. The issue is not whether the counsellor helps the client explore beliefs that are troubling, but rather whose agenda it is to explore those beliefs. If the client freely chooses to focus on values and is free to come to an independent decision based on the exploration, the counsellor can ethically explore these delicate subjects.

13.1.4 Justice (being fair)

The fourth ethical principle is justice, or fairness. Justice is a value at the core of democratic societies, and it demands that people be treated equally and that judgment about counselling goals and strategies must be based on the individual characteristics of the client, and not on discriminatory attitudes toward groups. Stereotyping and bias are unethical because they are unjust, regardless of whether the discriminatory attitudes are conscious or not. Justice demands that it is highly inappropriate for the counsellors to give differential treatment to their clients based on their hierarchy or status. Thus, when evaluating whether an action is ethical or not, a counsellor needs to ask whether that action is based on any factor other than the unique needs of the individual.

The principle of justice also helps guide the counsellor in responding to the parents of the college graduate who don't want their son dating a girl of a different caste, one of the examples presented at the beginning of this chapter. If the counsellor learns that the only attribute of the young women the parents find offensive is her caste, then justice demands that the counsellor refrain from involving himself in the situation in the way he wants. Counsellors cannot allow themselves to be put into the service of discrimination. The counsellor may work with the family to foster communication and help resolve the conflict, but to agree to try to dissuade the boy from dating the girl on the basis of her caste is unethical. Justice also demands that counsellors display respectful and unbiased attitudes when counselling client who are different in culture, background, lifestyle, or gender. This principle also requires counsellors to use counselling strategies appropriate to the culture of the client.

13.1.5 Fidelity (being faithful)

The fifth ethical principle is fidelity. One helpful way to think about the principle of fidelity is to use of the term 'promise keeping'. Counselling professional are taught attitudes and skills that help build the client's trust and encourage his or her self-disclosure. Promoting trust is the counsellor's main goal in initial counselling sessions because self-disclosure and trust are critical to the success of the counselling process. Once the counsellor has gained the client's trust, he or she becomes a powerful person who can do harm to the client. Because the counsellor engages in a set of actions designed for the sole purpose of promoting trust, it is particularly despicable when that trust is betrayed. When counselling begins, counsellors implicitly promise not to divulge what a client tells them unless there is some overwhelming reason that is ultimately in the client's or society's best interests. Research suggests that most clients assume that the counsellor will always maintain confidentiality about their discussions and will not share it with anyone (Miller and Thelen, 1986). However, confidentiality becomes limited based on the problem at hand. For example, if the counsellor gets to know about the child or the adult abuse that the client is going through, it would be harmful to keep this information confidential. Further, in the course of discussion, if the counsellor gets to know that the client is a source of threat either to self or to someone other; the information is required to be divulged to significant people in this situation. In addition, if a court orders a counsellor to testify about a client, confidentiality cannot be maintained. Thus, before clients disclose such information, they need to know the consequences of their disclosure.

Another way to think of fidelity is to use the word 'loyalty'. The principle of fidelity demands that counsellors be loyal to clients, to employers, and to the profession. Thus, current ethical standards prohibit the abandonment of a client in the midst of counselling. Clearly, there are good reasons why a counsellor may need to terminate counselling before the scheduled time. In these situation, however, the principle of fidelity assumes that the client be provided with appropriate referrals to be faithful to the initial promise to provide help. The principle of fidelity is also the reason why the codes of ethics include statements about responsibilities to employers and fellow professionals. To be ethical, counsellors must be faithful to the mission of their employer unless that mission interferes with the best interests of the clients. After all, counsellors accept salaries and other benefits from their employer with the implied promise to do what the employer expects. Similarly, counsellors enjoy the benefits of the professional status, so they must be loyal to the profession as well. Thus when trying to decide on the ethics of an action, the counsellor must ask, "Is this choice in keeping with the promises I have made, either implied or explicit?"

Personal Reflection

When have you acted in a way to avoid harm (non-maleficence)? When have you acted in a way that promoted good (beneficence)?

Using the ethical principles, think about the following case:

THE CASE OF SONAM

Sonam is a 49-year-old executive with a sports goods manufacturing company and has lived a full and rewarding life. She has won many recognitions and rewards in different types of competitions that she took part both as student as well as a working executive. She is associated with many charitable institutions, and has devoted a major portion of her time and money for the noble causes. As a part of her philanthropic attitude she has also adopted two orphan, children and is raising them up as her own. She has been diagnosed with advanced cancer recently, for which treatment is rarely successful. Therefore, she has decided to not to go for a complicated treatment, but live the fullest quality of life she can in the months available to her. She has come to counselling not because of worries about herself, but because of concerns about how her growing children and other family members will cope with her impending death. In the course of the conversation, she reveals to her counsellor that she intends to end her own life when the pain becomes intolerable and she becomes a burden to her children. She wants to save her family from watching her suffer even more than she wants to avoid the suffering herself. She asks the counsellor to help her family adjust to her illness and her choice about the end of her life.

> **FOR FURTHER THOUGHT**
> 1. Based on these facts, how do you think the counsellor should respond to Sonam's request for service under the circumstances?
> 2. How can the ethical principles and ethics codes help the counsellor decide what to do?
> 3. What emotions do you think the counsellor will experience as he or she wrestles with this request?
> 4. Discuss your responses with a fellow student to compare the factors each of you found most salient and most difficult in this case.

EDUCATING COUNSELLORS IN ETHICAL DECISION-MAKING

Counsellors need to be educated in making ethical decisions. They can be imparted training in ethics and the principles governing ethical decisions. These kinds of training to the prospective or existing counsellors may be instrumental in bringing significant changes in their attitudes and the level of awareness regarding the ethical concerns in the counselling profession (Coll, 1993).

Van House and Paradise (1979) have suggested a five stage developmental model to govern the ethical behaviours of counsellors. These are:

1. *Punishment orientation:* With this orientation, the counsellor measures his behaviour with certain external standards and is likely to be punished if found violating these standards.

2. *Institutional orientation:* Counsellors with this orientation follow the rules and regulation of the organization which employs them. They are not likely to challenge the system and base their decisions on these rules.

3. *Societal orientation:* Counsellors with this orientation, base decisions on societal standards. In case of a dilemma between the gain of an individual and the gain of the society, the society is always given priority.

4. *Individual orientation:* This orientation gives priority to individual needs. Though the counsellors are concerned about the system and its rules, but are mainly governed by the individual interests.

5. *Principle (conscience) orientation:* In this orientation, the internalized ethical standards take the priority and none of the external considerations are relevant.

13.2 Common Ethical Violations by Mental Health Professionals

Over the last two decades, much information has been gathered regarding the ethical practice of mental health professionals. Research has been conducted, and licensing boards and ethics committees have published summaries of the complaints presented to them each year. Taken together, these data provide a fairly clear picture of the kinds of ethical difficulties most frequently encountered by helping professionals. Ethics committees deal overwhelmingly with one type of ethics violation, such as dual relationships with clients, especially sexual intimacies with current or former clients. This violation is particularly troubling because of the clear evidence of harm coming to clients who have been sexually exploited by their counsellors (Bounhoutsos, et al., 1993). This kind of behaviour has been termed as a form of sexual assault and compared with incest in its devastating effects on clients (Pope, 1994). The personal difficulties that brought these clients to counselling in the first place are not cured; indeed, they are often worsened. Moreover, such clients often become averse to getting the therapy they need because of their victimization by a counsellor. So troubling are the consequences of sexual exploitation by mental health professionals that the American Psychological Association has published a brochure intended to help clients learn about their rights.

Counsellors are human, so it is not surprising that they sometimes feel sexual attraction toward a client. Experiencing such attraction is not unethical in itself. What is unethical is acting on it. The first step for a counsellor who experiences sexual feelings for a client is to consult with a supervisor or colleague to discuss the case and decide on an appropriate course of action. The frank discussion about the attraction is often sufficient to help the counsellor attend to the client's concerns. If the consultation does not refocus the counsellor's attention, referring the client to another counsellor is usually the wisest choice. If sexual attraction to clients happens persistently and frequently, the counsellor should seek counselling to better understand the personal issues that may be provoking this reaction. Obviously, a counsellor who is having persistent sexual thoughts about a client is likely to be distracted from the client's needs and concerns. Sometimes counsellors have responded to their attraction to a client by terminating the counselling relationship, referring the client to another professional, and then beginning social relationship with that former client. Such a 'solution' to the problem of sexual attraction to a client is unethical. The fact that counselling has officially ended does not immediately change the client's perception of the counsellor as a professional or diminish the problems that provoked that client to seek counselling in the first place.

Non-sexual dual relationships account for another large category of misconduct. Counsellors who borrow money from clients, employ their clients in their practices, or begin a close personal relationship with a current client have all been found guilty of misconduct. In such cases, the counsellor jeopardized the client's welfare by embarking on the additional personal contact with the client.

Other breaches of ethics that commonly come to the attention of licensing boards include other forms of unprofessional conduct (such as using counselling sessions to discuss the counsellor's problems), unethical billing practices, incompetent practice, fraudulent application for license, violations of confidentiality, misrepresentation of competence and violations relating to reporting of child abuse (Welfel, 1998). Pope and Vetter (1992) surveyed psychologists about the kinds of ethical issues they encountered in their work. Those who responded to the survey reported more ethical dilemmas about confidentiality than about any other issue. They expressed concerns about how and when to disclose confidential information and how to respond when one client has several caregivers or the same professional has clients who know each other. In addition, they also described ethical dilemmas about the definition of dual relationships that are not sexual and about payment, insurance, and the like. It is interesting to note that although confidentiality was the issue mentioned most frequently by the respondents in this survey, confidentiality violations are seldom reported to ethics committees. A national survey of certified counsellors revealed that the overwhelming majority saw sexual exploitation of clients and violations of informed consent, confidentiality, and voluntary participation in counselling as unethical. Counsellors were more uncertain about the ethics of charging and collecting fees for counselling and the ethics of non-sexual dual relationships (Gibson and Pope, 1993).

Which counsellors commit these ethical violations? No particular demographic characteristics have been associated with unethical practice. Experience, gender, type of degree and similar characteristics do not predict who will act unethically, with one exception. Complaints about dual relationships with clients, especially sexual intimacies with clients or former clients, have been largely made against male mental health professionals. The usual pattern is of an older male therapists and a younger female client. However, cases against women therapists have also been reported.

Some counsellors blunder into unethical actions because "they just didn't think about the ethical issues" or they weren't familiar with the code of ethics of the profession. Given the needs to establish a trusting relationship, to assess the client's concerns, and to develop appropriate strategies to assist the client, it is not altogether surprising that counsellors get distracted from otherwise obvious ethical issues. However, counsellors must maintain their attention to ethical issues even while attending to therapeutic concerns if they are to merit the title of professional.

Other counsellors act unethically because their primary motivation is self-interest or because they think codes of ethics are for professionals who are less experienced or gifted than they are. Such grandiose thinking has led to serious ethical violations and puts a counsellor at risk for a pattern of unethical behaviour with a number of clients. Although most helping professionals are dedicated to serving their clients, and seem to show interest in nothing but self-gratification.

Professionals sometimes act unethically because they are distracted by personal difficulties or are made especially needy by a personal crisis. A counsellor who is lonely and sad after a difficult divorce may step over the boundaries of the counselling relationship because of those personal needs. Such cases have come before ethics committees and licensing boards on numerous occasions. The codes of ethics all address this kind of circumstance, putting the responsibility to be aware of personal limitations on the counsellor. If unable to attend to the client's needs because of personal difficulties, the responsible counsellor must not attempt counselling until the personal issues are resolved. The power of the counsellor to do harm is too great to allow such a distortion of the counselling process to occur or continue. In this type of situation, counselling for the counsellor is the best solution. Some professional associations are beginning to develop resources to assist such distressed professionals in recovering their equilibrium.

13.3 Summary

Counsellors have ethical obligations to be loyal to the institutions and promote good reputation of the counselling professions. Some of the ethical principles that underline the counselling profession include respect for autonomy, beneficence, nonmalficence, justice and fidelity.

Some ethical violations by mental health professionals include dual relationship with the clients, especially sexual intimacies with current or former clients, borrowing money from them, employ the clients in their practices, and therefore, jeopardize the client's welfare. Other such violation include unethical billing practice, incompetent practice, fraudulent application of licence, violation of confidentiality and incidents relating to the reporting of child abuse.

There are various reasons for ethical violation but it needs to be checked and managed by the counsellor so that they do not indulge in it and harm the counselling services.

Review Questions

1. Why are ethics important in counselling? What are the important ethical principles which govern the counselling procedures?

2. List and discuss some of the ethical violations by mental health professionals.

3. How can counsellors be trained with respect to the ethical conduct in the counselling process?

Exercises, Cases and Role Plays

Exercise 1: Self-Disclosure (1)

In pairs complete the following statements:

1. Joining a new group makes me feel...
2. I like people to think I am...
3. When things are getting me down, I ....
4. At this moment I feel..
5. When I first met you, I thought..
6. This exercise..

When all the questions have been compiled, discuss and answer the following questions:

1. How did you feel doing the exercise?
2. Which questions were easiest to answer? Most difficult?
3. Did you use objective and factual information about yourself to answer the questions, or subjective and feeling information? Which is most revealing of you? Why?
4. What did you learn about yourself?

Exercise 2: Self-Disclosure (11)

In pairs complete the following sentences:

1. As a counsellor or helper I ....
2. I am becoming the kind of person who ....
3. My strengths are...
4. My weaknesses are ....
5. What I need most from people is...
6. What I give to people most of the time is......................................

233

Discuss and answer the following questions:

1. How open, searching and honest were you in your statements about yourself?
2. Which statements were the easiest to complete? Most difficult? Why?
3. What did you learn about yourself?

Exercise 3: Feedback

In pairs complete the following sentences:

1. As a counsellor or helper you ....
2. You are becoming the kind of person who ....
3. Your strengths are...
4. Your weaknesses are ....
5. What you need most from people is..
6. What you give to people most of the time is ....

Discuss the following questions:

1. How open, searching and honest were you in your statements about others?
2. Which statements were the easiest to complete? Most difficult? Why?
3. What did you learn about yourself?

Exercise 4: Attending Behaviours

Form groups of three students, let one be the helpee, one be the helper, and one be the observer. The helpee should think of some issue he or she would like to discuss with the helper. Instruct the helper to intentionally violate the principles of good attending described as the helpee presents his or her issue. The observer notes whatever occurs. Continue this pattern for three minutes. Then discuss what the helper's behaviour did to the process. Did the helpee show any non-verbal signs of his or her reactions? This is a time that the helpee can share directly how it felt to be ignored while trying to talk. If this exercise is done in a classroom setting, debrief the various triads to share experience across groups.

Repeat the same process (switching roles so that each participant eventually can serve as helper, helpee and observer) for an additional three minutes, with the helper practicing the best attending skills possible. Discuss the contrast with the first exercise.

Finally (after switching roles again), a helper and a helpee should engage in a discussion about something important to the helpee for longer period, say, seven minutes. The helper should maintain good attending and may offer brief verbal responses as appropriate. The observer will take written notes on the paralinguistic and attending behaviours of both the helper and the helpee. At the conclusion of the discussion, the observer will report his or her findings, and the triad will discuss the meanings they attach to the behaviours that were observed. Both the helper and the helpee are encouraged to be self-disclosing about how they felt when a particular behaviour was occurring in the session.

Exercise 5: Genuineness

Think of two people in your life. Person A is an individual you perceive to be genuine. Person B is an individual you do not perceive to be genuine. Develop a clear visual image of each person. Recall one or two significant experiences that you have had with each one. Now, while remembering these experiences, answer the following questions, writing down your answers or sharing them with another student.

Questions:

1. What specific observations have I made about person A that gives me the impression that her or she is a genuine individual?
2. What specific observations have I made about person B that gives me the impression that he or she is not a genuine individual?
3. What differences do I note in their way of relating to me?
4. How would I describe my inner experiences in the presence of person A, particularly my emotions?
5. How would I describe my inner experiences in the presence of person B, particularly my emotions?
6. From my personal experience, what principles about genuineness seem valid for me?

Exercise 6: Are You A Good Listener?

Read the following 14 statements and rate yourself on each by using the following scale:

A – Always
B – Almost Always
C – Usually
D – Sometimes
E – Rarely
F – Almost Never
G – Never

No.	*Statement*	*Rank*
1.	Do you let the speaker completely express his or her ideas without interrupting?	
2.	Do you become upset or excited when the speaker's views differ from your own?	

No.	Statement	Rank

3.   Are you able to prevent distractions from disrupting your ability to listen?

4.   Do you make continuous notes on everything the other person says?

5.   Are you able to read between the lines and hear what a person is saying even when there are hidden messages being conveyed?

6.   When you feel that the speaker or the topic is boring, do you find yourself turning out and start daydreaming about other matters?

7.   Are you able to tolerate silence by sitting quietly and allowing the speaker time to gather his or her thoughts and go on with the message?

8.   As you listen, do you find yourself trying to pull together what the speaker is saying by thinking of what has been said and what seems to be coming?

9.   As you listen to the speaker, do you note that person's body language and try to incorporate this into your interpretation of the message?

10.   If you disagree with what the speaker is saying, do you provide immediate feedback by shaking your head in disagreement?

11.   Do you move around a great deal while listening, changing your postures, crossing and recrossing your arms and/or legs, and sliding back and forth in your chair?

12.   When you listen, do you stare intensely into the speaker's eyes and try to maintain this direct contact throughout the time the person is speaking?

13.   When the other party has finished speaking, do you ask pointed and direct questions designed to clarify and amplify what was said?

14.   If the speaker has been critical to you, do you try to put down that person before addressing the substantive part of the message?

Interpretation of Are You A Good Listener

Take your answers provided for each question and using the scoring key below, determine the total number of points earned.

Question	A	B	C	D	E	F	G	Score
1.	7	6	5	4	3	2	1	
2.	1	2	3	4	5	6	7	
3.	7	6	5	4	3	2	1	
4.	1	2	3	4	5	6	7	
5.	7	6	5	4	3	2	1	
6.	1	2	3	4	5	6	7	
7.	7	6	5	4	3	2	1	
8.	7	6	5	4	3	2	1	
9.	7	6	5	4	3	2	1	
10.	1	2	3	4	5	6	7	
11.	1	2	3	4	5	6	7	
12.	1	2	3	4	5	6	7	
13.	7	6	5	4	3	2	1	
14.	1	2	3	4	5	6	7	

| | | | | | | | **Bonus point** | **+ 2** |

Total

Scoring interpretation:

90–100	Excellent	You are an ideal listener
80–89	Very Good	You know a great deal about listening
70–79	Good	You are an above average listener
60–69	Average	You are typical of most listeners
Less than 60	Below Average	You need to work on developing more effective listening habits

Exercise 7: Dealing with Problem Subordinates

Purpose

The purpose of this exercise is to help the manager become more aware of the challenges of managing the subordinate performance problems. By the time they complete this exercise, they will

1. Learn how to categorize typical performance problems
2. Develop strategies with which to manage such performance problems
3. Understand the challenges of managing subordinates

Introduction

If there is one universal truth among managers, it is that all of them have subordinates with performance problems. Motivating and leading ideal subordinates is a simple task, but coping with the realities of problem subordinates is an entirely different matter. In many cases, ignorance on the part of the manager of how to handle a problem subordinate causes the manager to neglect the problem. This, in turn, leads to exasperation, dissatisfaction, poor performance and depressed morale.

According to Veiga's (1988) article, Face Your Problem Subordinates Now! two recurring themes—job performance and interpersonal relations—emerged in his classification of problem subordinates. Employees who perform above job expectations but who are perceived as not working effectively with others are classified as *talented but abrasive*. Employees who perform below expectations and who are viewed as having difficulty working with others are categorized as *plateaued but indifferent*. Employees who works effectively with others yet perform below expectations are seen as *charming but unreliable*. Finally, employees who perform above expectations and work effectively with others are viewed as *ideal* subordinates.

It can be argued that a subordinate's classification into one of these categories may suggest levers for change. For example, if a manager is dealing with a talented but abrasive subordinate, coaching in terms of communication and political skills might be recommended. Plateaued but indifferent subordinates might benefit from career counselling or work redesign, while charming but unreliable subordinates might require additional technical training to help them perform job tasks more effectively. Veiga (1988) argues that there are no quick fixes or guarantees with problem subordinates. Managers must accept the fact that a pattern of coaching and feedback, supplemented with training, is necessary to improve performance.

These six case studies have been developed to help the student/manager recognize subordinate performance problems and determine strategies to manage them. Six cases of problem subordinates are being given to discuss and evaluate the solutions, independently and in groups. Their skills in diagnosis and implementation are tested so that they are able to not only categorize problem subordinates but also will be able to determine strategies to improve performance.

Instructions:

1. Read the management problems cases and complete them independently.
2. In a small group, discuss how you each independently classified subordinates in the six cases. Attempt to reach a consensus decision on each case.
3. Together as a group, prepare a development plan for performance improvement for each case.
4. Report out your group's strategies for dealing with selected cases to the class as directed by your instructor.
5. Participate in a class discussion on real-life problem subordinates.

Management Problems

CASE 1

Recently, you were promoted to the position of manager of your department. One member of your group who now reports to you, Ashish, is upset that you were given the promotion over him. Although he is known as the company expert on technical matters in his field, lately his work has been slipping. On more than one occasion he has left work early, arrived late and missed several deadlines on monthly reports. You are concerned because you consider him a valuable employee of your staff and an asset to the company. Since you are new to your position, you know that you must depend on his expertise to keep the group on track, as you require more time to learn more about your new responsibilities. Ashish has been known to be difficult to deal with and has developed a reputation as a scientific 'Prim Donna'. In a meeting the other day, several of your peers (and your boss) were joking about Ashish's occasional superior attitude toward others. His attitude and behaviour on the job are not consistent with the norms your company associates with its management staff. Ashish seems to believe that he's put in lot of his time, effort and energy in the company and that the company owes it to him to grant him a promotion. You believe he has the talent, skills and knowledge to make excellent contributions if his attitude improves.

Answer the following questions to find a solution to the existing problem.

1. If this situation were left unchecked, what category might this subordinate represent? Put a tick mark against the right option.

    _____ Talented but Abrasive   _____ Charming but Unreliable
    _____ Plateaued but Indifferent   _____ Ideal

2. How would you manage this situation?
3. What strategies would you use to coach and guide this subordinate's development?

CASE 2

Your assistant, Arpita, has been working for you over the past two years. During that time, you have learned to respect the clerical and word processing skills she demonstrates. However, you are concerned about other areas of her job that, in your view, reflect substandard performance. On several occasion, it seems that she does not hear your requests, or if she does hear, she does not follow them properly. Occasionally she performs tasks different from those you have assigned. For example, just take the case of yesterday when you asked that she make arrangements for a temporary to handle a special project. No temporary turned up this morning to take on the assignment. When you asked Arpita about the situation, she conveniently said that she forgot to make the phone call because she was busy preparing a lengthy mailing that you had given her the day before. You became frustrated by her response, as similar incidents had happened many times in the past. You wonder if the recent incidents like this which keep on happening are due to a lack of listening skills on her part or a result of poor time management skills. You have heard complaints from others who have worked with her from time to time, so you are confident that your judgment is accurate in this matter. Whatever the cause, you have decided that now is the time to discuss this with her.

Answer the following questions to find a solution to the existing problem.

1. If this situation were left unchecked, what category might this subordinate represent? Put a tick mark against the right option.

   _____ Talented but Abrasive   _____ Charming but Unreliable
   _____ Plateaued but Indifferent   _____ Ideal

2. How would you manage this situation?
3. What strategies would you use to coach and guide this subordinate's development?

CASE 3

For several months you have been upset that one of your staff members, Gaurav, has placed you in more than one embarrassing situation. The situation just described to you by a phone call from a former and valuable customer, however, takes the cake. This former customer wanted to know who in your group now had responsibility for handling his account. You went to great lengths to cultivate this customer when you were a member of the sales team; fortunately, through your efforts the company won a major share of his business. Several months ago you specifically assigned accounts responsibility for this customer to Gaurav. You chose Gaurav because he is very effective and impressive in meetings with customers due to his strong interpersonal skills. Reports from the field indicate that Gaurav is one of the most beloved salespeople that your company has to offer. When pursuing a new customer, Gaurav has been known to put on quite a sales show, taking new customers out for expensive dinners, providing them with theatre tickets, and driving them to the theatre in Opel Astra. However, Gaurav does not demonstrate strong customer follow-up skills, and he also has been known to neglect sales quota deadlines. You had asked Gaurav to follow up the arrangements with this particular customer; the phone call alerted you to the fact that the customer has not been contacted for follow-up. Fuming, you leave your office and head straight for Gaurav's desk.

Answer the following questions to find a solution to the existing problem.

1. If this situation were left unchecked, what category might this subordinate represent? Put a tick mark against the right option.

   _____ Talented but Abrasive   _____ Charming but Unreliable
   _____ Plateaued but Indifferent   _____ Ideal

2. How would you manage this situation?
3. What strategies would you use to coach and guide this subordinate's development?

CASE 4

It's Monday morning, and you have just returned to your office after travelling for two weeks. You check with each of your direct reports to discuss their activities in your absence. One member of your staff, Gagan, is frustrated and furious. After letting him vent his frustration, you discover the problem. While you were gone, your boss agreed to an arrangement with another function that will change record-keeping procedures significantly for your department. You will now have to organize information by project number instead of alphabetically by project name. Your boss decided not to tell your staff, preferring to wait for you to return so that he could talk to you and let you handle the announcement. From one point of view, the change makes sense. The new approach will make it much easier to track project costs by category. However, your people will now have to create and learn an entirely new system. This will require the reorganization of all existing files and records. Gagan heard rumours of the change late last Friday and became quite upset. He took it upon himself to confront your boss about the problem. A messy argument erupted in your absence. Now one of your best team members is angry and your boss is upset. This is particularly difficult situation for you as Gagan is one of your most talented subordinates and you had hoped he would be promoted soon.

Answer the following questions to find a solution to the existing problem.

1. If this situation were left unchecked, what category might this subordinate represent? Put a tick mark against the right option.

———— Talented but Abrasive ———— Charming but Unreliable
———— Plateaued but Indifferent ———— Ideal

2. How would you manage this situation?
3. What strategies would you use to coach and guide this subordinate's development?

CASE 5

Due to organizational restructuring, the members of your department will now be assigned responsibility for making regular telephone contact with customers to alert customers of the availability of new promotional material and to monitor local sales efforts. You are pleased with the change in assignments. However, when you discussed plans for the change with individual subordinates, one employee, Lillian, expressed a great deal of reluctance and uncertainty. You are concerned whether Lillian will be able to adjust to the change at all. She has grown comfortable with the administrative tasks she has performed over the years and is not happy about changing her job duties.

Lillian does not have the skills appropriate to the selling assignment, and she is not motivated to make the change. Lillian is an average but solid performer. She has strong interpersonal skills but is uncomfortable dealing directly with customers. If pushed, you are certain that Lillian would gain the confidence she needs to handle the new assignment, but you are not certain whether this is the right course of action. Somehow you must make a decision about her new role in the department.

Answer the following questions to find a solution to the existing problem.

1. If this situation were left unchecked, what category might this subordinate represent? Put a tick mark against the right option.

   _____ Talented but Abrasive   _____ Charming but Unreliable
   _____ Plateaued but Indifferent   _____ Ideal

2. How would you manage this situation?
3. What strategies would you use to coach and guide this subordinate's development?

CASE 6

One of the employees who reports to you, Suman is over confident and seems to think she is destined for great things at the company where you work. The problem is that you don't agree with Suman's assessment of her potential. Nor does your boss. Suman has an outgoing personality and generally gets along well with people. However, she has a tendency to get on everyone's nerves in the department with her hour-long personal phone calls. She also has a tendency to blow events out of proportion. For example, she was quite upset with the comments you made during her last performance review. You reviewed a number of her shortcomings concerning missed deadlines and substandard work, yet she had an excuse for every example offered. Since that discussion, she has avoided talking to you on matters that do not require your direct approval. Recently another staff member has informed you about what Suman has been spreading about you to others that you feel threatened by her and have reacted by giving her an unfair performance review. You are concerned about this news and feel that it is just another example of Suman's lack of readiness for promotion. Of particular concern is that of late her work has been slipping and she no longer is motivated to do her best.

Answer the following questions to find a solution to the existing problem.

1. If this situation were left unchecked, what category might this subordinate represent? Put a tick mark against the right option.

   _____ Talented but Abrasive   _____ Charming but Unreliable
   _____ Plateaued but Indifferent   _____ Ideal

2. How would you manage this situation?
3. What strategies would you use to coach and guide this subordinate's development?

Exercise 8: Typical Response Inventory

Based on the work of Carl Rogers, this inventory exercise is designed to find out what sort of responses you tend to give naturally in normal conversation. Read each statement and choose one of the five responses given which you think is most similar to the response you are likely to give in everyday conversation.

Statement 1 (from man, aged 35 years):

"I am a highly ambitious person. Every job I've had I've been successful at it, and I intend to be successful here even if it means walking over a few people to do so. I'm going to prove myself and really go places."

Choose one of the following responses:

(a) "You feel you are a very ambitious man, is that right?"
(b) "Why do you think you have such strong needs for success?"
(c) "That's good. You should soon get to the top with that attitude. Let me know if I can help you in any way."
(d) "It seems to me that your needs for success are so strong that they outweigh your needs to be popular."
(e) "It will make you very unpopular here if you maintain that attitude. That's not how we do things here at all."

Statement 2 (from woman, aged 26 years):

"Two years at business school have really equipped me to be a professional manager. Competing with men there has convinced me that women who get as far as I have are more than a match for most men. If this organization wants to keep me they'll have to fit in with my own career progression."

Choose one of the following responses:

(a) "A business school education is a great asset, but if you ask me it doesn't make you a good manager. You have to learn the hard way."
(b) "What difficulties do you foresee in being female in this organization?"
(c) "I'm sure you're right. We are really in need of people with your skills and drive. Let's get together next week and I'll help you plan out how you can get the experience you want in this department in the shortest possible time."
(d) "If I'm hearing you correctly, you feel that you are well equipped as a professional manager and you expect the organization to respect this."
(e) "It appears to me that you have some worries about being accorded the status you think you deserve."

Statement 3 (from man, aged 44):

"I used to be very ambitious person but as I grew older I realized that the success is not so important to me. I may not have been a success with the company, but I've put all my real effort into my family. I'm a very happy family man."

Choose one of the following responses:

(a) "That sounds like a very sensible attitude, after all, very few people get to the top. Is there any help I can give you?"

(b) "Yes, you've reached the point where you decided to switch goals- from your career to your family but you feel perhaps that something is missing?"

(c) "You're absolutely right. A man is a fool to keep struggling when nobody cares a damn. You did the right thing and I'd do the same in your position."

(d) "As you have got older, you find more and more satisfaction with your family."

(e) "Why do you feel that you weren't a success with the company? What do you mean by success?"

Statement 4 (from woman, aged 41):

"When I moved to this town I thought I'd make lots of new friends but people of this town aren't interested in socializing much. I think it must be me. I'm getting more closed up and into myself."

Choose one of the following responses:

(a) "Can you tell me more about how you go about making friends? Have you made any efforts recently to meet people?"

(b) "Living alone is all right if you have lots of friends, but without them it's very lonely. Is that what you're saying?"

(c) "It looks as though you may be really worried about the future. Perhaps you've lived alone for so long that you've dropped out of the habit of getting close to people."

(d) "That sounds really sad, to be lonely and without friends. What you've got to do is get out and make some. If I were you I'd get started straight away."

(e) "Well let's see. There are lots of ways in which you could get involved with the staff social club. Next month there's the annual outing and I could get you onto the organizing team. What do you think about that?"

Statement 5 (from man, aged 32):

"I'm telling you; Lewis has really got his knife into me. I got the blame for the whole of the Brown and Williamson affair and there were eight of us involved. Now, he's trying to insinuate that I'm falling down on the job. I had a good name in this office until he came here—he just doesn't like me and he's determined to bring me down."

Choose one of the following responses:

(a) "You are getting paranoid feelings about Lewis. Could it be that you are working out your frustrations at not getting the job you both applied for?"

(b) "You're right, he can really be a mean so-and-so when he chooses to, but I wouldn't go about it with your attitude."

(c) "Have there been any other occasions when he's tried to show you up in a poor light?"

(d) "If I understand you correctly, you feel persecuted by Lewis and think that he intends to ruin your reputation."

(e) "Right, you need to protect yourself from situations like this. Do you know that the union is becoming very strong among our grades? In fact, I've got some application forms here which I can help you to fill out."

Scoring:

The scoring grid is organized with the Situation No. 1 to 5 identified in the vertical column on the left, and response types identified in the top horizontal row. Moving row by row, circle your response letter for each situation. Next, add up the total number of responses circled in each column and put the totals in the bottom row.

Responses:

	E	*I*	*S*	*P*	*R*
Situation 1	E	D	C	B	A
Situation 2	A	E	C	B	D
Situation 3	C	B	A	E	D
Situation 4	D	C	E	A	B
Situation 5	B	A	E	C	D

Number of Responses

You should now have scores for all five types of responses. The total of your totals should add up to 5.

E = Evaluative response—(making judgments)

I = Interpretive response—(reading between the lines, making hunches)

S = Supportive response—(sympathy, agreeing, backing up, offering psychological and physical support)

P = Probing response—(questioning asking for more, often deeper information)

R = Understanding/reflecting response—(empathy, non-directive, non-evaluative response which reflects back to the speaker what was said)

Exercise 9: The Dynamics of Sitting

The purpose of this exercise is to help students appreciate how personality style may reveal itself even in apparently simple behaviours—such as where you choose to sit in a classroom. The facilitator tells students to get up from their seats (taking their belong-  ings with them) and move to the sides of the room. He further adds, "Now, pretend that it's the first day of a class. Sit down in a seat that would be the one you would probably choose—the one that feels most comfortable to you." After all the students have positioned themselves, the facilitator comments on the choices they made and how these choices depict about their personalities. Here are some of the ideas that often come up:

People who sit in the front may give the kind of impression that they want to be close to the teacher, like to be seen, be outgoing, be 'brown-posers', like to be upfront where all the action is (perhaps even to help them stay awake), want to be sure they hear everything that the teacher says (perhaps are grade-conscious?).

People who sit in the back may give the kind of impression that they like to sleep during class (are 'slackers'), like to see everything that's happening in the room (are 'observers'), dislike attention, or like the attention of having everyone turn around to see them when they talk, like the security of having their back against a wall, are oppositional or rebellious.

People who sit by the window are usually daydreamers, they like the 'freedom' of having wide-open space next to them (but often pay the price of being far from the door).

People, who sit by the door like having a quick way out of a situation, are often in a rush to do things.

People, who sit in the middle like to be inconspicuous, like to blend in with the crowd, are possibly shy people.

The loner avoids sitting near other people.

The changeling sits in various seats (likes variety, likes to see things from different perspectives, is indecisive, likes to experiment?)

Now students can take cue from the above account and observe the sitting pattern of the entire class and attempt to answer the following:

1. Does the class look cohesive or fragmented?
2. Are there subgroups?
3. Are people seated evenly across the room, or are there gaps? Are the gaps in the front of the room, middle, sides, back?
4. What might these patterns say about the class and its group personality?

Exercise 10: The Circulating Papers Technique

This technique provides a fairly anonymous way for EVERYONE in the group to give and receive feedback from other participants. It comes in very handy to collect views about almost any short writing that participants do—be it their reactions to a class topic, feedback about an exam or the course, a writing related to a group exercise, etc.

The participants are invited to express their written views on any given topic on a piece of paper and then the facilitator collects all the papers (including his/her own, for he/she also participate), randomly shuffle them, and then passes them back out to the group, keeping one for self. Now, everyone has someone else's paper, but they don't know whose paper it is (participants are instructed not to include their names on the page). Then you are required to read the paper you have received and then write on the page some useful feedback or reaction to the participant who wrote it. When you finish with that paper, you stand up and exchange papers with someone else who also has finished reading and reacting to the paper he/she received. Now, you and the other person have a second paper to read and write a response to. When you finish with that second paper, you stand up and find someone else who is also finished. Everyone keeps doing this—reading, writing, and exchanging papers—until everyone has read and written a response to approximately 5 to 10 papers.

The facilitator then collects all the papers, places them into two piles at the front of the room, and tells the participants to come up and collect their own paper. They then discuss as a group the results of the exercise.

The purpose of this exercise is that EVERYONE, including shy or non-verbal participants, gives and receives feedback from several peers. It also gives the facilitator a chance to find out what the participants are thinking, how the participants are reacting to each other, and to also helps them get individual feedback.

Exercise 11: Life Facts

It has been generally noticed that clients who indulge in a process of exploring their life story, usually at first, by describing the most important facts about themselves.

For this exercise, ask participants to write down four important facts about themselves and their lives—things that have happened to them, information about their family, facts about their personality or their history, etc. (participation is voluntary). Ask them to include on that list one item that is **a LIE**.

*Extra features for the exercise might involve asking participants to add to the list: (1) something their parents said about how they were as a baby (to explore early, perhaps temperament-determined aspects of self), and/or; (2) something important about one of their parent's or grandparent's life (to explore identification issues and cross-generational issues in the development of self-identity).

Then collect the papers and use the circulating papers techniques so everyone gets a chance to give and receive feedback from several others. Also instruct participants, when reading other participant's lists, to put a star next to the item in the list that they think is a lie.

Questions pertaining to some issues that can be discussed within the group are:

1. Is there a pattern to the list of life facts?
2. What does the list say about oneself?
3. Could people determine which item was the lie?
4. Is the lie meaningful and revealing of one's personality?
5. Is there anything important MISSING from the list?

Exercise 12. The Shadow Exercise

The aim of this exercise is to explore the suppressed feelings of the client and find a cure for that.

Instructions to the Client:

Think of someone you know whom you don't like very much. Maybe you even hate this person. On a piece of paper, write down a description of that person. Write down what it is about this individual's personality that you don't like. Be as specific as you can be.

When everyone in the group is finished writing, tell them to draw a box around what they have written—and at the top of the box write MY SHADOW.

Consider this, tell them. "What you have written down is some hidden part of yourself—some part that you have suppressed or hidden. It is what Jung would call your SHADOW. Maybe it's a part of you that you fear, can't accept, or hate for some reason. Maybe it's a part of you that needs to be expressed or developed in some way. Maybe you even secretly wish you could be something like that person whom you hate.

Invariably, the participants' reactions to this idea are mixed. Some immediately see the connection; some immediately reject the idea. When the facilitator asks the group how many of them have friends or romantic partners who fit the description of the *hated* person, many are surprised to see that this is indeed the case. The exercise always leads to interesting discussions about how we project suppressed parts of ourselves onto others, and about why we sometimes choose these *hated* people for our close relationships.

Performance Counselling Activity

Practical Exercises—Role plays

Objective. The purpose of this performance counselling activity is to help the managers as well as the subordinates to improve their overall performance and deal with only work related problems. The basic aim of performance counselling activity is to help the managers to deal with any ongoing problem be it a problem caused by a problem subordinate or a problem faced by a subordinate without wasting any time and energy, and seeing that the problem is solved without ugly outcome giving rise to ill-will among the staff and thus in the process also avoiding damage to the reputation of the organization or its work output. These practical sessions are conducted to make the managers well versed in problem solving techniques. To conduct these sessions successfully certain things are to be considered like the exercise should be attempted in an organized and easy to follow steps as mentioned below:

Step 1   Identifying the problem.

Step 2   Analyzing the forces influencing the behaviour.

Step 3   Planning, co-ordinating and organizing the sessions.

Step 4   Conducting the sessions using sincerity, compassion and kindness but remaining firm and in control.

Step 5   Determining what the worker believes is causing the counter productions labour and what will be required to change it.

Step 6   Maintaining a sense of timing when to use directive or non-directive counselling.

Step 7   Using all the facts to take a decision or to make any plan of action to correct the problem.

Step 8   Evaluating the worker's progress to find out whether the problem has been solved after the session is complete or not.

Procedure. The instructor should adopt such a procedure which will be easy to follow and will be able to teach the managers as well as subordinates whatever is being practically practiced in the class. Conduct a performance counselling session following the steps given below:

Step 1   Gather the class round and break the class into group of three.

Step 2   Give them each a problem case to read.

Step 3   Ask them to enact the roles of the people involved.

Step 4   Repeat the roles and rotate the roles among other groups.

Step 5   Observe them and collect feedback to discuss further.

Exercises to be attempted. There are five role plays being given below to the participants to attempt. According to the problem being discussed choose the players to enact the role of person in problem and the other person for solving problem. For example, one can be a supervisor performing the counselling session and the other can be an employee with a behavioural problem. Follow the above mentioned steps.

Most of the counselling sessions will be relatively easy. For example an errant employee breaks a rule such as being late or does not meet a performance standard such as not completing a task correctly. The majority of employees follow the rules and excels the standards but they are humans and make mistakes. The main concern should be to make him understand and in case if he or she fails to understand and the overall work output is adversely affected then to take an appropriate disciplinary action against him.

ROLE PLAY 1

Problem at hand:

Take a case of an excellent employee named Sandhya who has not needed performance counselling up to this point. But when her manager reviewed her time record for the previous day he noticed that she left office 15 minutes early without making a request. The manager checked to confirm and found out that she did not make a request to leave early and in the past also similar incidents have occurred.

Analyzing the problem:

So the main problem is that the employee left the work early without giving any notice. A good rule for being objective is, *if you are faced with a problem but cannot describe it in measurable terms, you do not have a problem, you just think you do*. Here in this case problem present is subjective which can be discussed and solved. So according to the step mentioned above try to plan, co-ordinate and organize the session to find a cure to Sandhya's problem. Conduct the session teaching the participants the value of sincerity, compassion, kindness and discipline. Try to understand what Sandhya believes caused the counter productive behaviour and what will be required to change it. Now, select the participants and distribute the roles accordingly and make observation and collect feedback.

The discussion between the manager and Sandhya can take the following direction:

Manager: *Sandhya I have been very pleased with your performance. But, yesterday you clocked out 15 minutes early, which is in violation of our company policy.* (After a brief pause), *"Could you please explain why you left early?"*

Sandhya: *I'm so sorry, when I looked at my watch, I thought it was quitting time. It was not until I was on my way home that I realized I left early.*

Manager:	(Giving a directive reply), *From now onwards, please double check the time before you leave.*
	(Giving a non-directive reply) *How do you plan to ensure this will not happen again?*
Sandhya:	*I will look at the time more closely to ensure I do not make the same mistake twice.*
Manager:	*Sandhya, I'm sure you will not let it happen again. Except for that one mistake, your performance has been great, your tasks are always at par and on time, and this is the first rule you have broken.*
Observation:	Since it was not a serious violation, no further action is needed and the counsellor has no reason to believe that it was nothing more than a human error.

After this session evaluate the worker's progress in future to ensure that the problem has been solved.

ROLE PLAY 2

Problem at Hand:

Take the case of Tushar who has been a valued employee for you for the last 18 months. But, when you review the production report for last week, you discover that he was not up to standards on both Thursday and Friday. The standard is to assemble at least an average of 12 kits per hour. For Thursday, his average was 10 kits per hour and for Friday it was 11 kits per hour. You check the schedule and note that he was not away from the assembly line for training, meetings, etc. Using the following guide, conduct a performance counselling session:

- Identify the problem.
- Analyze the forces influencing the behaviour.
- Plan, coordinate and organize the session.
- Conduct the session using sincerity, compassion, and kindness; but remain firm and in control.
- During the session, determine what the worker believes causes the counterproductive behaviour and what will be required to change it.
- Try to maintain a sense of timing of when to use directive or non-directive counselling.
- Using all the facts, make a decision and/or a plan of action to correct the problem.
- After the session and throughout a sufficient time period, evaluate the worker's progress to ensure the problem has been solved.

ROLE PLAY 3

Problem at hand:

Take the case of Sushma who has been working in the company for past three years and has been a very good employee. But, for the last three project meetings in which she is a key player, she has been coming late. This has caused the meetings to run late, because she brings some critical decision making information and also because she has to be brought up to date about the proceedings. The first time, you let the incident go by, while the second time you explain the situation to her as it is high time that this must be discussed.

Using what you have learned, conduct a performance counselling session. The only difference is, you want to use a more non-directive approach by having Sushma make a firm commitment to correct her behaviour. For example:

> Manager: (Giving a non-directive statement): *Sushma, this behaviour is very disruptive to the department. What are you going to do to correct it?*

ROLE PLAY 4

The next two exercises are more difficult than the previous three. In the last three exercises, the employees knew they made mistakes, took the counselling in stride, and moved on. In this one, the employee is walking on an extremely thin line. His performance has extremely disintegrated and he is about ready to get fired.

Problem at hand:

Shekhar has been an excellent employee since he started working in your department two years ago. However, in the last few weeks, he has not been performing up to standards.

He has been late three times. His production goals have been below standards on many occasions. Two of his coworkers have reported that he seems to be extremely agitated most of the time and in a very cranky mood. (You checked this out with some other employees and found it to be true.)

Today he was late for the fourth time. Finally, it is difficult to ignore the problem and you have called him into your office for a performance-counselling meeting.

Start the meeting:

First of all, the participants acting as the counsellor should start by being firm and confident.

> Manager: *Shekhar, I have called you in because there is a problem, and quite frankly the problem involves you. I have been going through the documentation on your performance over the last few weeks. Shekhar, you know that today is the fourth time*

you have been late and your production standards have not been up to standards. Recently it was reported to me that you have not been getting along with your coworkers. Your unacceptable performance cannot continue. We are here to find out what you are going to do about it." (Notice it is not **our** problem)

Use power base:

The power base is in the documentation that the manager has built from the previous counselling sessions. He should directly make use of these documentations in dealing with this errant employee.

This is the first time Shekhar may have the opportunity to manipulate the meeting. Shekhar may try to interrupt by making an excuse why he was late today, such as:

My car had a dead battery this morning and my neighbour had to help me jump start it.

The counselling manager should not let the employee interrupt or distract. He should firmly stress his point of view. For example,

Manager: *Excuse me Shekhar, I want to give you the opportunity to respond, but I feel it is important for you to see the entire picture. Once I lay out the pattern of your deterioration over the past few weeks then I certainly want to hear from you.*

The counselling manager should be objective and specific. Avoid 'you always' and 'you never' traps. *Remember if you have a problem but cannot describe it in measurable terms, you do not have a problem, you just think you do.*

To make the errant employee realize his mistakes the counselling manager should produce concrete proof. For example, show and explain to Shekhar the following documentation:

1. April 6   Production 5% below standard
2. April 17   30 minutes late
3. April 20   Production 12% below standard
4. April 24   Production 14% below standard
5. April 29   25 minutes late
6. May 5   35 minutes late
7. May 8   Yelled out to other worker that they were not doing their work correctly and was making his job harder to do
8. May 11   Production 10% below standard
9. May 20   Used profanity when telling a coworker how to set up a line
10. May 26   Production 15% below standard
11. June 1   30 minutes late (today)

When in doubt, return to the facts:

Shekhar becomes very defensive, examples, *I cannot meet my production goals because the other workers are getting in my way!* or *I have been having car trouble!*

In spite of efforts to remain in control, the counsellor manager might feel that he is being backed into a corner. He should take on the defensive if he feels his emotions taking over, or he is about to loose control. If any of these happens he or she should simply return to the facts. For example,

Shekhar*, you may feel that is important to the meeting, but the primary issue is...* Get back to your documentation...show a pattern, that is his **Power**.

Move to closure:

After the documentation and the issues have been covered, move to closure. The counsellor manager has to address three issues. First of all, he should make the employee *own* the problem, second inquire about the reason for the decline in performance and thirdly find out whether it is a personal problem. These can be handled in the following ways:

First, get the employee to own up the problem, for example: *Do you understand the problem I have just addressed?* This requires the subjective employee to become objective, for example, *Yes, I understand the problem as you have described it.*

Next, ask for the reason the performance has been poor, for example, *What is the reason for your decline in performance?* You will probably not get a good reason; you might only get a shrug, for example, *I don't know.*

The manager should not worry about the answer unless it is really explained to him. What he is doing is re-emphasizing the pattern of poor performance.

But if the employee does not explain to the counsellor in the step above, then he should express his concern about the problem, for example, *Is there a personal problem causing your performance to deteriorate?* Do not wait for a response, continue by saying, *Because if there is, we have assistance counsellors and programmes that can help.*

The counsellor might get a negative response to this question also. But, by asking this question, he shows the employee his concern about the problems underlying the poor performance.

Shekhar replies that he does not have any personal problems; he has just been having a string of bad lucks.

Commitment:

Now, after failing to get the desired response, it is time to apply the 'Principle of Pain'. This is a process in which people with a performance problem must make a choice between keeping their disruptive behavioural pattern or keeping their job. The pain of losing their job may be the pain that is necessary to make the choice.

For example:

> *Manager:* Shekhar, whatever the problem is that is causing your performance to deteriorate, there is help if you want to deal with it. I want you to know that we so value your potential here that you have a job if you want to deal with your personal issues. However, if there is no problem or you choose not to ask for help then you leave me no choice other than to fire you strictly for your unacceptable performance problem. What is your choice?

The counsellor manager may ask if the employee wishes to speak confidentially with a counsellor, or he wishes to postpone the issue by silently waiting for an answer. If the employee ask for time to think it over, then give it, but no more than one or two hours.

The manager should always try to couple his offer of help with a firm and precise outline of the performance based consequences.

ROLE-PLAY 5

Problem at hand

Take the case of Anita who started working for you three months ago. Since that time, you have counselled her on the following:

June 8	20 minutes late for lunch
June 23	Did not have a helmet on in the production area (health and safety violation)
July 14	45 minutes late for work
July 24	10 minutes late for break
August 5	Bumped into rack with a forklift (safety violation)
August 13	left 10 minutes early for lunch

Today, she left for her 15 minutes break and was gone for 25 minutes.

Using the following guide, conduct a performance counselling session:

Start the meeting (being firm and confident).

Use your power base (documentation):

When in doubt, return to the facts. (Anita comments, *I thought we were friends?* Note: If they play on friendship—real friends do NOT let their buddies self-exit out of an organization, real friends help.

Move to Closure:

Get the employee to own the problem.
Ask for the reason for the poor performance.
Is there a personal problem?

Get commitment!

References

Adler, A., *The Practice and Theory of Individual Psychotherapy* (1927), New York: Harcourt.

Aguilera, D.C., *Crisis Intervention*, 8th ed., St. Louis, MO: C.V. Mosby (1998).

Alexander, E.M., *Fundamentals of Psychoanalysis* (1963), New York: Norton.

Allen, C., *Modern Discoveries in Medical Psychology*, 2nd ed. (1949), London: Macmillan.

Association for Counsellor Education and Supervision, The Counsellor: Professional Preparation and Role, *Personnel and Guidance Journal* (1964), (42), pp. 536–541.

Bailey, M.B., and Fuchs, E., Alcoholism and the Social Worker, *Social Work* (1960), (4), pp. 14–19.

Bakalinsky, R., People vs. Profits: Social Work in Industry, *Social Work* (1980), November: (25), pp. 471–75.

Baker, E.L., *Psychoanalysis and Psychoanalytic Psychotherapy* (1985), in J.L. Lynn and J.R. Garske (Eds.), Contemporary psychotherapies, pp. 19–67, Columbus, OH: Merrill/Prentice Hall.

Beauchamp, T.L. and Childress, J.F., *Principles of Biomedical Ethics*, 4th ed., England: Oxford University Press (1994).

Beers, C.W., *The Mind That Found Itself* (1908), Kessinger Publishing.

Belkin. G., *Introduction to Counseling*, 2nd ed. (1984), Dubuque, Iowa: W.C. Brown.

Benjamin, L.S., Structural Analysis of Social Behavior, *Psychological Review*, (1974), (81).

Berenson, B.G. and Mitchell, K.M., *Confrontation: For Better or Worse!* (1974), Amherst, Mass.: Human Resource Development Press.

Blackham, G.J., *Counseling: Theory, Process and Practice* (1977), Belmont, Calif.: Wadsworth.

Blocher, D.H., *Developmental Counseling* (1966), New York: Ronald Press.

Bohart, A.C. and Greenberg, L.S., *Empathy Reconsidered: New Directions in Psychotherapy* (1997), Washington, DC: American Psychological Association.

Bordin, E.S., The Generalizability of the Psychoanalytic Concept of the Working Alliance, *Psychotherapy: Theory, Research and Practice* (1979), 16(3), pp. 252–260.

Bouthoutsos, J.C., Holroyd, J., Lerman, H., Forer, B., and Greenberg, M., Sexual Intimacy between Psychotherapists and Patients, *Professional Psychology: Research and Practice* (1983), (20), pp. 112–115.

Brammer, L.M. and Shostrom, E.L., *Therapeutic Psychology: Fundamentals of Counselling and Psychotherapy,* 4th ed. (1982), Englewood Cliffs, N.J.: Prentice-Hall.

Brammer, L.M., Abrego, P.J., and Shostrom, E.L., *Therapeutic Counseling and Psychotherapy*, 6th ed. (1993), Upper Saddle River, N.J.: Prentice-Hall.

Broverman, I.K., Broverman, D.M., Clarkson, F.E., Rosenkrantz, P. and Vogel, S.R., Sex role stereotype and clinical judgments of mental health. *Journal of Counseling and Clinical Psychology* (1970), (34), pp. 1–7.

Burke, J.E., *Contemporary Approaches to Psychotherapy and Counselling: The Self-regulation and Maturity Model* (1989), Pacific Grove, CA: Brooks/Cole.

Burns, D.D., *Feeling good: The New Mood Therapy*, New York: New American Library (1980).

Carkhuff, R.R., *Helping and Human Relations: A Primer for Lay and Professional Helpers*, Vol. I, Selection and Training (1969), New York: Holt, Rinehart and Winston.

Cartwright, S. and Cooper, C., *No Hassle: Taking the Stress out of Work* (1994), London: Century Business Books.

Chaikin, A.L., Derlega, V.J. and Miller, S.J., Effect of Room Environment on Self-disclosure in a Counseling Analogue, *Journal of Counseling Psychology* (1976), (23), pp. 479–481.

Chusmir, I., Characteristics and predictive dimensions of women who make non-traditional vocational choices. *Personnel and Guidance Journal* (1983), 62(1), pp. 43–47.

Cocks, G., *Psychotherapy in the Third Reich* (1985), New York: Oxford University Press.

Coll, K.M., Student attitudinal changes in a counseling ethics course, *Counseling and Values* (1993), (37), pp. 165–170.

Combs, A., Soper, D. Gooding, C. Benton, J., Dickman, J., and Usher, R., Florida, *Studies in the Helping Professions* (1969), Gainerville: University of Florida Press.

Combs, A.W. and Soper, D., The Measurement of Self-concept and Self-report. *Educational and Psychological Measurement* (1963), (23), pp. 493–500.

Committee on Women in Psychology, If Sex Enters into the Psychotherapy Relationship, *Professional Psychology: Research and Practice* (1989), (20), pp. 112–115.

Cook, E.P., *Women, Relationships, and Power: Implications for Counseling.* Alexandria, VA: American Counseling Association (1993).

Cook. T., The Influence of Client-counsel or Value Similarity on Change in Meaning during Brief Counseling, *Journal of Counseling Psychology* (1966), 13, pp. 77–81.

Cooper, A., *Cooper's Comprehensive Environmental Desk Reference,* edited by André R. (1995).

Corey, G.R., *Theory and Practice of Counseling and Psychotherapy*, 5th ed. (1996), Pacific Grove, CA: Brooks/Cole.

Cormier, L.S. and Cormier, W.H., *Fundamental of Skills and Cognitive Behavioural Intentions*, 4th ed. (1998), Pacific Grove, CA: Brooks/Cole.

Cunningham, R.J., The Impact of Christian Science on American Churches, 1880–1910, *American Historical Review* (April 1967), 72(3), pp. 885–905.

De Luca, J.M. and McDowell, R.N., Managing Diversity: A Strategic Grass-Roots Approach, in S.E. Jackson and Associates (Ed.), *Diversity in the Work Place* (1992), New York: Guilford Press, pp. 227–347.

Dewey, J., *How We Think* (1910), Published by Dover Publications in 1997.

Dodgson, M., *The Management of Technical Learning,* (1991), Berlin: De Gruyter,

Dollard, J., and Miller, N.E., *Personality and Psychotherapy: Analysis in Terms of Learning, Thinking, and Culture* (1950), New York: McGraw-Hill.

Drag, R.M., Self-disclosure as a Function of Group Size and Experimenter Behavior. *Dissertation Abstracts International* (1969), 30(5-B), p. 2416.

Drucker, P., The Coming of New Organization, *Harvard Business Review* (Jan.–Feb. 1988), pp. 48–53.

Dryden, W., 'Counselling under Apartheid: An Interview with Andrew Swart, *British Journal of Guidance and Counseling* (1990), 18(3), pp. 298–320.

Dustin, R., and George, R., *Action Counseling for Behavior Change*, 2nd ed. (1977), Cranston, R.I.: Carroll Press, p. 77.

Egan, G., *The skilled helper: A Model for Systematic Helping and Interpersonal Relating* (1975), Monterey, California: Brooks/Cole.

_____, *The skilled helper: A Problem Management Approach to Helping,* 6th ed. (1998), Pacific Grove, CA: Brooks/Cole.

_____, *Working the Shadow-side: A Guide to Positive Behind the Scenes Management* (1994), San Francisco: Jossey-Bass.

Eisenberg S. and Delaney, D.J., *The Counseling Process*, 2nd ed. (1977), Chicago: Rand McNally.

Ellis, A., *Reason and Emotion in Psychotherapy*, New York: Lyle Stewart (1962).

Erikson, E., *Childhood and Society*, 2nd ed. (1963), New York: Norton.

Eysenck, H.J., The effectiveness of psychotherapy: An evaluation, *Journal of Consulting Psychology* (1952), (16), pp. 319–324.

_____, The Effects of Psychotherapy: An Evaluation, *Journal of Consulting Psychology* (1952), (16), pp. 319–324.

Faiver, C. Eisengart, S. and Colonna, R., *The Counselor's Interns Handbook*, 3rd ed. (2004), Pacific Grove, CA: Brooks/Cole

Figley, C.R., *Compassion Fatigue: Coping with Secondary Traumatic Stress Disorder in those who Treat the Traumatized*, New York: Burner/Mazel (1995).

Ford, D.Y., Harris, J.J., III, and Schuerger, J.M., Racial identity development among gifted Black students, *Journal of Counseling and Development* (1993), 71, 409–417.

Foster, S., Characteristics of an effective counselor, *Counseling Today* (1996, December), 21.

Fromm, E., *To Have or to Be* (1976), New York: Harper and Row.

Frykman, J., *The New Connection* (1971), San Francisco: The Scrimshaw Press.

Gaushell, H. and Lawson, D., *Counseling trainee family-of-origin structure and current intergenerational family relationships: Implications for counselor training*, Paper presented at the Southern Association of Counselor Education and Supervision Convention, Charlotte, NC (1994, November).

Gazda, G.M., Asbury, F.S., Balzer, F.J., Childers, W.C., and Walters, R.P., *Human Relations Development: A Manual for Education,* 3rd ed. (1991), Boston: Allyn & Bacon.

Giannandrea, V., and Murphy, K.C., Similarity Self-Disclosure and Rreturn for a Second Interview, *Journal of Counseling Psychology* (1973), 20(6), pp. 545–548.

Gibson, W.T., and Pope, K.S., The Ethics of Counseling: A National Survey of Certified Counselors, *Journal of Counseling and Development* (1993), (71), pp. 330–336.

Gilliland, B.E., and James, R.K., *Crisis Intervention Strategies,* 3rd ed. (1997), Pacific Grove, CA: Brooks/Cole.

Gladding, S.T., *Counseling as an Art: The Creative Art in Counseling*, 3rd ed., Alexendria, VA: American Counseling Association (2004).

Glatt, M., Pittman, D.J., Gillespie, D.G., and Hills, D.R., *The Drug Scene in Great Britain: Journey into Loneliness* (1967), London: Arnold.

Goodyear, R.J., Termination as a loss experience for the counselor, *Personnel and Guidance Journal* (1981), (59), pp. 347–350.

Grosch W.N. and Olsen, D.C., *When Helping starts to Hurt*, New York: Norton (1994).

Guy, J.D., *The Personal Life of the Psychotherapist*, New York: Wiley (1987).

Haase, R.F., and Mattia, D.J., Spatial Environments and Verbal Conditioning in Question Counseling Interview, *Journal of Counseling Psychology* (1976), (23), pp. 414–421.

Hackney, H. and Cormier, L.S., *The Professional Counselor: A Process Guide to Helping*, 4th ed., Boston: Allyn & Bacon (2001).

Hall, E.T., *The Hidden Dimension* (1966), Garden City, New York: Doubleday and Company, Inc.

Handy C., *The Age of Unreason* (1990), Arrow Books.

Hayman, P.M. and Covert, J.A., Ethical dilemmas in college counselling centers in college counseling centers. *Journal of Counseling Development* (1986), (64), pp. 318–302.

Hendricks, C.F., *The Rightsizing Remedy* (1992), Homewood, IL: Business Irwin.

Herlihy, B. and Corey, C., *ACA Ethical Student's Casebook*, 6th ed., Alexandria, VA: American Counseling Association (2006).

Hersh, J.B., 'Interviewing college students in crisis', *Journal of Counseling and Development* (1985), (63), pp. 286–289.

Hobbs, N. and Seeman, J., Counseling, *Annual Review of Psychology* (1955), (6), pp. 379–404.

Hoffman, R.M., Gender self-definition and gender self-acceptance in women intersections with feminist, womanist, and ethnic identities. *Journal of Counseling and Development* (2006), 84(3).

Hoppock, R., *Job Satisfaction* (1935), New York: Harper.

Hubble, M.A., Duncan, B.D., and Miller, S.D. (Eds.), *The Heart and Soul of Change: What Works in Therapy*, Washington, DC: American Psychological Association (1999).

Huffman, S.R. and Myers, J.E., Counseling women in mid-life: An integrative approach to menopause. *Journal of Counseling and Development* (1999), 77(3), pp. 258–266

Ivey, A.E., *Intentional Interviewing and Counselling: Facilitating Client Development in a Multicultural Society,* 3rd ed. (1994), Pacific Grove, CA: Brooks/Cole.

_____, *Micro Counseling: Innovations in Interviewing Training* (1971), Springfield, Ill.: Charles C. Thomas Pub. Ltd.

James, R.K. and Gilliland, B.E., *Crisis Intervention Strategies*, 4th ed., Pacific Grove, CA: Brooks/Cole (2001).

Jourard, S.M., and Jaffee, P.E., Influence of an Interviewer's Self-disclosure on the Self-disclosing Behavior of Interviewees, *Journal of Counseling Psychology* (1970), (17), pp. 252–257.

Jung, C.G., *Collected Works: The Practice of Psychotherapy* (1954), New York: Pantheon.

Kaul, T.T., Kaul, M.A., and Bedner, R.L., Counselor Confrontation and Client Depth of Self-exploration, *Journal of Counseling Psychology* (1973), 20(2), pp. 132–136.

Kazdin, A.E., *Behavior Modification in Applied Settings,* 5th ed. (1995), Pacific Grove, CA: Brooks/Cole.

Kelly, G.A., *The Psychology of Personal Constructs,* Vol. 1 (1955), New York: Norton.

Kitchener, K.S., Intuition, Critical Evaluation and Ethical Principles: The Foundation for Ethical Decisions in Counseling Psychology, *The Counseling Psychologist* (1984), (12), pp. 43–55.

Kitchener, K.S., Teaching Applied Ethics in Counselor Education: An Integration of Psychological and Philosophical Analysis, *Journal of Counseling and Development* (1986), (64), pp. 306–310.

Kleinke, C., *Common Principles of Psychotherapy*, Pacific Grove: Brooks/Cole (1994).

Kolbe, D.A., Rubin, I.M. and McIntyre, J.M., *Organizational Psychology: An Experiential Approach* (1984), Englewood Cliffs, NJ: Prentice-Hall.

Kottler, J.A., *On Being a Therapist*, San Francisco: Jossey-Bass (1993).

Krumboltz J.D., Behavioral Goals of Counseling, *Journal of Counseling Psychology* (1966), (13), pp. 153–159.

Krumboltz, J.D. (Ed.), *Revolution in Counseling* (1966), Boston: Houghton Mifflin.

Krumboltz, J.D. and Thoreson, C.E. (Eds.), *Counseling Methods* (1976), New York: Holt, Rinehart, and Winston.

Lambert, M.J. and Barley, D.E., Research summary on the therapeutic relationship and psychotherapy outcome. In J.C. Norcross (Ed.), *Psychotherapy Relationships that Work*, New York: Oxford (2002), pp. 17–32.

Lambert, M.J., and Bergin, A.E., The Effectiveness of Psychotherapy, In A.E. Bergin and S.L. Garfield (Eds.), *Handbook of Psychotherapy and Behavior Change,* 4th ed. (1994), New York: Wiley, pp. 143–189.

Lambie, G.W., The contribution of ego development level to burnout in school counselors: Implications for professional school counseling, *Journal of Counseling and Development* (2007), (85), pp. 82–88.

Lane, D., Counseling Psychology in Organizations, *The Psychologist* (1990), (12), pp. 540–44.

Lazarus, A.A., *The Practice of Multimodal Therapy* (1989), Baltimore: Johns Hopkins University Press.

Lodge, D., *Nice Work* (1988), London: Penguin.

Lofquist, L.H., and Dawis, R.V., *Essentials of Person—Environment—Correspondence Counselling* (1991), University of Minnesota Press.

Lowenstein, S.F., Helping family members cope with divorce. In S. Eisenberg and L.E. Patterson (Eds.), *Helping clients with special concerns*, (1979), pp. 193–217. Boston: Houghton Mifflin. Reissued. Prospect Heights, IL: Waveland Press (1990).

Marx, J.A. and Gelso, C.J., Termination of individual counseling in a university counseling context. *Journal of Counseling Psychology* (1987), (34), pp. 3–9.

May, R., Remen, N., Young, D. and Berland, W., The Wounded Healer, *Saybrook Review* (1985), (5), 84–93.

McAuliffe, G. and Lovell, C., The influence of counselor epistemology on the helping interview: A qualitative study, *Journal of Counseling and Development* (2006), (84), pp. 308–317.

Mehrabian, A., *Non-verbal Communication* (1972), Chicago: Aldine Publishing.

Meichenbaum, D., *Cognitive Behavior Modification: An Integrative Approach* (1977), New York: Plenum.

Miller, D.J. and Thelen, M.H., Knowledge and beliefs about confidentiality in psychotherapy. *Professional Psychology: Research and Practice* (1986), (17), pp. 15–19.

_____, Knowledge and Beliefs about Confidentiality in Psychotherapy, *Professional Psychology: Research and Practice* (1986), (17), pp. 15–19.

Miller, G.A., Britton, T.P., and Gridley, B.E., A framework of understanding the wounding of healers, *Counseling and Values* (1998), (42), pp. 124–132.

Morton, J.E., *On the Evolution of Manpower Statistics* (1969), W.E. UpJohn Institute of Employment Research, p. 113.

Mowrer, Hobart, *The Crisis in Psychiatry and Religion* (1961), New Turk: D. Van Nostrand Company, Inc.

Nahrwold, S.C., Why Programs Fail, in James Manuso (Ed.), *Occupational Clinical Psychology* (1983), New York: Praeger, pp. 105–15.

Nelson-Jones, R., *Practical Counseling and Helping Skills: Text and Activities for the Life Skill Counseling Model*, 5th ed. (2005), London: Sage Publications.

Neulinger, J., Schillinger, K. Stein, M.I., and Welcowitz, J., Perception of the optimally integrated person as a function of therapist's characteristics. *Perceptual and Motor Skills* (1970), (30), pp. 375–384.

Newton, T., *Managing Stress: Emotions and Power at Work* (1995), London: Sage.

Nonaka, I., Creating Organizational Order out of Chaos: Self Renewal in Japanese Firms. *California Management Review* (1988), 30(3), pp. 57–73.

Nystul, M.S., *The Art and Science of Counseling and Psychotherapy*, 2nd ed., New York: Macmillan (2003).

O'Leary, L., Fitness at work – is it worth it? *Occupational Health Review* (March/April 1994), pp. 14–16.

_____, Mental Health at work, *Occupational Health Review*, September/October 1993.

Oberer, D. and Lee, S., The Counseling Psychologist in Business and Industry: Ethical Concerns, *Journal of Business and Psychology* (1986), (12), pp. 148–162.

Okun, B.F., *Effective Helping: Interviewing and Counseling Techniques,* 5th ed. (1997), Pacific Grove, CA: Brooks/Cole.

Orlans, V., Counselling Services, *Organizational Personnel Review* (1986), 15(5), pp. 19–23.

Patterson, C.H., The Place of Values in Counseling and Psychotherapy, *Journal of Counseling Psychology* (1958), 5, pp. 216–23.

Patterson, L.E. and Welfel, E. R., *The Counseling Process*, 5th ed., Pacific Grove, CA: Brooks/Cole (2000).

Patterson, L.E., and Eisenberg, S., *The Counseling Process*, 3rd ed. (1983), Boston: Houghton Mifflin.

Pedler, M., Boydell T. and Buryogne J., Towards the Learning Company, *Management Education and Development* (1989), 20(1), pp. 1–8

Pittman, D.J., Drug Addiction and Crime, In D. Glaser (Ed.), *Handbook of Criminology* (1974), Chicago: Rand McNally, pp. 209–232.

Pope, K.S. and Vetter, V.A., Ethical Dilemmas Encountered by the Members of the American Psychological Association: A National Survey, *American Psychologist,* (1992), (47), 397–411.

Pope, K.S., Sexual Involvement with Therapists: Patient Assessment, Subsequent Therapy, *Forensic* (1994), Washington, D.C.: American Psychological Association.

Puder, M., Credibility, Confidentiality, and Ethical Issues in Employee Counselling Programming, in James Manuso (Ed.), *Occupational Clinical Psychology* (1983), New York: Praeger, pp. 95–103.

Rae, Leslie, *The Skills of Interviewing: A Guide for Managers and Trainers* (1988), New York: Nicholas Publishing Company.

Rao, S.N., *Student's Performance and Adjustments* (1967), Tirupati: S.V. University.

Roberts, A.R., How to Work with Clients' Strengths in Crisis Intervention: A Solution-focused Approach. In A.R. Roberts (Ed.), *Crisis Intervention Handbook*, New York: Oxford, (2000), pp. 31–35.

Rogers and R.F. Dymond (Eds.), A Therapist's View of the Good Life, *Humanist* (1961), (17), pp. 291–300.

Rogers, C.R., *A Way of Being* (1980), Boston: Houghton Mifflin.

_____, *Client Centered Therapy* (1951), Boston: Houghton Mifflin.

_____, Client-centered Therapy, In E. Shostrom (Producer), *Three Approaches to Psychotherapy* [Videotape], (1986), Orange, CA: Psychological Films, (Original film produced 1965).

_____, *Counseling and Psychotherapy* (1942), Boston: Houghton Mifflin.

_____, *On Becoming a Person* (1961), Boston: Houghton Mifflin.

_____, The Necessary and Sufficient Conditions of Therapeutic Personality Change, *Journal of Consulting Psychology* (1957), 21, pp. 95–103.

Rokeach, M., and Regan, J.F., The Role of Values in the Counseling Situation. *Personnel and Guidance Journal* (1980), 58(9), pp. 576–582.

Rosenthal, D., Changes in Some Values Following Psychotherapy, *Journal of Consulting Psychology* (1955), (19), pp. 431–436.

Samler, J., Change in Values: A Goal of Counseling, *Journal of Counseling Psychology* (1960), (71), pp. 32–39.

Sanderson, C., *Counseling Adult Survivors of Child Sexual Abuse,* 2nd ed. (1995), London: Jessica Kingsley.

Schlossberg, N.K. and Pietrofesa, J.J., Perspectve on counseling bias: Implications for counselor's education. *Counseling Psychologist* (1978), 4(1), pp. 44–54.

Seligman, M.E.P., The Effectiveness of Psychotherapy: The Consumer Reports Study, *American Psychologist* (1995), (50), pp. 965–974.

Senge, P.M., *The Fifth Discipline: The Art and Practice of Organizational Learning* (1990), New York: Doubleday.

Shertzer. B., and Stone. S.C., *Fundamentals of Counseling*, 2nd ed. (1980), Boston: Houghton Mifflin.

Shulman, L., *The Skills of Helping*, 2nd ed., Itasca, IL: Peacock (1984).

Skinner, B.F., *Beyond Freedom and Dignity* (1971), New York: Knopf.

Söderlund, John, Your Tired, Old Ideas About Hypnosis will Begin to Grow Heavy... *New Therapist* 10, (Nov./Dec. 2000), The Hypnotic Edition.

Sonnerberg, F.K., 'The Age of Intangibles', *Management Review* (Jan. 1994), pp. 48–53.

Sreedhar, K.P., Current Trends in the Practice of Counseling, **www.Psychology4 All.Com** (2001).

Stewart, N.R., Winborn, B.B., Johnson, R.G., Burks, H.M., Jr., Engelkes, J.R., *Systematic Counselling* (1978), Englewood Cliffs, NJ: Prentice-Hall.

Sullivan, H.S., *The Interpersonal Theory of Psychiatry* (1953), New York: Norton.

Swanson, C.D., Ethics and the counselor. In J.A. Brown and R.H. Pate, Jr. (Eds.), *Being a counselor*, Pacific Grover, CA: Brooks/Code (1983), pp. 47–65.

Tennyson, W.W. and Strom, S.M., Beyond professional standards: Developing responsibleness, *Journal of Counseling and Development* (1986), (64), pp. pp. 298–302.

Thomas, R.R., Jr., Managing Diversity: A Conceptual Framework. In S.E. Jackson and Associates (Ed.), *Diversity in the Work Place* (1992), New York: Guilford Press, p. 307.

Toffler, A., *Future Shock* (1970), New York: Bantam.

Tomasko, R.M., *Rethinking the Corporation* (1993), New York: AMACOM.

Van House, W.H. and Paradise, L.V., *Ethics in Counseling and Psychotherapy*, Cranston, RI: Carroll (1979).

Viega, John, F., *The Academy of Management Executive*, Vol. 2 (1988), (2), 145.

Ward, D.W., Termination of individual counseling: Concepts and strategies, *Journal of Counseling and Development* (1984), (63), pp. 21–26.

Watts, A.G. (Ed.), *Counseling at Work* (1977), Plymouth: Bedford Square Press.

Weinberg, G., *The Heart of Psychotherapy*, New York: St. Martin's Press (1984).

Weiss, R.S. (Ed.), *Loneliness*, Cambridge, MA: MIT Press (1973).

Welfel, E.R. and Patterson, L.E., *The Counseling Process: A Multi-theoretical Integrative Approach*, 6th ed., Belmont, CA: Thomas Brooks/Cole (2005).

Welfel, E.R., *Ethics in Counseling and Psychotherapy: Standards, Research, and Emerging Issues* (1998), Pacific Grove, CA: Brooks/Cole.

_____, *Ethics in Counseling and Psychotherapy: Standards, Research, and Emerging Issues*, 2nd ed., Pacific Grove, CA: Brooks/Cole (2002).

WHO Expert Committee on Addiction Producing Drugs, Technical Report Series No. 273, (1964), Geneva: World Health Organization.

Wikerson, K. and Bellini, J., Interpersonal and organizational burnout among school counselors, *Journal of Counseling and Development* (2006), (84), pp. 440–450.

Williamson, E.G., Values Orientation in Counseling, *Personnel and Guidance Journal* (1958), (37), pp. 520–28.

Wirth, L., Clinical Sociology, *American Journal of Sociology* (1931), 37(1), pp. 49–66.

Witmer, J.M. and Young, M.E., Preventing counselor impairment: A wellness model, *Journal of Humanistic Education and Development* (1996), (34), pp. 141–155.

Wolberg, Lewis R., *The Technique of Psychotherapy* (1977), New York: Grune and Stratton, p. 3.

Wolpe, J., *Psychotherapy by Reciprocal Inhibition* (1958), Stanford, CA: Stanford University Press.

_____, *The Practice of Behavior Therapy* (1990), Elmsford, New York: Pergamon.

Wrenn, C.G., *World of Contemporary Counselor* (1973), Boston: Houghton Mifflin.

Index